Six Days

The Age of the Earth and the Decline of the Church

KEN HAM

First printing: November 2013

Copyright © 2013 by Ken Ham. All rights reserved. No part of this book may be used or reproduced in any manner whatsoever without written permission of the publisher, except in the case of brief quotations in articles and reviews. For information write:

Master Books®, P.O. Box 726, Green Forest, AR 72638
Master Books® is a division of the New Leaf Publishing Group, Inc.

ISBN: 978-0-89051-789-5
Library of Congress Number: 2013951724

Cover by Diana Bogardus
Cover artwork by Dan Flynn

Unless otherwise noted, Scripture quotations are from the New King James Version of the Bible.

Please consider requesting that a copy of this volume be purchased by your local library system.

Printed in the United States of America

Please visit our website for other great titles:
www.masterbooks.net

For information regarding author interviews,
please contact the publicity department at (870) 438-5288

Master Books®
A Division of New Leaf Publishing Group
www.masterbooks.net

Acknowledgments

I want to especially thank Answers in Genesis researcher/writer Steve Golden for the many hundreds of hours spent helping me to put this important work together. I also want to thank staff member (and my son-in-law) Bodie Hodge for assisting Steve in a number of areas as this book was mapped out. And thanks to my wife for her patience in putting up with the many hours I spend writing and speaking so others will understand the importance of not compromising biblical authority. Without her total support and love, I would never have been able to accomplish the many things I have been a part of in ministry over the years.

Contents

Introduction

For if the trumpet makes an uncertain sound, who will prepare for battle? (1 Corinthians 14:8)

In a world that is increasingly in rebellion against God and in a society where the authority of the Word of God is being eroded out from under us, the Church stands as a light in the darkness. God's people are called together to share the gospel and love of Jesus Christ with the world — using the Word of God as their foundation of wisdom and knowledge.

With the Scriptures, we can speak with authority about the issues of our age, just as Christ spoke with authority to those to whom He ministered:

> And they were astonished at His teaching, for He taught them as one having authority, and not as the scribes. (Mark 1:22)

But, readers, the Church has a problem. There is an uncertain sound coming from many in the Body. How can we be discerning? Think about it! When many Christian academics, Bible scholars, and church leaders and pastors are asked what they believe about Genesis, they will likely offer one or more of the following responses:

> "There is a gap of millions of years between the first verses of Genesis."
>
> "We don't know what the days of Genesis mean."
>
> "The Flood was a local event. Fossils are probably millions of years old."

"God used evolution to create Adam and Eve."

"Genesis 1 is a poem."

"Genesis is not about our origins."

"Adam and Eve weren't real people."

"Genesis 1 represents the temple, not material origins."

This is just a short list. The point is, there are several positions (which I assert are compromise positions) on Genesis that permeate the Church today. And all these views have one thing in common — they try to accommodate what secularists believe about origins, particularly the idea that the earth is millions of years old.

Most children in Christian homes attend public schools where, by and large, their textbooks and lectures give our young people a very specific history. Here is what they are almost always taught as fact:

> The universe began with a big bang 15 billion years ago. The stars formed 10 billion years ago. The sun formed 5 billion years ago and the molten earth 4.5 billion years ago.
>
> Water formed on the earth 3.8 billion years ago. And over millions of years, life formed from nonlife and then evolved to fish, then amphibians, to birds and mammals, then ape-like creatures, and then man — a process involving death over millions of years.

Secular museums, documentary programs on television, secular professors at universities, most public school textbooks — they all give the same basic view of origins. They are unified. They have a very certain message.

And these ideas are not just taught in the science classroom! A new history curriculum is being piloted in schools across the country, and its distinctive is that it does not just teach recorded history from a secular perspective — it supposedly starts at the "beginning," some 13 billion years ago.[1]

Secularists insist they know what happened in the unobservable past. They claim to know the true history of the universe. They believe and preach their worldview with zeal.

But Christians have the benefit of a very specific history that has been revealed to them by Someone who was there at the beginning and throughout

---

1. Stephen Beale, "New Gates History Curriculum Closes Young Minds to God," *Crisis Magazine*, http://www.crisismagazine.com/2013/new-gates-history-curriculum-closes-young-minds-to-god.

history — and that Someone does not lie. This specific history is revealed to us in the first chapters of the first book of the Bible — Genesis. Yet many believers are not sure what God said in Genesis! And the reason they are not sure is because they have been influenced by the secular views of origins. As a result, many Christians, including Christian leaders, have adopted secular beliefs about origins and reinterpreted God's Word in Genesis in an attempt to get them to "fit" together.

No wonder there is a mass exodus of young people from our churches! They begin to doubt the Bible in Genesis, based on the compromised teachings of church leaders (or the absence of biblically based apologetics), reject it as God's Word, and then leave the Church. The Bible declares, "For if the trumpet makes an uncertain sound, who will prepare for battle?" (1 Corinthians 14:8). The Church does not have a unified view on origins, because so many want to be unified around man's beliefs in evolution and/ or millions of years — instead of being unified on what God's Word teaches so clearly in Genesis.

In many sectors of Christian academia and in many churches, there is an uncertain sound being blared. Young people and adults are hearing and often heeding this uncertain sound about the accuracy of the Bible from its very start. They are being taught that parts of the Bible are untrustworthy, that death, disease, and suffering have always been in the world, and thus that God has called obviously bad things "very good." They are being taught to accept man's ideas and to reinterpret God's Word. The result is that many Christians are not really sure about what they believe regarding origins (and thus what they believe about the first eleven chapters of Genesis), because they have been taught that they cannot trust the Bible at the beginning.

What's more, even parts of the modern-day homeschool movement are being impacted by such compromise. An article in *The Atlantic* declared, "Evangelical Homeschoolers Embrace Evolution."[2] The writer explains that while the majority of homeschooled students are part of Christian families, "a growing number of their parents are dismayed by these textbooks [that teach a young-earth perspective]." I have even seen reports from Christian school teachers who have embraced an old earth or theistic evolution in their

---

2. David R. Wheeler, "Old Earth, Young Minds: Evangelical Homeschoolers Embrace Evolution," *The Atlantic*, March 8, 2013, http://www.theatlantic.com/national/archive/2013/03/old-earth-young-minds-evangelical-homeschoolers-embrace-evolution/273844/.

science and Bible courses! How has such compromise become so common in the Church, and how is it now even beginning to invade what were once very conservative sectors, such as homeschooling?

What has happened is that many Bible scholars and Christian leaders are no longer reading Scripture in the first chapters of Genesis to glean answers from it, known as *exegesis*. Instead, they are reading man's ideas *into* Scripture, a problem known as *eisegesis*. In many instances, man's fallible view of origins (based on evolution and millions of years) has been given authority over the Word of God. And it is the views of these compromised scholars, who train our pastors, and then these compromised pastors, who teach church attendees, that have resulted in these doubts being filtered down to many Christian families.

In the midst of the Church's wavering on origins, the secular world is speaking with authority and unity, leading many unsure believers astray as they authoritatively indoctrinate them to believe their secular views!

God has given us a very specific history from the Old Testament to the New Testament. This history is the foundation of all doctrine, including the gospel (in Genesis 3). It is the true history of the world that tells us where we all came from, what our problem is (sin), and what the solution is — salvation through Christ.

When people begin to understand the foundational nature of Genesis, they typically come to realize the importance of taking God at His word in the first 11 chapters of Genesis. This book is about how the Bible is intended to be read (exegesis, not eisegesis), and about how compromise on Genesis has become so rampant in the Church today — leading to a generational loss of believing in biblical inerrancy and authority. I pray that this book challenges the minds and hearts of pastors, laypeople, scholars, and students alike. My prayer is that as a result of this book, many more Christians (including Christian leaders) will speak with authority and give that "certain sound" concerning God's Word beginning in Genesis.

Although this book is written with many examples from the US and specific examples from the United Kingdom, it is just as applicable to our whole Western world. The Church and culture in the West are suffering from the same basic problems — and they need the same basic solution!

Chapter 1

 # Shepherds Leading
the Sheep Astray

Once, after I had spoken at a conference, a man walked up to me and said, "Thank you for your stand on the Word of God." At this point, he burst into tears, saying, "Your teachings and materials saved my sons. Years ago, what you taught about Genesis influenced me, and I was able to be a godly influence on them. Thank you." He had apparently never heard someone teach about biblical creation, about taking Genesis in a straightforward way — as it is meant to be taken. Another couple approached me and asked, "Do you know of any churches in our area that hold to a literal Genesis and a young earth? We can't find one, and our current pastor refuses to teach these things." In fact, I get that question at almost every conference.

The Church is reaching a crisis point. Really, the Church has already reached it — and we are witnessing the tragic results of compromise on the authority of God's Word. More and more pastors, church leaders, and Bible scholars are choosing either not to take a stand on Genesis or to teach some form of evolution and/or millions of years in their churches, Sunday schools, or college courses. Many of them will unfairly characterize biblical creationists as people who deny the value of what they term as "science." Others try to convince those who sit under their teachings that Genesis is symbolic or somehow millions of years can be fit in, or that God really did use evolution to create the universe.

What has happened is that many in our churches, including many of our young people, do not understand the connections between the gospel and the history presented in Genesis chapters 1–11. They do not comprehend that every major doctrine, like marriage, sin, why we wear clothes, and so on, is founded ultimately in the Book of Genesis. Many pastors and church leaders do not bother to teach Genesis anymore, saying, "It doesn't matter," or "It's a secondary issue." It is not uncommon to hear Christian leaders claim that as long as we believe that God created, it does not matter how or when He did it. The literal history of Genesis 1–11 is under attack — and the attacks are coming from within the Church!

The Genesis 3 Attack of Our Day

What we are seeing in the Church today is not very different from the temptation in the Garden of Eden. We read in Genesis chapters 1 and 2 that God, in His goodness, created a "very good" world and placed the first man and the first woman, Adam and Eve, in the garden. They were to tend and keep it (Genesis 2:15), and to be fruitful and multiply, to fill the earth and subdue it (Genesis 1:28). Adam and Eve were given everything they could ever need, including access to every tree in the garden:

> And the LORD God commanded the man, saying, "Of every tree of the garden you may freely eat. (Genesis 2:16)

But God also gave Adam a command, the one prohibition in the garden:

> but of the tree of the knowledge of good and evil you shall not eat, for in the day that you eat of it you shall surely die. (Genesis 2:17)

Now, if you have read Genesis — and I hope you have! — you know that Adam and Eve broke that command. While working in the garden, Eve encounters the serpent, who is Satan (2 Corinthians 11:3; 1 Timothy 2:14; Revelation 12:9). In fact, it's very interesting what transpired between Eve and the serpent that day:

> Now the serpent was more cunning than any beast of the field which the LORD God had made. And he said to the woman, "Has God indeed said, 'You shall not eat of every tree of the garden'?" And the woman said to the serpent, "We may eat the fruit of the trees of the garden; but of the fruit of the tree which is in the midst

of the garden, God has said, 'You shall not eat it, nor shall you touch it, lest you die.' " (Genesis 3:1–3)

In that first verse, Satan casts doubt about God's Word. He asks, "Did God really say . . . ?" (NIV), thus questioning the trustworthiness of the plain meaning of God's command. Eve explains what God commanded, though she adds the bit about not even being able to touch the fruit. The serpent's attack continues:

> Then the serpent said to the woman, "You will not surely die. For God knows that in the day you eat of it your eyes will be opened, and you will be like God, knowing good and evil." (Genesis 3:4–5)

Here, Satan casts doubt on the truthfulness of God's Word. When He gave Adam the command not to eat the fruit of the tree of the knowledge of good and evil, God very clearly said that if he did, he would "surely die." There is no question about what God meant — if Adam and Eve ate the fruit, they would eventually experience death. But Eve is deceived by the serpent's twisting of God's Word, and she and Adam eat from the one tree God had forbidden them to — an event known as the Fall of man. And as a consequence, sin and death entered the once-perfect "very good" world.

When I read the account in Genesis 3, I am struck by the fact that the attack on the Word of God has not changed. Even today, about 6,000 years later, we are seeing man question the authority of Scripture, calling into question the trustworthiness and truthfulness of what God has said — especially in Genesis 1–11. When it comes to the creation account in Genesis 1–2, we hear the same question: "Did God really say . . . ?" When we talk about a literal Adam and Eve and the Fall, the question crops up: "Did God really say . . . ?" When the account of Noah and the Ark is brought up, the Genesis 3 attack is not far behind: "Did God really say . . . ?"

You see, the Apostle Paul warns readers in 2 Corinthians 11:3 that "as the serpent deceived Eve by his craftiness, so your minds may be corrupted from the simplicity that is in Christ." The Apostle Paul knew that Satan would attempt to use the Genesis 3 attack on us just as he did to Eve, because he wants us to disbelieve the Word of God.

I have talked about creation and evolution/millions of years for nearly 30 years, because evolutionary ideas are one of the main forms of the modern-day Genesis 3 attack. The idea of long ages (i.e., millions and billions of years) I believe is the major Genesis 3 attack of our day. But these beliefs of evolution and/or millions of years speak to a deeper issue that involves an attack on Christianity. The real attack is on the authority of Scripture. For this reason, I do not want Answers in Genesis (AiG) to be known as just a "creation ministry." Answers in Genesis is an evangelistic *biblical authority* ministry dedicated to calling the Church back to the Word of God. Our focus cannot be simply evolutionary ideas or millions of years, because those are just fruits of the deeper problem: the loss of regard for the authority of the Bible. Thus, we also specialize in creation and biblical apologetics to deal with this attack on the authority of God's Word.

When sinful man believes the lie that God's Word cannot be trusted, he has effectively declared that he knows better than God. When sinful human beings believe the lie that God's Word is not authoritative, they put themselves in a position of authority over God, disregarding and even rewriting His Word. Our culture is answering the question "Did God really say . . . ?" with a resounding "No!" Those who question His Word are denying the full authority and accuracy of the Bible from its very first verse. This has had devastating effects on our culture and on the Church.

The Consequences of Compromise

In 2009, we published *Already Gone*, detailing data as to why around two-thirds of young people are leaving the Church in America by the time they reach college age. For the research behind the book, Answers in Genesis contracted with America's Research Group to find out why these two-thirds are walking away from the Church. Britt Beemer, who heads America's Research Group, and his team created a study composed of questions such as, "At what age did you begin to really question contents in the Bible?" Of the two-thirds who have left the Church, 40 percent had started to question the Bible by the end of middle school, and another 45 percent by the end of high school.

Another question asked was, "If you don't believe the Bible, when did you first have doubts?" The results were the same: Of the two-thirds, 40 percent first had doubts by the end of middle school, and another 45 percent by the end of high school.

The research revealed that we are losing these kids at a young age. They are starting to doubt (the Genesis 3 attack) the Bible at a young age. Why? What is really going on? To summarize it, by and large in our churches and in our Christian homes, what we tend to do is teach Bible stories. What do I mean by "Bible stories"? Jonah and the big fish, feeding the five thousand, the Apostle Paul's missionary journeys, Jesus on the Cross, Noah and the Ark, Adam and Eve, and so on.

I believe all these accounts are true — so what is wrong with teaching them? It is the way we teach them. For instance, many people use the word *story* in reference to these accounts. But what has the word *story* come to mean today? Fiction. And yet we say, "Children, let me tell you a story. I'm going to tell you a wonderful Bible story." The children get the idea that they get "stories" at home or church — but what they are taught at school is real! Now around 90 percent of these children from church homes attend public schools.

Even though there is a minority of Christian teachers as missionaries in the public education system, as I was, the schools have by and large thrown out God, the Bible, prayer, and biblical creation. They teach evolution and millions of years as fact. Biology textbooks claim that scientists can explain the whole of reality by natural processes — a universe and all it contains came into existence without God. That is naturalism, which is atheism.

Many people, including Christians, have this idea that when we do not argue using the Bible, we are on "neutral" ground. But it is not neutral. Christ

Himself explained, "He who is not with Me is against Me, and he who does not gather with Me scatters abroad" (Matthew 12:30; Luke 11:23). We are either for Christ or against Him. We either walk in the light, or we walk in darkness. Because of a "neutral ground" mentality, what is happening is students have the idea that they are taught real history at school and on television, but they are

taught religious "stories" at home and in church. At the same time, many parents think what their students are taught at public school is neutral — but in reality if it is not for Christ, then it is against Him. Christians need to wake up to the fact there is no neutral position and their students are really being indoctrinated into an anti-God religion in the public schools.

Another thing America's Research Group found was that most churches and most Christian homes do not teach apologetics. Most Bible colleges, most seminaries, and most Christian colleges do not teach apologetics. What do I mean by that? We can have all the knowledge in the world, but if we are not prepared for where the culture is and to answer their skeptical questions, then the culture will likely have more influence on us than we will on it.

The word *apologetics* comes from the Greek word *apologia,* which means an "answer" or a reasoned defense. First Peter 3:15 tells us, "But sanctify the Lord God in your hearts, and always be ready to give a defense to everyone who asks you a reason for the hope that is in you, with meekness and fear." We have to teach our children how to answer the basic questions of the age. We have to prepare ourselves and generations of children with solid training in apologetics, but instead we mostly teach "stories" in our Christian homes and churches. We might teach great doctrine. We might have great amounts of knowledge. But if we do not know how to defend our faith, we are not going to survive in the world. And sadly, Christians for the most part simply are not teaching apologetics to their children.

But if the Church is not teaching apologetics, then who is? Actually, the public school system and television shows are. They offer evidence for why the Bible is not true, for millions of years, for the big bang, for why there never was a global flood, and on and on. In fact, they do such a great job that they can put it on educational television stations, where they can communicate their brand of apologetics to the layman, to the average person. And to our children (and many parents) it can sound very convincing.

Readers, most of the Church is not doing what the secular world is doing — teaching students apologetics to defend the beliefs they teach them. We can become very proud of our knowledge and our doctrines, but if we do not know — if our children do not know — how to defend the faith, what is going to happen? It will be as Psalm 11:3 says:

If the foundations are destroyed, what can the righteous do?

We have, as a result, trained up generations who have been led by the world to doubt and disbelieve the Word of God. Now we are suffering the consequences.

What Is Being Taught in "Christian" Colleges?

A particular area of concern within the Church is Christian colleges, Bible colleges, universities, and seminaries. Sadly, many of these educational institutions cannot be trusted to teach a message that is consistent with Scripture's account of the Creation, Fall, and Flood.[1]

In June 2011, *Christianity Today* concentrated on the fact that increasing numbers of Christian academics — Christian scholars in America — no longer believe in a literal Adam and Eve.[2] In 1987, when my book *The Lie* was first published, I argued that if the Church does not stand on the authority of the Word of God beginning in Genesis and if it continually starts to add millions of years to Genesis or embraces theistic evolution,

---

1. For a detailed analysis of what is being taught in these Christian institutions, see Ken Ham and Greg Hall, *Already Compromised*, with Britt Beemer (Green Forest, AR: Master Books, 2011).

2. Richard N. Ostling, "The Search for a Historical Adam," *Christianity Today*, June 2011, p. 23–27.

eventually the Church will give up Genesis all together. Today, that is exactly what is happening.

John Schneider, retired professor of religion at Calvin College in Grand Rapids, Michigan, is quoted in *Christianity Today* as saying that Eden "cannot be a literal description of how things really were in the primal human past."[3] Daniel Harlow, professor of religion at Calvin College was also quoted in the article:

> Harlow proposed that understandings of the Fall may need to be "reformulated" and the church must be willing to "decouple original sin from the notion that all humans descended from a single pair."[4]

Once believers "reformulate" their understanding of the Fall, there is no gospel message. Why are humans sinners? Where did we come from? What exactly is the gospel all about?

Baker Publishing Group in 2012 published the book *The Evolution of Adam* by Peter Enns. Enns, former fellow with BioLogos and a theistic evolutionist, writes, "Evolution demands that the special creation of the first Adam as described in the Bible is not literally historical."[5] As far as evolution is concerned, Enns is correct — evolutionary ideas were intended to explain the world without God. So of course there is no room for a literal Adam.

But the Bible demands that Adam is literally historical. In a lecture at Westmont College, a Christian college in Santa Barbara, California, Enns put forth a view that has become typical of many Christian colleges across the nation:

> I'm just giving you my opinion. Who knows if it will change in the years to come. I'm still thinking about it. All the Jesus stuff and all the sin and death stuff are still real, but personally I don't need a historical Adam to make all that happen.[6]

---

3. Ibid., p. 26.
4. Ibid.
5. Peter Enns, *The Evolution of Adam: What the Bible Does and Doesn't Say about Human Origins* (Grand Rapids, MI: Brazos Press, 2012), p. xvi.
6. Enns, "Lecture: Erasmus Lecture — Peter Enns, Feb. 9, 2011," WestmontTV (YouTube channel), http://www.youtube.com/watch?v=36T3tbygQgA&safety_mode=true&persist_safety_mode=1.

At this point, I would ask, if we do not have a historical Adam, but we still believe in sin, then what exactly is *sin*? Where did it come from? Why are we sinners? Enns's assertion undermines the foundation of the gospel of Jesus Christ. And he is not the only professing Christian making these claims!

Tremper Longman III, professor of religious studies at Westmont College, explained in a presentation why he believes Adam is not a historical figure:

> My understanding of Genesis 1 and 2 as high style literary prose narrative, leads me to conclude that it's not necessary that Adam be a historical individual for this text to be without error in what it intends to teach.[7]

What happens when professors begin teaching generations of students in Christian colleges that there is no literal Adam and Eve and no literal Fall? What happens when the Church embraces evolution and/or millions of years? I would suggest that the majority of young people (and research shows it is at least two-thirds) will walk away from the Church by the time they reach college age.

In fact, Longman commented on what Westmont College is teaching its students about the Bible:

> It's equally important to send a message to the youth in the church that the Bible is not at odds with what they are learning in their biology classes about evolution in school.[8]

That is what this Westmont College professor (and presumably other professors at this college) is telling their students. In fact, that is true of most Christian colleges. It is true of many churches and church leaders. We have already done the research on that and published it in the ground-breaking books *Already Gone* and *Already Compromised*.[9]

Another Christian college professor and former president of BioLogos, Dr. Darrel Falk, who teaches biology at Point Loma Nazarene University in

---

7. Tremper Longman, "What Genesis 1 and 2 Teaches (and What It Doesn't)," YouTube, http://www.youtube.com/watch?v=iL88e5fVArU.

8. Ibid.

9. For more information, see Ken Ham and Britt Beemer, *Already Gone*, with Todd HIllard (Green Forest, AR: Master Books, 2009) and Ken Ham and Greg Hall, *Already Compromised*, with Britt Beemer (Green Forest, AR: Master Books, 2011).

San Diego, California, shared what he would tell a student who asked him about the age of the universe:

> The age of the universe is around 13 billion years old. And I would talk to them a little bit, and I would say that the age of the earth is 4.3 billion years old. I've got various books I can refer them to, and I would go through and say, "Here's the kind of data that shows the age of the universe." And I would kind of lead them through that process that the role astronomy that demonstrates so clearly how old the universe is. The age of the rocks, which tells us how old the earth is. And how these are two totally different ways of looking at age. One of them involves looking at stars and using some instruments and ways of measuring it which have absolutely no relationship whatsoever to the age of rocks. And I would say, "Here's what it says. It says it's 14 billion years old."[10]

These are professors in Christian universities — and they are not even willing to defer to Scripture when responding to students about the creation account. Notice what Dr. Falk says he would tell his students: He would look at sinful man's fallible dating methods and say, "Here's what it says." He does not even mention biblical authority here.

And what is happening as a result? Students are walking away — statistical research establishes this is so. There is a whole series of videos on the Internet of people — many young people — telling their "de-conversion" stories. One young man explained that a lack of apologetics training in his youth led to his "de-conversion":

> How I became an atheist. I was born into a Christian family and indoctrinated growing up as a kid. That next year was freshman year of high school and I started learning about evolution in my biology class. That's where I realized I had never seriously questioned or thought about my religious beliefs. So as I learned about evolution and started thinking philosophically about it, I realized that there couldn't be a God. So I became an atheist.[11]

---

10. Darrel Falk, "How Old Is the Universe?" Test of Faith, http://www.testoffaith.com/resources/resource.aspx?id=328.

11. "How I Became an Atheist," YouTube, http://www.youtube.com/watch?v=iJTjpWgc-jXE&feature=BFa&list=PL0B322B60D6CF6308 (accessed May 2012).

Sadly, this is typical of the testimonies we hear today. Many of the leading atheists in America will say that they were brought up in Bible-believing homes — church homes, in other words.

Losing Our Foundation

President Barack Obama, before he was elected, made a statement about our country. He made a similar statement in his first inaugural address, in his book *The Audacity of Hope*, and even to the president of Turkey. President Obama claimed:

> We are no longer a Christian nation, at least not just. We are also a Jewish nation and a Muslim nation and a Buddhist nation and a Hindu nation and a nation of non-believers.[12]

President Obama's statement rings true (but sadly he champions this change): whatever we once were as a nation, we are no longer. Most of the founding fathers — not all, but most of them — were Christians who built their thinking on the foundation of the authority of the Word of God. That is why Christian absolutes permeated the nation. But if we do not build our thinking on God's Word, there is only one other foundation — man's word. There are only two religions in the world. We can start with God's Word or man's word (that was really the battle that began in Genesis 3). When we build our thinking on man's word and abandon God's Word, then things will be as they were in the Book of Judges:

> In those days there was no king in Israel; everyone did what was right in his own eyes. (Judges 21:25)

We would expect to see moral relativism pervading the culture — and that is exactly what we are seeing today.

There has been a battle ever since Genesis 3. The battle is one of worldviews, between God's Word and man's word. Between moral absolutes and moral relativism. Christianity is based upon God's Word because God is the ultimate authority. But the culture has given up God's Word — and it has not just been given up in the culture but also in parts of the Church. Actually, we could say the spiritual state of this nation currently reflects the spiritual state of the Church!

---

12. President Barack Obama, "Obama: We Are No Longer a Christian Nation," YouTube, http://www.youtube.com/watch?v=tmC3IevZiik.

When we add man's word to God's Word, our starting point is no longer God's Word — it becomes man's word, because now fallible ideas have been inserted into the infallible Word. And that is what many churches are teaching the coming generations to do. If we remove the foundation of the absolute authority of the Bible, we will see the collapse of Christian morality and increasing moral relativism. I believe we are seeing much of that played out in our culture before our very eyes.

Here is how I explain it in my book *The Lie: Evolution/Millions of Years*:

On the left, we see the foundation of man's word. The castle built upon it represents the secular humanistic worldview. Out of this worldview come the social issues (gay marriage, abortion, and so on) we have been discussing. On the right, we see the foundation of God's Word, and built upon that is the castle representing the biblical worldview (doctrines, gospel, and so on). As part of the foundation of God's Word is attacked (by both the secularists and Christians who compromise God's Word with evolution/millions of years), the structure starts to collapse. On the Christian structure, the cannons are either aimed at each other, aimed nowhere, or aimed at the social issues.

Many might even agree to fight against such issues as abortion, gay marriage, sexual immorality, pornography, and so on. But if we attack only at the level of these issues and not the motivation for their popularity, we are not going to be successful. Even if the laws are changed in our society to outlaw abortion and gay marriage, the next generation, which is more secularized, will simply change the law again. One really cannot legislate morality — such is dependent on their hearts and minds. If the Church wants to be successful in changing society's attitudes toward abortion and gay marriage, it is going to have to fight the issue at a foundational level.

It is important to understand that these moral issues are really the symptoms — not the problem. This does not mean that one should not deal with these moral issues, but the battle cannot be fought only at the symptom level. Christians in the United States have spent millions of dollars trying to change the culture (deal with these social issues), but it has not worked. Why not? Because the Bible does not say to go into all the world and change the culture. The Bible gives a different command:

> And He said to them, "Go into all the world and preach the gospel to every creature." (Mark 16:15)

> Go therefore and make disciples of all the nations, baptizing them in the name of the Father and of the Son and of the Holy Spirit, teaching them to observe all things that I have commanded you; and lo, I am with you always, even to the end of the age. (Matthew 28:19–20)

The point is, it is hearts and minds that change a culture. Proverbs 23:7 says clearly of man, "For as he thinks in his heart, so is he."

The secularists certainly understand this. Because the majority of students from church homes are enrolled in the secular education system, these students are being indoctrinated by the world in secular ideas. Churches in the main have concentrated on trying to teach young people the message of Jesus and Christian doctrines — while the education system has been changing their thinking from starting with God's Word to making man's word the starting point. Over time, the student's worldview changes to a secular one, and the more this happens, the more such people cease being light and salt — and the culture changes.

Christians think the battle is with the culture and the moral issues — but ultimately the battle is a foundational one concerning God's Word versus man's word. The majority of Christian leaders, according to our experience and research, have in some way compromised Genesis with the evolutionary/millions-of-years beliefs of the day — thus contributing toward this change in the foundation of the next generation. This is also why many Christians do not understand the battle — because in reality, they have been helping the enemy.

Christians are fighting a war, but they do not know where to fight it or how to aim their guns. This is the real problem. If we want to see the structure of secular humanism collapse (which any thinking Christian must), then we have to re-aim the cannons at the foundation of man's word. It is only when the foundation is destroyed that the structure will collapse. In other words, we need to raise up generations who will stand boldly, unashamedly, and uncompromisingly on the authority of the Word of God. They need to know what they believe and why they believe what they do. They also need to be taught how to defend the Christian faith against the secular attacks of our day (taught general Bible and creation apologetics). This second "castle diagram" illustrates the solution.

The world has attacked God's Word, but that is nothing new. In fact, it started in Genesis 3. There have been many ways the Genesis 3 attack has manifested itself down through the ages. In the first century, there was a particular attack on Christ — on who He is and what He accomplished on the Cross. At the time of the Reformation, there was an attack on justification by faith.

But what is new is the Genesis 3 attack of our age (involving the teaching of evolution and/or millions of years) has particularly been an attack on the first 11 chapters of Genesis — and even much of the Church has succumbed to that attack. Some in the Church say they do not need the first 11 chapters of Genesis, but that they will keep the rest. But just like a building, if you do not have the whole foundation, the structure will collapse.

As the moral fiber of our culture begins to collapse, many say, "Woe is me! Look at the *problems* in the culture. Abortion! Same-sex marriage!" Church, we have to stop calling them the "problems." They are not the problems — they are the symptoms. They are the symptoms of a deeper problem. Think about it: we spend millions of dollars of Christians' money in America trying to change the culture. But has it worked? No. And why not? The Bible does not say, "Go into all the world and *change the culture*." It says to go into all the world and preach the gospel and make disciples (Matthew 28:19–20).

Scripture also reminds us that as a man thinks in his heart, so is he (Proverbs 23:7). Readers, hearts and minds change a culture. But what we have done as God's people is handed generations of children over to the world. Instead of capturing their hearts and minds and teaching them about origins and the history given in the Bible, young people in the Church have been taught to question God's Word in Genesis. They have been told to just trust in Jesus (whatever that means to them), without receiving any training in apologetics or any answers to their questions. But for many, parents and Christian leaders allowed the world to capture their hearts and minds and rebuild their thinking from a different foundation. Now we see a change in the worldview of the culture because there has been a change foundationally. The battle is not at the issue level — the battle is at the foundation level.

Imagine what would happen if Christians started to raise up generations of children who know what they believe and why they believe what they do. Imagine if the young people in our churches built their thinking on the Bible, knew how to answer the skeptical questions of this age, and could go out and preach with authority because they believed the authority from which it comes. Imagine generations who knew how to deal with the symptoms and the foundational problem. Church, we could change the world. God would change America, Australia, the United Kingdom, Europe — the world.

I believe the solution to America's problem (and, in fact, our Western nations) has to do with the Church. If the problems are in the Church, then the solution begins in the Church:

> . . . if My people who are called by My name will humble them-
> selves, and pray and seek My face, and turn from their wicked ways,
> then I will hear from heaven, and will forgive their sin and heal their
> land. (2 Chronicles 7:14)

I would suggest that unless Christian leaders and academics in this country who have compromised on God's Word (and the majority of them have) get on their knees before a holy God and repent of that sin of compromise, we are not going to see a change in this nation. The shepherds have led the sheep astray. Not all of the shepherds, but many of them. And without the foundation of the absolute authority of God's Word, the Church will be weak and will not produce much good fruit.

Chapter 2

 # Without Its Foundation, the Church Cannot Stand

One of the core topics I deal with in my talks is the necessity of Genesis for the Church. More specifically, I speak on the necessity of a Genesis that is understood in the way it was intended to be, as historical narrative teaching literal history. Of course, some people respond to this by saying, "What's the big deal? Believing in a young earth isn't necessary for salvation. It's a secondary issue."

What *is* the big deal? Why should Christians care about how Genesis, the age of the earth, and evolution are handled in their churches and Christian colleges?

To illustrate why the Church's view of Genesis does matter, I like to turn to Psalm 11:3: "If the foundations be destroyed, what can the righteous do?" (KJV) Think about it — if we were to remove the foundation from a building, what would happen? The building would collapse. Because nothing would be left to hold it up, the structure would become unstable and collapse.

That collapsing building represents the collapsing moral fabric of our Western nation, and the increasing moral relativism. Our foundation — the authority of the Word of God — has come under attack. In this day and age, the part of God's Word that is particularly being attacked is the foundational book of the Bible, the Book of Genesis.

I would argue that every major doctrine of the Church is founded (directly or indirectly) on the Book of Genesis. For example, when Jesus was asked about marriage, what did He say?

> And He answered and said to them, "Have you not read that He who made them at the beginning 'made them male and female,' and said, 'For this reason a man shall leave his father and mother and be joined to his wife, and the two shall become one flesh'? So then, they are no longer two but one flesh. Therefore what God has joined together, let not man separate." (Matthew 19:4–6; see also Mark 10:5–9)

Here, Jesus quotes from Genesis chapters 1 and 2 in the same passage where He talks about the doctrine of marriage. The doctrine of marriage is founded on the Book of Genesis.

It is not just the doctrine of marriage that is rooted in Genesis. Why did Jesus die on the Cross? Why is He called "the last Adam"? Why is there death in the world? Why is there sin? Why do we wear clothes? Why do we have a seven-day week? Why do we need a new heavens and a new earth? The answers to all these questions are found in Genesis 1–11.

During one conference at a church in Florida, I asked the audience, "Can you name one doctrine that ultimately — either directly or indirectly — is *not* founded on Genesis 1–11?" One of the attendees stood up and said, "What about the doctrine of election?" Well, I responded, "You wouldn't need such a doctrine if man hadn't fallen. Genesis 1–11."

Not a Salvation Issue

It is important to deal with the issue of whether belief in a literal Genesis is necessary to salvation. Sometimes when people write about us at Answers in Genesis, whether they are Christian or non-Christian, they will claim that we teach that a person cannot be a Christian unless he believes in six literal days and a young earth. I have never taught that in my life.

What does the Bible have to say about salvation? Does it say that if you confess with your mouth the Lord Jesus and believe in your heart God has raised Him from the dead *and believe in a young earth and six literal days* you will be saved? Does Scripture say that? No. Salvation is not conditional upon what you believe about the age of the earth; it is conditional on faith in Christ. Then some people will ask, "So you agree that a person can believe in millions of years and still be a Christian?" There are many Christians who believe in millions of years. A person can also believe in evolution and still be a Christian. There are many Christians who believe in evolution.

But should we say that our belief about the origin of the universe does not matter? No, because it does matter. If you are a Christian, then you believe that Jesus Christ bodily rose from the dead. But how do you know Jesus Christ bodily rose from the dead? You might respond by saying that there were witnesses and evidence. But how do you ultimately know you can trust these? How can you ultimately say you know for sure? Ultimately, it is because of the authority of the Word of God.

One well-known atheist claims that a man cannot rise from the dead, so should the Church believe what he says and reinterpret the Resurrection accordingly? No. But sadly, most of the Church does that with what evolutionary scientists say about our origins. Much of the Church chooses to believe in the supposed big bang, millions of years, and evolution, and reinterprets the Book of Genesis to make these false ideas fit in. Why shouldn't the Church do that with the Resurrection as well?

If I were able to question the congregations of many churches today, I imagine that most of them would affirm that Jesus walked on water, because the Bible says He did. They would affirm that Jesus miraculously fed thousands of people, because the Bible says He did. They would agree that the Israelites crossed the Red Sea and the Jordan by a miracle of God, because the Bible says so. They would also agree that the Israelites wandered in the desert for 40 years and that their clothes and shoes did not wear out, because the Bible says so. And they would affirm that a man named Jonah was swallowed by a great fish and after three days was spit out on the shore, because the Bible says so.

But would they affirm that God created the universe and everything in it in six, approximately 24-hour days, as the Book of Genesis recounts? Most of our churches, Bible colleges, and seminaries would say no. In fact, some of them would say God likely used the big bang to create the universe. Others would say He took millions of years to create the world. And still others are willing to say outright that God created man and the animals by using evolution. They take what secular scientists believe about origins as the truth and reinterpret Genesis. They tell their students and congregation members, "We don't really know how God created the universe — and it doesn't matter anyway. Or maybe God used evolution or created over millions of years. Who knows! Just trust in Jesus."

Much of this change in the Church began in the 1700s and 1800s in England, when the idea of millions of years, which came out of naturalism, was popularized to try to explain the fossil record without God. Some church leaders proposed a "gap" between Genesis 1:1 and 1:2, and decided to take the idea of millions of years and fit it in this supposed "gap." Some churches reinterpreted the days of creation and claim they represent millions of years, an idea known as the day-age theory. Some churches claimed the Flood was a local or regional event, rather than global. Then along came Charles Darwin. The Church took Darwin's ideas and claimed that God used evolution to create.

At this point, a door was unlocked. A door was unlocked in the Church that said we do not have to take God's Word as written from the beginning. It said that we can consider the word of man, who was not there, who does not know everything, who is fallible, and who knows nothing compared to what God knows, to be infallible. It said that we can make God's Word fallible, and that we can tell the next generation, "This part of the Bible doesn't matter. Just trust in Jesus."

Progressively, that door has opened farther and farther. Now we have generations of people who no longer believe the whole Bible. It is an issue of authority. It is not just about the age of the earth and creation or evolution. It is an issue of authority. Who is the authority, God or man? Isn't that the battle from Genesis 3? The Church is reaping the consequences of rampant compromise with the pagan religion of the age. Evolution and millions of years are attempts to explain life without God, and the Church is just like the Israelites, who took the pagan religion of the Canaanites and incorporated it into their own way of thinking. The main difference is that we call our pagan religion "science." Now, do not misunderstand me. Biblical creationists believe in science! But there is a big difference between observational science that builds our technology (and biblical creationists and evolutionists/old-earth creationists can all agree on this science) and historical science (which involves beliefs about the past — where biblical creationists and evolutionists/old-earth creationists disagree).

The Old-Earth View and Scripture

One of the key problems for the Christian who wants to embrace evolution-ary ideas is death. I speak at many conferences each year, so I travel quite a lot. Sometimes, on the way, we will see an accident. And sometimes, people die in those accidents. Is that God's fault? One of the questions I am asked the most is whether I believe in a loving God. How do we explain a loving God and all the death and suffering in the world?

I want to suggest something to my readers. If you are a Christian and you believe in millions of years, you have to take all the death, disease, and suffering, and all the horrible things happening in the world, and you have to attribute these to God. If you accept millions of years, then you have to say, "Isn't God good? He calls death, suffering, and disease very good." That is because (as I detail below) the idea of millions of years comes from the belief that most of the fossil layers (containing dead creatures with evidence of diseases) were laid down millions of years before man.

But if we interpret Genesis as literal history, in the same way Jesus inter-prets Genesis, as over and over in the New Testament Genesis is understood, then the conclusion is that the origin of death is Adam and Eve's sin (Gene-sis 3). Without original sin, death has always been here.

The Bible describes death as an enemy. It is an intrusion. If we do away with original sin, then man is not responsible for death — God is. We are just like Adam; we do not want to take the blame. In fact, I believe the first death was when God killed an animal and clothed Adam and Eve (Genesis 3:21). This was the origin of clothing. Otherwise, why do we wear clothes?

One of my favorite exhibits at the Creation Museum is of what we believe was the first blood sacrifice, covering Adam and Eve's sin. Remember what Scripture says:

> And according to the law almost all things are purified with blood, and without shedding of blood there is no remission. (Hebrews 9:22)

Man forfeited his life because he rebelled against God. So a life has to be given to pay the penalty for sin. If there was shedding of blood for millions of years before Adam sinned, what does the shedding of blood have to do with remission of sin?

If a Christian believes in millions of years, there are other issues to consider. The fossil record itself is a record of death and disease. There are many examples of animals eating each other within the fossil record. But how could that be in light of Genesis 1:30?

> "Also, to every beast of the earth, to every bird of the air, and to everything that creeps on the earth, in which there is life, I have given every green herb for food"; and it was so.

We were told here to eat fruit. Man was not told to eat meat until after the Flood, when God said, "Every moving thing that lives shall be food for you. I have given you all things, even as the green herbs" (Genesis 9:3). That is why today we can eat hamburgers, hot dogs, chicken, and many other types of meat — God allowed it after the Flood.

We find other types of evidence for death and suffering in the fossil record. There are dinosaur brain tumors, cancer, and arthritis — supposedly existing millions of years before man. Wait a minute — God said that everything he made was "very good." But if a Christian accepts millions of years, then he is saying that God called brain tumors "very good," because they would have existed millions of years before man. There are also thorns in the fossil record, which are said to be hundreds of millions of years old. The Bible, however, clearly says thorns came after the Curse (Genesis 3:18). Those two things cannot be true at the same time.

When the Christian who believes in millions of years stands on the edge of the Grand Canyon and looks at all the layers, he has to say that all the dead things in the rock layers were buried millions of years before sin. This view stands in opposition to what the Bible says. The Book of Genesis tells us that there was a global Flood. And if there was such a global Flood, we would expect to find billions of dead things buried in rock layers, laid down by water all over the earth. And that is exactly what we find. Yet in the secular world and even in some parts of the Church, the very evidence of the Flood is being used to convince people of the false idea of millions of years.

What Happened to the Starting Point?

One of the problems with both Christians and non-Christians in understanding the real nature of this battle of worldviews is that most people do not really understand where their worldview (the way they look at the world) comes from. They do not understand that because there are ultimately only two religions (or two starting points), there are ultimately two worldviews that can be built, based on the foundation or starting point they have to build their way of thinking about reality. The battle is not in essence one of worldviews, but one of starting points.

Sadly, many Christians do not think they have a starting point. The problem is the way the Bible is taught in some churches. The Bible is mostly not approached as a foundation to build a worldview to explain reality. Believers do not really understand that we have a revelation from the One who knows everything to give us a basis for understanding reality. Some churches leave topics like science to the school system, rather than helping their congregations understand the true nature of science — historical science and observational science, as we will discuss in detail later.

That is why people — especially kids — love the Creation Museum. At the museum, we take God's Word and walk visitors through the Seven C's of History: Creation, Corruption, Catastrophe, Confusion, Christ, Cross, and Consummation. And as guests walk through the museum, they learn from God's Word and through beautiful artistic recreations of scenes from Genesis that show why we see death, disease, and suffering in the world, and

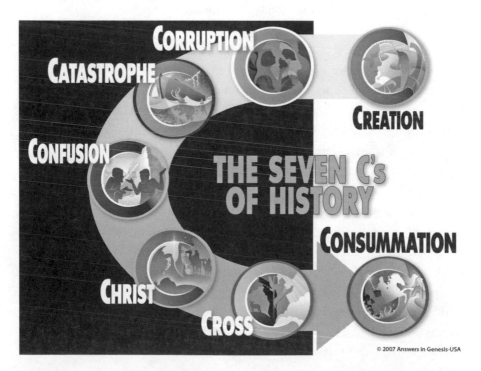

© 2007 Answers in Genesis-USA

why man needs a Redeemer. What we are teaching at the Creation Museum is that there is a revelation from God on which to build our worldview. Furthermore, we are saying that as creation scientists in the present study genetics, geology, and so on, their research confirms that what the Bible says is true. People (including even young kids) understand how the Christian worldview hangs together — and it is because of the foundation of history as revealed in the Bible.

However, because of the way the Bible is taught in most churches, the Christian worldview does not hang together. By and large, many people in the Church just look on various topics (marriage, dinosaurs, death, fossils, tragedies, and so on) as a somewhat disconnected group of items, instead of looking at how they are all encompassed by a worldview based on Scripture. So why this disconnect? Well, it is because of what really happened when the idea of millions of years was popularized in the late 1700s and early 1800s, when leaders in the Church chose to add millions of years to the Bible. Then with the rise of the idea of Darwinian evolution, many Church leaders chose also to add that to the Bible. With the popularization of the supposed big bang, many Church leaders then decided to add this into the Bible. All the while, these Church leaders are reinterpreting God's Word to fit millions of years, evolution, and the supposed big bang into Scripture.

As a result of this compromise, what eventually happened was that many churches were really disconnecting the Bible from the real world. The Church basically gave up the history in Genesis and began to emphasize spiritual and moral things. In essence, the Church leaders said, "You know what, kids, you can believe what you hear about millions of years and evolution from the TV or the public schools — as long as you trust in Jesus."

Thus, in reality, these leaders told the public school system, "You can teach our children the history of millions of years, evolution, and the big bang. We'll tell them about Jesus." And so people have the idea today that a church should deal only with spiritual and moral issues, and not with earthly or scientific matters. They dismiss the fact that the Bible is a book of history (really, a book of historical science). It is real history, not just a book of stories. The Bible is a revelation to us from the One who knows everything, and it enables us to have the right foundation on which we can build proper thinking and understand reality correctly. Because the Church mostly disconnected the Bible's history from the Christian worldview, this opened the door for the secular world to teach generations its false history of evolution and millions of years, and eventually to build a secular worldview, thus capturing the hearts and minds of the generation.

Another mistake Christians make is trying to argue from so-called "neutral" ground (as discussed in the previous chapter), without the Bible. People have come to me and said, "I've been talking to a friend, and he doesn't believe the Bible. Can you give me some evidence that Christianity is true without using the Bible?" This is an issue we have to think about in terms of starting points. If a Christian gives up his starting point — the Bible — then there is only one other starting point left: man's word. When a Christian gives up the Bible, then who has won the debate? The other side has. Many people have heard of Dinesh D'Souza. D'Souza is the former president of The King's College and a well-known author and commentator. He has done much writing on his particular brand of apologetics, and he has debated atheists. But D'Souza's claim to fame is that he would debate people without using the Bible. As one news report put it, "D'Souza has gained national notoriety for winning debates against fierce atheists by arming himself with science and philosophy, not scripture, to make the most effective case for today's Christians."[1]

How is an argument that does not use the Bible the "most effective" argument for Christianity? It isn't. God has given us the best case for Christianity in His Word. And Christ is clear about the issue of where we stand — there is no neutral ground:

> He who is not with Me is against Me, and he who does not gather with Me scatters. (Luke 11:23)

What's more, if we do not walk in light, then what do we walk in? Darkness (see Acts 26:18). I remember when Dinesh D'Souza debated Michael Shermer, a founder of *Skeptic* magazine and a leader of the humanist movement in America. The debate was held at the National Religious Broadcasters convention in 2008. Because Michael Shermer is an atheist, the first thing that happened was D'Souza stated that when debating an atheist such as Michael Shermer, who does not believe the Bible, that the Bible cannot be used in the debate. At that point, I may as well have left, because the secular humanist had already won.

---

1. "The Great God Debate: Making a Case for Christianity," Christian News Wire, http://www.christiannewswire.com/news/402955817.html.

But instead I stayed for about 15 minutes. As they started to present their cases, I did not know what the difference was between what D'Souza believed and what Shermer believed, because they both believed in evolution. They believed in the big bang and in millions of years — and the Bible was not mentioned. The one difference I could gather was that D'Souza believed in some sort of god, but I was not sure what god because he did not tell his audience.

Readers, that is how many Christians argue in today's world, and we wonder why we are not successful. When we give up our starting point, we have already lost the battle because we suddenly have no foundation. The only foundation that is left is man's word — man's fallible word. And remember this: faith comes by hearing and hearing by what? The Word of God (Romans 10:17).

D'Souza is not the only person to try to defend Christianity without the Bible. I often quote from Romans 1 in my talks, where the Apostle Paul explains that God has revealed Himself to man through general revelation:

> For the wrath of God is revealed from heaven against all ungodliness and unrighteousness of men, who suppress the truth in unrighteousness, because what may be known of God is manifest in them, for God has shown it to them. For since the creation of the world His invisible attributes are clearly seen, being understood by the things that are made, even His eternal power and Godhead, so that they are without excuse. (Romans 1:18–20)

Does Romans 10 conflict with Romans 1? Of course not. Romans 1 explains that it is obvious from the evidence that there is a God. (But it is not saying we can find out about our origins or the purpose and meaning of life from the creation.) So does that provide support for the idea that we do not have to use the Bible when giving a defense of our faith? I would suggest that it does not.

The Intelligent Design Movement

The idea of taking supposed neutral ground and arguing without using the Bible has manifested itself in many forms. For instance, consider the Intelligent Design movement. There are many Christians who think that the answer to the problem of creation in schools is to take a supposedly neutral position. We are not allowed to talk about God and the Bible, so that is where Intelligent Design comes in. The idea is that those teaching Intelligent Design are somehow neutral. They can talk about Intelligent Design arguments and solutions, and many people think that what the Intelligent Design movement is doing is something new. But Intelligent Design arguments are not new — Christians have been using them throughout the ages. What is "new" in a sense is that the Intelligent Design movement took God and His Word out of the argument. Thus they claim they are being neutral. However, this assumes man is "neutral," but he is not. It also assumes there is a "neutral" position — but as we have stated and is clear from the Bible, that is not so either.

When biblical creationists explain God's intricate design of DNA, *that* is an intelligent design argument. When we talk about how God has structured the eye, *that* is another intelligent design argument. Now while biblical creationists teach God's design in creation and how it proclaims the glory of the God of the Bible, many who teach Intelligent Design have taken God out of the equation and do not identify who the Designer is! It is an unnamed designer.

That is an incredible problem. We need to understand that the Intelligent Design movement is not a Christian movement. There are many Christians in the movement, but there are also many non-Christians, too. It is perceived as neutral because they do not talk about God or religion. But what did Christ say in Luke 11:23? If you are not for Christ, you are against Him. There is no neutral position. You are either walking in light or darkness. I would submit that the Intelligent Design movement potentially is a very dangerous movement for the Church.

Why do I believe that? If I understand Scripture correctly, the condition of man is very clear:

> The heart is deceitful above all things, and desperately wicked; who can know it? (Jeremiah 17:9)

> As it is written: "There is none righteous, no, not one; there is none who understands; there is none who seeks after God." (Romans 3:10–11)

The point is that man is *not* neutral. Many times, Christians seem to think that non-Christians are neutral. They claim that we are the biased ones because we believe in God. Unbelievers do not, so they are neutral. But that is simply not true.

From conception, our hearts are against God. The Psalmist wrote, "Behold, I was brought forth in iniquity, and in sin my mother conceived me" (Psalm 51:5). That is our sin nature. We do not want the true God. So what does that mean? It means that if we convince people that there is an intelligent Designer, but do not direct them to the Word of God, we could be opening their hearts to go after the Muslim god, a Hindu concept of god, a New Age god, or all sorts of other false gods because they in their sin natures do not want the true God. Remember — it is God's Word that convicts. It is God's Word that is "sharper than any two-edged sword" (Hebrews 4:12).

A Beautiful World?

As Romans tells us, "So then faith comes by hearing, and hearing by the word of God." There is another aspect to this that is so important. Some Christians tell people, "Just look at the creation. Can't you see there's a God?" How many times do we see some of our Sunday school literature and even children's books that tell kids to look at this "beautiful" world? They are taught that we can tell there is a God by looking at all the beauty out there. But I have news for people who teach this — it is *not* a completely beautiful world. In fact, our world is in many ways a very ugly world. In the beginning, it was all beauty — it was "very good" — but now it is marred by sin and the Curse.

Believers sometimes give non-Christians the wrong idea when they try to argue for the existence of God based on the "beauty" of the world. In reality, what do we see all around us? People are dying from disease or in tragic shootings; people are starving to death; tsunamis and earthquakes are claiming numerous lives; terrorists are bombing populated areas to kill people. It is only when we start with the history revealed to us in God's Word that we understand that this is a fallen world — *not* a world of nothing but beauty — because of sin. It is a groaning world because of sin as described in Romans 8:22:

> For we know that the whole creation groans and labors with birth pangs together until now.

Furthermore, do we get the gospel by looking at a tree? Do we get the gospel by looking at rocks? No, we get the gospel from Scripture. The Apostle Paul exhorts us to share the gospel:

> How then shall they call on Him in whom they have not believed? And how shall they believe in Him of whom they have not heard? And how shall they hear without a preacher? . . . So then faith comes by hearing, and hearing by the word of God. (Romans 10:14, 17)

That is where the gospel comes from — the Word of God. In light of this truth, how can we live our lives believing that we do not need to use the Word of God to reach people for Christ? If we are not with Christ, we are against Him. If do not gather, then we scatter. Friendship with the world is war with God.

An Uncertain Sound Rings Through the Church

The Bible says that men suppress the truth in unrighteousness (Romans 1:18) and that the carnal man is at war with God (Romans 8:7). Biblically speaking, there is no neutral position, despite what people believe. I would suggest that this is one of the reasons why we have not been very successful in fighting same-sex marriage and abortion, because the Church has been indoctrinated to accept that if believers talk about the Bible in a courtroom, they will lose. The attorneys will tell us we cannot use the Bible, or we will lose. But this attitude does not honor God's Word.

Is the Church prepared to honor God's Word or to be indoctrinated into this false idea of neutrality? Will we fight using the weapon God gave us — the Bible — or will we throw down our swords and surrender because of a belief in neutrality? It is foolish to believe that by leaving the Bible out of it, we are somehow going to come over onto neutral ground. In doing so, we are actually coming over onto the secularists' ground — and then they have already won.

A couple of years ago in Australia, a Christian named Steve Fielding, who was at that time a member of parliament, appeared on national TV. He was on a panel that included famed atheist Richard Dawkins. What an opportunity Fielding had to witness to the people of Australia, on one of the most popular television programs in Australia. But instead, he tried to be neutral. Dawkins asked Fielding, "Do you believe the world is less than 10,000 years old?" and Fielding responded:

Look, I think that there are a lot of questions in this area and I think people will come to their own conclusions. I don't want to force people into one way or the other. . . . Look, I think that the science today will discover more and more but I think that most Australians come to a view. They either believe that we evolved or we came from creation and I think that, you know, people — you can believe whatever they like on that issue. I'm not trying to force that issue onto anyone.[2]

Did Fielding's response offer a defense using the Bible? No, it did not. In fact, he did not even really answer the question! The moderator asked Fielding, "So where did human beings come from?" And Fielding, placing his hands on Dawkins's arm, replied, "Well, you may well ask this guy. He's got firm views on that perspective from there."[3] So according to this Christian, the atheist has "firm views" — but the Christian does not?

This is sad. But what's worse than the way that Fielding acts here is the way I see Christians acting in America and around the world. The first time I heard this exchange, a verse of Scripture came to mind:

For if the trumpet makes an uncertain sound, who will prepare for battle? (1 Corinthians 14:8)

Readers, many in the Church are making an uncertain sound concerning Genesis 1–11, which could very well lead to an uncertain sound about Scripture as a whole. If believers are willing to deny God's clear Word in Genesis, why should they believe God's Word concerning the miracle of the Resurrection or the Virgin Birth?

The mixture of millions of years and evolution with Scripture stems from secular ideas and philosophies. If we were to ask an evolutionist what he believes about the origin of the universe, he would likely tell us that there was a big bang 14 billion years ago, that 4.5 billion years ago there was a hot molten blob that formed into the earth, and that the solar system then formed. He would tell you that billions of years ago life formed in the oceans and then as life came out on land, one kind of animal changed into

2. Steve Fielding and Richard Dawkins, interview by Tony Jones, "God, Science, and Sanity," *Q&A: Adventures in Democracy*, ABC1 (Australia), March 8, 2010, http://www.abc.net.au/tv/qanda/txt/s2831712.htm.

3. Ibid.

another, resulting in the many species we see today. He might even show you an evolutionary tree, and tell you that ape-like creatures eventually became human, that writing was invented in the course of human evolution, and that man learned to grunt before he learned to speak.

All of this is considered dogmatic, evolutionary fact — and that is how an evolutionist would treat it in his explanation. And think about it: the public school science texts and most of the teachers, the university textbook and professors, many secular television programs and evolutionary scientists all give the same basic message concerning origins. They are unified. They give their "certain sound."

But if we were to ask the average Christian leader or pastor, or the average Christian academic or Christian college professor in America, or even just the average Christian, what they believe when it comes to the origin of the universe, they are not unified — they do not give a "certain sound." Church leaders, church academics, and the average churchgoing person will give a variety of positions on Genesis — theistic evolution, progressive creation, gap theory, day-age theory, cosmic temple view, and many others. Some will say they do not believe in a literal Adam or Eve or a literal Fall, or that Noah's Flood was just local, and so on. Others will give all sorts of combinations of ideas. And the reason there are so many different views is because these people are trying to fit man's ideas about origins into the Bible. And every one of these compromise positions tries in some way to fit in the supposed millions of years.

The reason there can be so many different views of Genesis to fit in the supposed millions of years is because none of them work! The only view that makes sense is what Genesis clearly states.

There is an uncertain sound that permeates through much of the Church. It is the secularists who are saying, "We know what we believe." The Christians are saying, "Well, we don't know, but we'll accept what you believe and try to fit it in the Bible somehow." That is what is happening, and we wonder why we have a problem.

When you think about it, the secularists by and large are unified around man's beliefs about origins. The Christians want unity around man's beliefs, which is why they are not unified on what God's Word says. We need to be unified on God's Word and take it in its natural sense as it is meant to be taken, and then judge man's fallible ideas accordingly.

Will the Church Stand on the Authority of God's Word?

As believers, we need to be in the world standing uncompromisingly, boldly, and unashamedly on the authority of the Word of God. One of the reasons why many Christians are not really interested in standing on God's Word is that they are not equipped to answer the skeptical questions of our age. As soon as believers stand up and say, "Because the Bible is true, that is why same-sex marriage is wrong. Because the Bible is true, abortion is wrong," they are asked how they know the Bible is true. Who wrote the Bible? What about all the evidence that supposedly contradicts the Bible? What about science — doesn't it contradict the Bible? Most Christians are not prepared to answer. They do not know how to answer. And so they shrink back or just do not get involved and let the world continue on its destructive Christianity attack course. That is why I believe the Lord has raised up ministries like Answers in Genesis. Apologetic ministries equip believers with answers to many of the skeptical questions of our day.

Another problem is that many Christians do not really know or understand what they believe. They do not understand that the Bible is supposed to be their starting point. As noted above, faith comes by hearing, and hearing by the Word of God. The Word of God is living and powerful, and sharper than a two-edged sword. It is God's Word that goes forth from His mouth and shall not return unto Him void (Isaiah 55:11).

When people come up to me and ask me questions, but then ask me to give up the Bible in my responses, I have a problem with that. In fact, the whole idea of asking the Christian to give up the Bible while also defending Christianity is backward. We should be the ones saying, "Come on, what are your questions? Come on, what are they? I'm not giving up God's Word. What's your problem?" But many believers do not want to do that because they are not equipped to answer the questions of skeptics. Many Christians do not understand that the Bible is their starting point, so they do not think it matters to not use the Bible. And they falsely believe they can be neutral by not using the Bible. In reality, they are giving up their sword and surrendering to the enemy.

Unfortunately, what is happening today is that many are going out and saying, "Trust in Jesus. We don't trust the Book of Genesis; it's not true or it doesn't matter. How did Noah get all those animals on the Ark anyway? Science has disproved Genesis as literal history. But don't worry about that — just trust in Jesus." And we wonder why we are not effective. The other problem the Church has is that many believers are not using the Bible. For example, in dealing with abortion or same-sex marriage in court, we are not allowed to use the Bible, because otherwise we are imposing our religion on the culture. But when believers give in to the idea that they can stand on supposedly neutral ground and give up the Bible, they have just allowed the non-Christians to impose their own religion on the culture — and on believers as well.

Why is it mainly atheists who threaten lawsuits regarding the teaching of creation in public schools, or against Christian symbols like crosses, or against Nativity scenes or the Ten Commandments in public places? It is because they want to impose their anti-God religion on the culture. So when crosses are removed from public places, or students are not allowed to pray in schools, the situation is not neutral — now Christianity has been forced out and atheism has been imposed on the culture. It is a clash of two worldviews because it is a clash of two starting points — God's Word versus man's word.

The point is that if you as Christians are equipped to defend the Christian faith against the attacks of our age, and if you understand the Genesis 3 attack of our day, then you will be ready for these attacks when they occur. Also, Christians need to understand they should never give up their starting point of God's Word — that is surrendering to the enemy. This is why the Answers in Genesis ministry publishes and sells apologetics resources — they are really "weapons" to equip believers for the Genesis 3 attack of our day. What's more, Christians must study God's Word. If you want to be equipped to be able to answer the skeptical questions of our day, study your Bible and then go out and do your best — never giving up your starting point, and always standing on the authority of God's Word. The Church should never be ashamed of that and should do its best to convince people of the truth of the Bible. Christians should powerfully confute, and argue, pointing people to the Word of God and the gospel of Jesus Christ, while answering the questions thrown at them. Then we can stand back and say, "Holy Spirit, bring the harvest."

Chapter 3

 What Is
Science?

For years, evolutionists have used a clever tactic to convince people that evolutionary ideas are supposedly proven — they have equivocated on the word *science*. Before we can address the specific types of eisegesis going on in the Church, we need to answer an incredibly important question: What is science? Now, many people, especially theistic evolutionists (and others who hold compromise positions on Genesis, such as progressive creation, the framework hypothesis, and so on) and secularists, talk about science and the Bible. And typically they claim that there is a conflict between science and the Bible. Secularists say that if someone accepts what the Bible says about the history of the universe, he is rejecting science. Theistic evolutionists, on the other hand, argue that they can show people how to mix science and the Bible by accepting evolutionary ideas. Others claim they can fit science into the Bible by adding millions of years. But the problem with these claims is that they have conflated two different types of science: operational (or observational) science and historical (or origins) science.

This confusion of operational and historical science is even seen on television shows. For instance, I was once watching one of those forensic crime shows that are prolific on TV these days. On this particular fictional crime show, the detective interrogates a man who they say just happens to own the largest creation museum in the United States. This was clearly a reference to the real Creation Museum, owned by Answers in Genesis, which has gained some notoriety over the years.

In the course of the episode, the writers marginalized Christianity and treated Christians very poorly. During the detective's interview with the creation museum's owner, the writers portray the owner as a "Bible basher" — meaning that Christians only answer with the Bible and that they do not have evidence for their beliefs. Furthermore, the characters in the episode actually talk about how these Christians destroy evidence.

The idea that many secularists present is that there is an abundance of evidence that contradicts biblical creation, and that creationists do not have evidence and do not engage with evidence. But here is the problem with this viewpoint: when it comes to the topic of origins, everybody has the *same* evidence! They have the *same* facts, because we all live in the same universe. The difference is in how people interpret those facts in relation to the past — analogous in a sense to forensic scientists interpreting the same evidence left at a murder scene but giving different scenarios of how they think the murder occurred, as we will discuss further on.

Understanding Science and Evidence

As I said above, a common tactic among secularists is to convince people that if they reject evolutionary ideas, they are rejecting "science." But another tactic that is gaining traction among secularists is to claim that parents who teach their children biblical creation are committing a form of "child abuse." One example of this is from an interview with Lawrence Krauss, an atheist and professor of physics at Arizona State University:

> If you think about that, somehow saying that while anything goes, we shouldn't offend religious beliefs by requiring kids to know, to understand reality. That's child abuse. And if you think about it, teaching kids or allowing the notion that the earth is six thousand years old to be promulgated in schools is like teaching kids that the distance across the United States is seventeen feet. That's how big an error it is.[1]

The things that Krauss and other atheistic evolutionists can say and get away with are absolutely incredible. People can measure the distance across the

---

1. Lawrence Krauss, "Teaching Creationism Is Child Abuse," Big Think (YouTube), http://www.youtube.com/watch?v=UTedvV6oZjo.

United States. It may not be an easy task, but it can be done, and in fact has been accomplished to a high degree of accuracy. However, no one can simply "measure" the age of the earth using our five senses in the present. The assumptions that underlie dating methods are fallible, full of problems, and involve extrapolating into the past where we cannot directly observe and repeatedly test the evidence. What Krauss and others are saying about evolution, millions of years, and biblical creation illustrates the main issue — people do not understand evidence and the nature of science.

An important passage of Scripture that relates to this topic is Romans 1:20, where the Apostle Paul tells us that God has made Himself plain to man:

> For since the creation of the world His invisible attributes are clearly seen, being understood by the things that are made, even His eternal power and Godhead, so that they are without excuse . . .

Even in nature, man can clearly see God's attributes. This verse does not give an indication that nature will provide us a detailed account of origins — only that if someone does not believe in God, they are without excuse. And having seen evidence for God in nature, if man chooses not to believe, he is willfully ignorant. Another verse that I want to highlight also comes from Romans:

> So then faith comes by hearing, and hearing by the word of God. (Romans 10:17)

It is important to understand how the Bible and evidence relate. Our faith is rooted in the fact that God has revealed Himself to us through general revelation (Romans 1:20) and in His Word (Romans 10:17). To place our faith in something or someone indicates that the person is reliable. We can have faith in God because He has proven Himself faithful — He never fails.

The issue of origins (historical science) is very different from the observational science used to build a car, to send a spaceship to Mars, or to build computers. The issue of origins deals with the past — when we were not there to witness it. The thing is, we are here in the present — hopefully we're all in the present! — and we can, for example, look at the stars. But what happened in the past (when we were not there) to put the stars in space?

Furthermore, what happened in the past to put people on earth? What happened in the past to put animals on earth? What about the dinosaurs?

What happened in the past that caused there to be dinosaurs to roam the earth? Why is there death in the world? Why do we see a world with life and death and love and hate all at the same time? How do we explain fossils?

What about the Grand Canyon? We were not there to see the Grand Canyon form. We were not there to see the layers being laid down. What about all the different species of dogs? How did they come about? How do we explain the so-called "races" of people? Why is it the Australian aborigines have stories that sound like Genesis in many ways, stories about a global flood, a forbidden tree, and a woman made while man was asleep? How do we understand these things? How do we connect the past to the present?

I like to explain it this way. It is like being a forensic scientist. If there has been a murder, a forensic scientist will be called in. Now, he has the evidence that is present at the scene, but here is the trouble: the forensic scientist was not there to see the murder committed. So what he has to do is try to reconstruct the crime. And you know what would really help? A witness. Of course, he has to be able to trust the witness. What if the witness does not tell the truth? What if the witness did not see everything that occurred, and thus missed a vital piece of information that had great bearing on understanding what actually happened?

Forensic scientists have to do their best using circumstantial (limited) evidence. But there is a problem with that. Have you ever watched a mystery show, such as Sherlock Holmes? The plots typically have a common point: halfway through the episode, viewers know who committed the crime. It was the butler! Three quarters of the way through, it is even more obvious that the butler did it. And then, just before the end of the movie, Sherlock Holmes, or whoever the detective is, gathers all the people in the room and goes around one at a time. Viewers say, "It's obvious the butler did it! I was right, the butler did it." And then suddenly, a new piece of evidence that had been withheld throughout the whole episode is revealed — the butler did not do it after all. It was somebody viewers completely did not suspect. Makes one frustrated, doesn't it?

This highlights the problem at hand. I like to say it this way: "No matter how much we know, there is an infinite amount more to know. And that means that no matter how much we know, we do not know how much more there is to know! Which means that no matter how much we know, we do not know how much we do know or do not know in relation to whatever there is to know, whatever that is, which means we just do not know much at all, do we?"

In the Book of Job, we see this problem presented in the questions God asks Job:

> Where were you when I laid the foundations of the earth? Tell Me, if you have understanding. (Job 38:4)

What does God do to Job here? He basically asks Job, do you know this or do you know that? Job wanted to argue with God but — to paraphrase it — after God questions Job about how much he really knows, Job falls down in dust and ashes and basically says, "Lord, I hardly know anything. You know everything."

The problem is, if we do not have access to someone who has all information, we could come to the wrong conclusion about things, just like in a murder mystery. In fact, we see this happening before our very eyes today. How many times have we seen someone jailed for a crime, and then years later scientists say they are now able to analyze DNA from the crime scene and the supposed criminal (something they could not do previously) and determined that this person actually was innocent? They realized that somebody else committed the crime, all because they found a little piece of evidence that they did not have before.

Many times, people have come up to me after I have given a talk and asked, "I know what you're saying about the Bible, six days, and everything else, but how can you believe in a young universe? Surely it takes light millions of years to get from the farthest star, so how do you explain that?" I then respond, "Let me ask you a question: do you know everything there is to know about light? Do you know everything there is to know about space? Is it possible that there's something we don't know about light or space that could totally change our conclusion?"

And really when it comes to the speed of light issue, one of the things that we need to understand is that the secularists have the same problem that Christians do, because they can only get light about halfway across the universe with their big-bang belief system. As a result, they have to come up with inflation theories, super inflation theories, and all sorts of ideas to try to get that light out there. There are some things that we just do not have definitive answers for because we do not have all knowledge — but that is no reason to doubt God's Word! However, biblical creation scientists have come up with some interesting suggestions to help give understanding to this issue.[2]

Many times I wonder why it is that we can see so clearly what the Bible says, but when somebody — a fallible human who was not there, who does not know everything, and does not have access to all information — presents an idea that contradicts the Bible, we are so quick to believe what this person says (I believe this is because our sin nature makes us biased against God's Word), and to say, "We can't trust what the Bible states here — we have to reinterpret it."

Why do we do that? I would suggest that it is because we would rather trust man than trust God — that is the basic sin nature we inherited from Adam. I praise the Lord that my father taught me that when it comes to man's word versus God's Word — that when something contradicts the Bible — to make sure I read the Bible carefully and interpret it in the way it was meant to be interpreted, whether it is historical narrative, or a parable, or speaking with phenomenological language, and so on. But if man's word contradicts God's Word, then there is something wrong with what man is saying — even if we do not know what it is. And we are not going to have all the answers. In fact, we will never have all the answers, because if we did, we would be God. We should never knowingly doubt or change God's infallible Word to try to fit in man's fallible understanding of things.

Do you know what it means when Scripture says that God is infinite in knowledge and wisdom compared to us? Psalm 8:4 says, "What is man that You are mindful of him, and the son of man that You visit him?" And talking about Jesus Christ, we read, "in whom are hidden all the treasures of wisdom and knowledge" (Colossians 2:3).

The point is this: The only way we could ever have the ability to build a worldview, to come to the right conclusion about things, is if we start with someone who knows everything, who does not lie, and who has revealed to us what we need to know.

Does anyone have access to someone like that? What does God's Word claim to be? It claims to be the Word of One who knows everything, who has always been there, and who does not lie. *That* is the only starting point for building a worldview. *That* is the starting point that gives us the ability to interpret evidence correctly. If we do not start with God's Word, then

---

2. Dr. Danny Faulkner and Bodie Hodge, "What about Distant Starlight Models?" in *The New Answers Book 4*, Ken Ham, gen. ed. (Green Forest, AR: Master Books, 2013), p. 255–264.

ultimately there is only one other starting point — man's word. I often say that there are only two religions in the world, going back to Genesis 3: We either trust God, or we become our own god (Genesis 3:5). There are only two starting points: God's Word or man's word.

Time and Death

The late Carl Sagan, a well-known cosmologist, once wrote something that really sums up the evolutionary/millions of years philosophy:

> The cosmos is all that is or ever was or ever will be.[3]

That is the philosophy that permeates our public education system, too. Even though there may be some Christian teachers who act as missionaries in the system, public schools have mostly thrown God and the Bible out. Instead, students are taught evolutionary history, which claims that 15 billion years ago there was supposedly a big bang, 10 billion years ago the stars came to be, 5 billion years ago the sun formed, and 4.5 billion years ago a molten earth appeared. And how do evolutionary scientists know all of this? From digital photographs? Of course not! Do you understand the problem? These scientists were not there — they did not take actual photographs. This is their story (and that is all it is — a man-made story) to supposedly explain what happened in the past to bring the present into being.

Often, skeptical people have challenged me, asking, "Why couldn't God have used the big bang to create the universe?" The answer is simple. God was there, and those who promote the big-bang idea were not! And God did not use the big bang, because that is not what His Word says.

The idea of the big bang is scientifically untenable anyway, as many creation scientists have explained in articles on the Answers in Genesis website (AnswersInGenesis.org), and in technical papers and books.

The story of evolution continues, teaching that around 3.5 billion years ago the first oceans supposedly formed. Then somehow, matter is able to produce an information system and a language system to produce life. Then over millions of years one kind of animal supposedly changes into another.

A man named Charles Darwin noticed that animals change — and by the way, he was correct, animals do change. Dogs change. They change into dogs. Cats change. They change into cats. But Darwin said that, given

---

3. Carl Sagan, *Cosmos* (New York: Random House, 1980), p. 4.

enough time, these little changes that are observed are part of a mechanism that supposedly would see one kind of creature change into a totally different kind (e.g., reptiles supposedly changed into birds). That is why long ages are so important to secularists. They have to have *time*. The late George Wald, an American scientist and Nobel laureate, confirmed the evolutionists' need for long ages in an article:

> Time is in fact the hero of the plot. The time with which we have to deal is of the order of two billion years. What we regard as impossible on the basis of human experience is meaningless here. Given so much time, the "impossible" becomes possible, the possible probable, and the probable virtually certain. One has only to wait: time itself performs miracles.[4]

Evolutionary ideas teach people that, given enough time, a "miracle" will happen — one kind of animal will change into another! Evolutionists will believe this, but they look at the miraculous creation account of Genesis with derision. By the way, even with all the time in the world, the sort of changes Darwin proposed (one kind evolving into a totally different kind) simply will not (and cannot) happen. But the average person has been brainwashed into thinking, *Oh, well, given all that time, it could happen. Supposedly ape-like creatures could have turned into people.* The evolutionary view of time and change is also a process of death, bloodshed, disease, and suffering over millions of years.

Carl Sagan once said, "The secrets of evolution are time and death."[5] Time and death. The evolutionary/millions-of-years view conflicts with God's Word. The Bible puts sin and death together, not time and death.

According to the secularists, layers like those in the Grand Canyon were laid down over millions of years. They have constructed what they call a geologic time scale, where they place what they call the oldest layers on the bottom and the youngest layers on the top. In most instances, biblical creationists would agree that the oldest layers are on the bottom and the youngest are on the top. But biblical creationists would say that, because of the event of Noah's Flood around 4,300 years ago, those top layers are younger by maybe a few months, not millions of years. These are different interpretations of the same evidence.

---

4. George Wald, "The Origin of Life," *Scientific American* (August 1954).
5. Carl Sagan, *Symphony of Science*, video 4, "The Unbroken Thread"; Carl Sagan, *Cosmos* (New York: Random House, 1980), p. 3.

Purpose and Meaning in Evolutionary Philosophy

Now it is also important to understand that one's worldview not only determines how a person will interpret the evidence available to us, but it also defines how we look at purpose and meaning in life. For Christians, our purpose and meaning is found in Jesus Christ. The Apostle Paul wrote about the believer's identity in Christ in the Book of Romans:

> For you did not receive the spirit of bondage again to fear, but you received the Spirit of adoption by whom we cry out, "Abba, Father." The Spirit Himself bears witness with our spirit that we are children of God. (Romans 8:15–16)

If a person has believed the gospel of Jesus Christ, that He is Lord and was raised from the dead, he is a child of God. And Christians live their lives with the purpose of sharing the gospel and living lives that are pleasing to God. When we die, we know that we will join the Father in heaven.

So what does the secularist have to say about purpose and meaning? Such people actually have a statement on "purpose" and "meaning." Richard Dawkins was asked about this topic, and he gave a very telling answer:

> Well, the answer to the question of what's going to happen when we die depends on whether we're buried, cremated or give our bodies to science. . . . The brain is what we do our thinking with. The brain is going to rot. That is all there is to it.[6]

That's it. We are going to rot. Doesn't that make atheism appealing? If you are an atheist, when you die, you will not know you ever existed. When people who knew you die, they will not know they existed, and you will not know they existed — and eventually everything dies. The whole universe dies. So ultimately no one will know anything ever was. The atheistic worldview lacks purpose and meaning

And yet, this is the message that is being given in the secular education systems of the world today. There is no God. Everything happens by natural process. Man has no purpose or meaning, so become an atheist. No wonder coming generations have such a sense of meaninglessness and purposelessness, and resort to drugs, sex, suicide, and so on. It's so sad.

---

6. Richard Dawkins, interview by Tony Jones, "Religion and Atheism," *Q&A: Adventures in Democracy*, April 9, 2012, http://www.abc.net.au/tv/qanda/txt/s3469101.htm.

The Bible is so very different. It starts, "In the beginning God created . . ." (Genesis 1:1). The Bible gives us a very specific history — the same history visitors walk through at the Creation Museum — that God created a perfect world. He created everything in six days and rested for one. (By the way, that is why we have a seven-day week.) Because it was a perfect world, there was no death of creatures with a life spirit (the word *nephesh* is used for such in Genesis). All the animals and man were vegetarian (Genesis 1:29–30). In fact, there was no death, bloodshed, diseases, or suffering (of animals or humans) before sin. But when the first man Adam rebelled against God, sin and death (physical and spiritual) entered the world. That is why the Bible calls death an "enemy" (1 Corinthians 15:26).

There could not have been billions of dead things in the fossil record (which contains numerous examples of animals having eaten other animals, diseases like brain tumors/cancer, and thorns) supposedly millions of years before Adam sinned. But if there really was a global Flood, we would expect to find billions of dead things buried in rock layers laid down by water all over the earth. And that is exactly what we find. The Bible says there was a time after the Flood when man rebelled against God again. At the Tower of Babel, He confused the people's languages and caused them to split up and form different people groups. This explains why we have distinct cultural groups today, yet all humans belong to one race.

Even the researchers on the Human Genome Project determined when they mapped the human genome that there is only one race. J. Craig Venter, head of the Celera Genomics Corporation, made this pronouncement in 2000:

> Dr. Venter and scientists at the National Institutes of Health recently announced that they had put together a draft of the entire sequence of the human genome, and the researchers had unanimously declared, there is only one race — the human race.[7]

For some, this is a startling revelation: there is only one race. That would explain why the Australian aborigines and other cultures around the world have flood legends that sound similar to that in the Book of Genesis, because they have handed them down from Noah. These cultures changed

---

7. Natalie Angier, "Do Races Differ? Not Really, DNA Shows," *New York Times*, http://partners.nytimes.com/library/national/science/082200sci-genetics-race.html.

the accounts, but the real record of history God has preserved in the Bible. God's Word also tells us that because man is fallen, God's Son, Jesus Christ, stepped into history to live a perfect life, die on the Cross, and be raised from the dead:

> For God so loved the world that He gave His only begotten Son, that whoever believes in Him should not perish but have everlasting life. (John 3:16)

And the Apostle Paul wrote that "if you confess with your mouth the Lord Jesus and believe in your heart that God has raised Him from the dead, you will be saved" (Romans 10:9). The Bible also teaches us that one day there will be a new heavens and a new earth.

Wow, what a completely different understanding of things to that of the secularists! The Bible gives us real meaning and purpose and a way to receive a free gift of eternal life with God.

Two Worldviews: What Do They Have in Common?

The secular view and the Bible's record give two totally different accounts of the origin of the universe. Compare them:

Evolution	Creation
big bang	no big bang
billions of years of history	thousands of years of history
no purpose and meaning	purpose and meaning
man and woman from an ape-like creature	man from dust and woman from his side
no global Flood	global Flood
death has always been here	death is an intrusion and an enemy because of sin

They are totally different, aren't they?

I have had young people ask me, "How can you have two totally different accounts of the universe?" Well, whether people are Christians or non-Christians, do they have the same earth or a different earth? Same earth. Do they have the same fossils or different fossils? Same fossils. Do they have the same animals or different animals? Same animals. Do they have the same canyons and rock layers or different canyons and rock layers? Same canyons and rock layers. In fact, Christians and non-Christians even have the same dinosaur fossils and observe the same animal death, and have experienced or will experience the same human death.

What this means is that it does not matter whether you are a Christian or a non-Christian, an atheist or an evolutionist — when it comes to the origins issue, we all have the same facts. Now some Christians will say, "We need to have more facts than the evolutionist so we can win the debate." And evolutionists often say, "We have more evidence than the creationists, so our view is correct." But none of this is correct.

The battle concerning origins is really one over the *same* facts. We are examining the same evidence, but interpreting it in a particular way in relation to the past.

The issue in the origins debate is understanding how the past connects to the present. We exist in the present, and we have all this evidence in the present, just like a forensic scientist. But what happened in the past to put the present here? Ultimately, there are only two ways of trying to understand that. You either start with God's Word, or man's word. You can start with Genesis, a revelation from the One who knows everything that tells us what happened in the past. If that is true — which it is — then we should be able to build a worldview that will make sense of the evidence observed in the present — and it does. And observational science confirms this interpretation of the evidence.

If we do not begin with God's Word, then there is only one other way forward: Somehow, fallible man, who has not always been there and does not know everything, has to try to figure out what he thinks happened. Fallible man has to come up with a story about the past. Millions of years and evolutionary ideas are man's attempts to understand the evidence of the present and connect it to the past. And observational science does not confirm this interpretation of the evidence. The battle is one of two different starting points — thus two different worldviews — but examining the same evidence.

For instance, look at DNA. DNA is a molecule of heredity. The secularist would claim this complex molecule came about by natural processes. But does observational science confirm that? DNA makes up our genes, our chromosomes, our inner cells, and contains the information that builds a human, a dog, a cat, and so on. If the Bible is accurate, that in the beginning God created, we would expect to see evidence of an intelligence behind life. And we do, because DNA is an information system and a language system. Languages only come from intelligence. Information only comes from information. DNA confirms — cries out! — "in the beginning God," not "in the beginning hydrogen." Thus, observational science confirms the Bible is the right starting point!

When we study genetics, we find that there can be great variation within a kind, such as within the dog family or dog kind, but there is no mechanism to change one kind into another (e.g., dogs cannot change into a totally different kind). The Book of Genesis tells us that God created animals and plants according to their kinds (Genesis 1). And that is exactly what we find. When we examine the science of genetics, it confirms the Bible's account of history. It does not confirm Darwin's idea that one kind changes into another totally different kind (even though there can be great variation within a kind).

What about the human kind? What kind of variation do we find? I can tell you what we do not find — we do not find different races. Darwin, in addition to claiming that one kind could change into another, also believed there were different races: lower races, higher races, primitive races, and advanced races. This is incorrect, and even the Human Genome Project found, using observational science, that there is only one biological race of humans. This does not in an ultimate sense (from a human perspective) prove the Bible is true, but it confirms the Bible's truthfulness. It confirms the account that we are all descendants of one man and one woman.

Observational science once again confirms God's Word as the correct starting point, not man's word concerning molecules-to-man evolution.

The more we observe the fossil record and other geological structures on the earth (such as canyons and so on), the more we see evidence of catastrophism consistent with the Flood of Noah's day, but not consistent with man's ideas of slow processes forming these layers and structures over millions of years.

The Bible also accounts for why we see life, death, joy, sorrow, love, and hatred all at the same time — because the world was once "very good," but sin has marred it.

The Bible is the right starting point. It is the true account of history that God has revealed to us, so it does explain the world. Often, after I have explained all of this, people will ask, "But doesn't science tell us that the Bible's account in Genesis is not true? Doesn't science say that we have to believe in evolution and millions of years?" Actually, science does not say anything — it is the scientists who say something. But the key here is understanding what is meant by the word *science*.

What Is Science?

A very common claim today, as I stated earlier, especially within parts of the Church, is that there is a conflict between science and the Bible. When anyone begins to speak to me about science and scientific views, I stop them right in their tracks and ask them what they actually mean by the words *science* and *scientific*.

Most people do not understand that they are using the word *science* incorrectly. According to the Merriam-Webster's Dictionary, the root meaning of science is a "state of knowing." Basically, it means "knowledge." There is a difference between what is called *observational* or *operational* science and what is called *historical* or *origin* science.

Operational science deals with knowledge that is gained by observation and repeated testing in our present world. Whether scientists are Christian or non-Christian, they can all perform the same operational science. Operational science is what enables us to build technology, such as computers and airplanes. It is what enabled us to send man to the moon and to put the rover *Curiosity* on Mars.

As soon as a scientist starts talking about the origin of Mars, however, we have to remember that he was not there to see that. That is different.

That is in the area of historical science. Historical science deals with history — the past. What happened in the past? Most people, especially children, do not understand the difference between operational and historical science. They are usually not taught in the public school system how to distinguish between operational science, which builds up technology, and historical science, which deals with beliefs about the past.

There are occasions when I give presentations to students in schools on this topic, and I try to help them understand the differences by giving specific examples. For instance, we can go to the Grand Canyon and look at the Coconino Sandstone. We can see the sandstone. We see it is a *sand stone*. It is a sedimentary rock in the present. That is observational science.

Now, what if somebody said to you that the Coconino Sandstone was supposedly laid down over millions of years? Which type of science is that? That is historical science. We were not there to see it being laid down.

If we are talking about the fact that we can see and study apes today, and we can see and study people, that is operational science. But if somebody claims that millions of years ago ape-like creatures turned into people, what is that? That is historical science. What if we said that God made Adam from dust, what is that? That is historical science, too.

Scientists can observe radioactive decay in a laboratory — that is operational science. But then when they extrapolate backward and try to date something, they have to assume many factors about what happened in the past—what was there at the beginning—decay rates and so on. That is historical science.

See the difference? It is very important that, as Christians, we understand the difference and teach it to our children. The role of operational science is this: when we apply operational science, for instance, to DNA, it confirms "in the beginning God." It does not confirm a slow process because of properties supposedly inherent in matter over millions of years. When we apply operational science to the study of genetics, it confirms created kinds. There can be great variation within the kinds. For example, different species of dog and different species of elephants may form, but that is not evolution in the Darwinian sense because dogs remain dogs and elephants remain elephants.

When we apply operational science to fossils and rock layers, it confirms catastrophism consistent with the Flood of Noah's day. It does *not* confirm millions of years. When we apply operational science to the human kind, it confirms that there is only one race, which is exactly what the Bible teaches. It all comes down to the starting point — and the Bible is the correct starting point.

Can Creationists Be Good Scientists?

I want to deal with a trend that is becoming more and more noticeable in the culture today. Many evolutionists regularly confuse operational and historical science in an attempt to brainwash people into believing that evolutionary ideas are proven, and some Christian academics and church leaders have even joined the secular world in confusing these two types of science. They use the one word *science* when discussing both observational and historical science. This is why so many are confused and why generations are brainwashed into believing evolutionary ideas. People recognize the great strides scientists have made in our modern technology, and they often think that if they do not believe in evolution and/or millions of years, then they are denying the reason for the technology they use! But the science used to develop technology is observational science — evolution and millions of years come under the heading of historical science. We have to educate people on these matters so they will understand we can honor scientists, whether Christians or atheists, for the technology they develop — but we do not agree with scientists (no matter how brilliant they are at developing technology) concerning their evolutionary views of origins. Sadly, many Christians have been led astray because they do not understand the difference between observational (operational) science and historical science.

For example, the organization BioLogos answers the question, "How are the ages of the Earth and universe calculated?" by appealing to man's word and by treating historical science as though it is operational science:

> Many different and complementary scientific measurements have established with near certainty that the universe and the Earth are billions of years old. Layers in glaciers show a history much longer than 10,000 years, and radiometric dating places the formation of the Earth at 4.5 billion years. Light from galaxies is reaching us billions of years after it left, and the expansion rate of the universe dates its age to 13.7 billion years. These are just a

sampling of the types of evidence for the great age of the Earth and the universe.[8]

In the present, scientists can use various dating methods that involve something that changes with time — but they must rely on assumptions concerning those changes in the past when they were not there. The answer that BioLogos has provided conflates operational and historical science and treats the *interpretation* of evidence as though it is evidence itself for the supposed millions of years. BioLogos is teaching readers that it is appropriate for the fallible interpretation of the evidence (based on numerous fallible assumptions) to conflict with what Scripture (the absolute authority of the Word of God) teaches.

What BioLogos is teaching about the age of the earth is just a step away from the fallacy that many prominent secularists have been committing recently: that a belief in creationism leads to a denial of and inability to practice operational science. In *Scientific American,* writer Jacob Tanenbaum, a fourth- and fifth-grade science teacher, expresses his concern for the American population:

> The danger is that 40 percent of the American electorate [referring to his earlier claim that 40 percent of U.S. adults believe that Genesis is literal] seems to have forgotten what science is. Considering that our nation put a man on the moon and invented the airplane and the Internet, this development is extraordinary.[9]

Did you catch the problem with his statement? Men on the moon, airplanes, and the Internet all fall under the category of operational science — none of this has anything to do with historical science. Both evolutionists and biblical creationists can practice good operational science — in fact, biblical creationists really have a far better foundation for it (a basis for the laws of logic and the laws of nature as a result of creation, not random processes). I would hate to fly in a plane built based on chance, random processes! But evolutionary scientists do not lay out all the parts of the plane (which they had to design anyway) on the runway, and wait for them to come together

---

8. "How Are the Ages of the Earth and Universe Calculated?" BioLogos, http://biologos. org/questions/ages-of-the-earth-and-universe.

9. Jacob Tanenbaum, "A Science Teacher Draws the Line at Creation," *Scientific American,* http://www.scientificamerican.com/article.cfm?id=science-teacher-draws-line-creation.

over long ages to form a plane. They know better — their view of origins does not affect their ability to perform operational science.

But secularists still seem unwilling to admit this. Bill Nye, a former children's television show host, claimed that a lack of belief in evolution is equivalent to scientific illiteracy:

> And I say to the grownups, if you want to deny evolution and live in a world that's completely inconsistent with everything we observe in the universe, that's fine, but don't make your kids do it because we need them. We need scientifically literate voters and tax-payers for the future. We need people that can — we need engineers that can build stuff, solve problems.[10]

Once more, scientific literacy does not require a belief in millions of years or evolutionary ideas. Nye continually attempts to claim that a Christian's historical science will stop people from doing operational science — but this is nonsense!

Now, if there is any doubt about whether our children are being taught this distorted view of science, have a look at Zach Kopplin. Kopplin is a college student and science education activist who has advocated for the repeal of a law in Louisiana allowing the critical examination of evolutionary ideas and the presentation of other views of origins in the classroom. Kopplin fears that belief in biblical creation will cripple students' chances in the job market and prevent scientific research:

> "Creationism confuses students about the nature of science," he says. "If students don't understand the scientific method, and are taught that creationism is science, they will not be prepared to do work in genuine fields, especially not the biological sciences. We are hurting the chances of our students having jobs in science, and making discoveries that will change the world."[11]

Kopplin, like Nye, is not distinguishing between historical science and operational science. He himself is confused and thus confuses others. He is a

---

10. Bill Nye, "Creationism Is Not Appropriate for Children," Big Think, http://www.youtube.com/watch?v=gHbYJfwFgOU.

11. George Dvorsky, "How 19-year-old Activist Zack Kopplin Is Making Life Hell for Louisiana's Creationists," io9, http://io9.com/5976112/how-19+year+old-activist-zack-kopplin-is-making-life-hell-for-louisianas-creationists.

product of an education system that has not taught him to understand science correctly. What Nye, Kopplin, Tanenbaum, and other skeptics who make this fallacious claim are really arguing against is the biblical worldview and starting point — and they do it by mixing historical science and operational science together and using the one word *science*.

Which Worldview Will Win?

Our culture today has embraced the worldview of moral relativism. It has lost regard for the authority of God's Word and the biblical foundation on which this once very Christian nation was built. And this loss of regard has been fueled by evolutionary ideas and millions of years, which call into question the truthfulness of the Word of God.

Two starting points, two different worldviews. What we are seeing in the culture today is the clash of those two worldviews: moral absolutism versus moral relativism. Which one is going to win? The one that has the foundation to stand upon. The one that has the starting point the culture builds on.

What has happened in America? Many of the founding fathers of this nation were Christians who built their worldview (which permeated the culture) on the starting point of God's Word. By and large, people increasingly have been rejecting God's Word as the foundation for their worldview, thus changing their starting point to man's word

Over the years, the nation increasingly has changed starting points in the government, in the education system, and in the culture as a whole. But the saddest realization of all is that we have really changed starting points in the Church — by adopting man's fallible ideas (such as evolution/millions of years) into God's Word.

As more of the Church adopts man's pagan religion of evolution and millions of years into the Bible and changes God's Word, and as more of the Church introduces man's fallible ideas into God's infallible Word, the starting point becomes man's word. That is why we are seeing such a catastrophic worldview change in America (in fact, in our whole Western world) — a change in starting points and thus a change in worldviews.

So what is the answer? Christians, we must call the Church back to the authority of the Word of God and stand without compromise.

Chapter 4

Exegesis — What Does God's Word Say?

Many Christians do not understand that they have a starting point on which they should build every area of their thinking — the Bible. Because of the way the Bible is taught in many churches, basically as a collection of "stories" containing spiritual and moral truths, many Christians do not understand that their entire worldview must be built on God's Word. The Church largely concentrates on teaching spiritual, moral, and relationship matters — sort of connected to the Bible, but by and large not with the understanding of a worldview built solely upon God's Word. In fact, I have spoken at churches where older members of the congregation have told me, "You can't talk about dinosaurs — this is church. Christianity is about Jesus and spiritual matters."

Yes, Christianity is about Jesus, and moral and spiritual truths — and relationships. But the truth concerning these is founded in real history — on God's Word beginning in Genesis — as should all of our thinking

in every area. For instance, the Bible also has everything to do with understanding dinosaurs correctly. The Bible is a history book that connects to dirt;

it connects to death and disease; it connects to thorns; it connects to the Grand Canyon; it connects to the sun, moon, and stars; it connects to the different people groups; it connects to the animal kinds; and yes, it even connects to dinosaurs. But sadly, much of the older generation of professing Christians seems to have this false idea that the Bible only has to do with spiritual and moral truths. Why? In many ways I believe it is because of the influence of millions of years and evolution.

Today, the Church has mostly given up the history in Genesis — the history that is foundational to all doctrine — foundational to one's world-view to understand the universe and life correctly. Many pastors have not taught on Genesis because they are unsure how to treat it or how to answer questions. I believe this is largely because churches and Christian institutions have not taught apologetics to defend Christianity beginning in God's Word — and the influence of evolution and/or millions of years has either been adopted by most pastors or has confused them.

Establishing Our Starting Point

When believers talk with non-Christians, they falsely think they do not have a starting point for their thinking. They start with man's word — regardless of whether they acknowledge it or not. Generations of children are deriving their starting points on origins from secular school curricula. What exactly do textbooks teach? They basically teach that scientists in white lab coats, who are supposedly completely objective and unbiased, start with evidence and develop their theories from there. But this is entirely incorrect. For example, some of you may be familiar with a woman named Eugenie Scott. Scott, who will retire from her post in 2014, is the executive director of the atheistic National Center for Science Education. The organization particularly opposes creationists.

A few years ago, she sat in my office to interview me for the BBC about the opening of the Creation Museum. The conversation went something like this. She asked me if I start with the Bible. I said yes. She wondered if I would be prepared to change my thinking on Creation, the Fall, the Flood, and so on. I told her no. She said that was religion, and that real scientists like her start with evidence and develop theories, and as new evidence comes along they are prepared to change their theories. She insisted that this was real science — being prepared to change as new evidence is understood. She went on to indicate that biblical creationists are not prepared to change, and thus what they teach is religion, not science.

Of course, biblical creationists are not prepared to change what the Bible states clearly, for example, about a global Flood, the creation of Adam from dust and Eve from his side, and the entrance of death because of sin. The Bible reveals that the eternal God created the universe and everything in it in six days (we will discuss the issue of six days in more detail later on). The Bible then gives a very specific history concerning Creation, Corruption, Catastrophe, Confusion (creation account, entrance of sin and death, Flood of Noah's Day, Tower of Babel) — and then Christ, Cross, and Consummation (the gospel based in that history). That is my starting point for when I examine the evidence. And I am not prepared to change any of this as it is revealed in God's Word.

So I asked Eugenie Scott whether she believed in God. She said no. She confirmed she was an atheist. I asked whether she would be prepared to consider the account of Creation, Fall, and Flood in the Bible — but she said absolutely not! I then asked her if she was prepared to change her belief — which she was not prepared to do!

What I really did in the course of that conversation was show her that she does indeed have a starting point — that the Bible and its account of origins are not true and not even to be considered when understanding the evidence of the present. She may insist that as a scientist she starts with the evidence, but really she starts with the belief that there is no God (she states she is an atheist) and the Bible's creation account is not true — and only natural processes (not supernatural) explain the evidence of the present. Thus, the Bible is not at all relevant to the discussion for her. No matter what evidence she examines, she is going to interpret it on the basis of her atheistic starting point.

What I was doing in my answers and questions to her was to separate out historical science from observational science, and illustrate that we both have starting points. We are both prepared to change our models (worldviews) built on our starting points — but the battle is ultimately over starting points, not evidence.

Once we understand this, that a person will interpret the evidence based on their starting point or worldview, then we can begin to address the foundational problem. Remember, the battle is not ultimately at the worldview level. Issues like abortion, gay marriage, or polygamy are concerning, but they are manifestations of the real problem — a starting-point problem. The battle is over the foundation. For Eugenie Scott, her foundation (whether she acknowledges it or not) is man's fallible opinions, while for the believer, the foundation should be the unchanging Word of God. When interacting with people whose foundation is something other than the Bible, we have to help them see the difference is with their starting point.

How do we do that? We know that we are called to give a reasoned defense for our faith:

> But sanctify the Lord God in your hearts, and always be ready to give a defense to everyone who asks you a reason for the hope that is in you, with meekness and fear; having a good conscience, that when they defame you as evildoers, those who revile your good conduct in Christ may be ashamed. (1 Peter 3:15–16)

But the Bible also says that we were "dead in trespasses and sins" until Christ made us alive (Ephesians 2:1), and that "there is none righteous, no, not one" (Romans 3:10). The Apostle Paul reminds us that it is "by grace you have been saved through faith, and that not of yourselves; it is the gift of God, not of works, lest anyone should boast" (Ephesians 2:8–9).

Essentially, there is nothing that we, man, can do to change our starting point. It is God who changes our starting point. Romans 10:17 tells us that faith comes by hearing and hearing by the Word of God. It is God (by His Word) who raises the dead — physically and spiritually — back to life. On the other hand, some might argue that it is not God's will that any should perish but that all should come to repentance (2 Peter 3:9). Others might point to Romans 10:14:

> How then shall they call on Him in whom they have not believed? And how shall they believe in Him of whom they have not heard? And how shall they hear without a preacher?

How do we make this all work together then? As believers, we should go into the world and be like the Apostle Paul, bold for the faith, powerfully arguing and correcting error, giving a defense and answers. But we must also remember that we were saved *by grace* — God's grace — through faith. It was not of ourselves, but the gift of God. Because there is no one righteous, a non-Christian is dead in trespasses and sins.

One analogy I like to use when explaining these seemingly contradictory positions from Scripture is that of Lazarus. In fact, this really sums up what the ministry of Answers in Genesis is all about, what apologetics is all about. Some people may object to my view, saying that if it is God who changes our starting points, then why does the evidence matter at all? Church, we must think biblically, recognizing we can never understand the mind of the infinite Creator God. Consider when Jesus came to the tomb of Lazarus.

Lazarus was dead physically, just like an unbeliever is dead spiritually. My late brother Robert used to say that non-Christians were "walking dead people." When Jesus arrived at the tomb, He said, "Take away the stone" (John 11:39). Now, Jesus could have moved the stone with just a word, yes? But instead He asked humans to do what they can do. We are capable of taking the stone away, so we should do that.

But what can humans not do? They cannot raise the dead to life again. Jesus Christ is the Resurrection and the life, and it is by His power and Word that the dead are raised to life. In John 11:43, Christ gives the command, "Lazarus, come forth!" And he does!

Here is how I apply this. When we talk with unbelievers, we are talking with walking dead people. Only God's Word can raise that dead person to life.

> So then faith comes by hearing, and hearing by the word of God. (Romans 10:17)

But I, a mere human, can roll the stone away. I can do what the Bible tells me to do — give a defense, give an answer — never giving up my starting point, but always pointing people to the Word of God and the gospel.

When I was in my interview with Eugenie Scott, one of the things that hit me was that we need to be doing what we can as humans. I could do my best to answer her questions, so I did. I gave her all the evidence I could to point her to God's Word — all without giving up my starting point. I made sure I pointed her to God's Word and the message of the saving gospel. It is God's Word that convicts, and faith comes by hearing, and hearing by the Word of God. The goal is to share the gospel with the unbeliever, and then step back and say, "God, I've shared your truth, but you're the one who changes hearts."

> For the word of God is living and powerful, and sharper than any two-edged sword, piercing even to the division of soul and

spirit, and of joints and marrow, and is a discerner of the thoughts and intents of the heart. (Hebrews 4:12)

Some have said to me, "I feel like a failure because I've been trying to witness to this person for years." But it is not our job to do the converting, only the sharing! The actual conversion is the work of the Holy Spirit. God is the one who makes the new creation. Our job is to do what God has called us to do: preach the gospel, defend the faith, give answers and stand boldly, unashamedly and uncompromisingly on the Word of God. This is where it all comes together, rolling the stone away (giving answers — defending the faith) and preaching the Word (that raises the "dead"). But part of having the correct starting point is knowing how to properly read and interpret God's Word and knowing the answers to defend the Christian faith. In the Church, erroneous doctrinal views creep in because people try to the read the Bible from the perspective of man's opinions, rather than as the inerrant Word of a holy God.

I believe there are two reasons why many Christians are not bold in their witnessing, or are reticent to enter into arguments with non-Christians:

1. Most Christians do not understand they have a starting point from which to build their way of thinking. For instance, in one of my talks I explained how I would answer someone who came up to me and said, "I'm a homosexual." I explained that I would not immediately say that homosexual behavior is a sin and he needs to repent. (I know some Christians would do this). I first of all would share with the person where my thinking comes from — the Bible. I would tell this person about my starting point and what it teaches, and why I hold the worldview I do — my views on homosexual behavior are not my opinion. I then will talk to the person who made the statement to find out what they believe about the Bible and why they believe the way they do. What I am attempting is to get the argument down to the starting point (the foundational level). This takes much of the emotionalism out of the discussion. I would explain that if someone does not build their thinking on the Bible, I can understand why they would accept homosexual behavior — they are being consistent with the foundation of their worldview. (If this person claims to believe the Bible, then I will show from the Bible that it is an inconsistent position).

2. Most Christians have not been taught the answers to the skeptical questions of the age (creation apologetics and general biblical apologetics) and thus they know that when people ask them tough questions, they do not know how to answer. So they do not want to interact and admit they cannot defend the Christian faith as they should! There is an incredible lack of teaching apologetics in our churches, as we demonstrated in the research for the book *Already Gone.*[1]

Historical-Grammatical Hermeneutic

In this chapter, I want to also define and demonstrate exegesis from a historical-grammatical hermeneutic.[2] Now, I know that sounds like a highly technical term, but what it really means is reading Scripture "naturally." Because God is the all-powerful, all-knowing Creator of the universe, He is entirely capable of giving man a text that can be understood and accurately interpreted for all time. Some people say that they read the Bible "literally" — as long as "literally" means "naturally." Let me explain!

While the Bible is generally plain in its meaning, interpreting it properly still requires careful study. And it is not always easy to understand! The Bible was written over about a 2,000-year period by approximately 40 authors in three languages (Hebrew, Aramaic, and Greek). The authors had different personalities, cultural backgrounds, and social standings. But because "all Scripture is God-breathed" (2 Timothy 3:16, NIV), we can trust that what these men wrote is the inspired, inerrant, and infallible Word of God.

In order to properly understand and interpret Scripture, we have to make use of six important principles[3]:

1. Observe the text
2. Context
3. Clarity
4. Compare Scripture with Scripture

---

1. Ken Ham and Britt Beemer, *Already Gone*, with Todd Hillard (Green Forest, AR: Master Books, 2009).

2. For a fuller explanation of the historical-grammatical hermeneutic, see Tim Chaffey, "How Should We Interpret the Bible, Part 1: Principles for Understanding God's Word," Answers in Genesis, http://www.answersingenesis.org/articles/2011/02/22/interpret-the-bible-1-principles.

3. These principles were taken from Tim Chaffey's previously cited article, "How Should We Interpret the Bible, Part 1."

5. Classification
6. Church's historical view

1. Observe the Text

The historical-grammatical hermeneutic requires us to look for the intended meaning of the author. A biblical passage means what its author intended it to mean. Think about it: if we could not trust the words on the pages of Scripture to mean what they say, why bother to write them at all? If readers are just going to take away whatever meaning they want from the text, then reading Scripture becomes pointless.

What's more, we must consider the historical and cultural setting of the passage we are studying. Because the Bible was written by authors from many different cultural and historical backgrounds, our understanding of Scripture will be better if we take the time to learn the circumstances in which it was written.

But the most obvious point is this: look at what the text actually says. Many people, because they want to find scriptural support for a particular idea, try to claim that the Bible says things it does not. Others simply have not read the text very closely and subscribe to ideas that are not actually found there.

2. Context

Many times, the meaning of a word is defined by its context. This is especially true in biblical Hebrew, but we see it in the English language as well. For example, the word *day* has multiple meanings. It could mean a 24-hour day, the daylight portion of a day, or a certain period of time. If I said, "The drive home took two full days," the context makes it clear that the meaning of *day* there is a 24-hour period of time. But in the sentence, "We worked all day long," the context tells us that *day* is only referring to the daylight portion of the day. And if I said, "Back in my father's day," the context indicates that *day* is referring to a historical time period.

In the Bible or any document, the context helps us understand the meaning of words, phrases, and sentences. Furthermore, we need to know how the particular bit of Scripture we are studying fits into the Bible as a whole. Without knowing the context of a passage of Scripture, coming up with an accurate interpretation becomes incredibly difficult, if not impossible.

3. Clarity

Scripture can be understood! Proverbs 8:9 tells us that the Word of God is "plain to him who understands, and right to those who find knowledge." Now, God has given His Word to man, so does it make sense that He would make it impossible to understand? Of course not. If God gave it to us, then He has also given us the ability to accurately read and interpret it, if we are serious about learning the truth.

Will there be parts of Scripture that are difficult to understand? Yes, and we must still read our Bibles and carefully study God's Word daily if we expect to gain clarity on it. We should also look at Scripture with the assumption that it is generally clear — not assuming that it is full of hidden meanings.

4. Compare Scripture with Scripture

This principle is often known as interpreting Scripture with Scripture. The author of Hebrews writes that "it is impossible for God to lie" (Hebrews 6:18), so we can trust that no passage of Scripture will ever contradict another passage of Scripture. Allowing Scripture to interpret Scripture means that we can interpret a passage that is difficult to understand, and then compare our interpretation to the other passages on the topic. If we find that they all seem to teach the same truth, then we can consider our interpretation to be accurate.

5. Classification

The classification of a book of the Bible is based on its genre (poetry, history, prophecy, and so on). Now, when we read a passage of Scripture, it is important that we understand it in terms of its literary style. For example, a historical book is going to recount historical events and should be fairly straightforward. Genesis is a historical book — it recounts the creation of the universe, the Fall of man, the global Flood, and so on. Knowing the genre of the text aids greatly in our interpretation of it. For more on this, see the chart and accompanying discussion in Appendix A.

6. Church's Historical View

The last principle of the historical-grammatical hermeneutic is recognizing what the views of the Church have been historically on various passages.

Of course, the thoughts of past Christian leaders on different doctrines are not equivalent to the inspired Word of God. But many doctrines have been discussed and debated throughout Church history, so we can look to see what conclusions other Christian leaders have reached about portions of Scripture we may be unsure about.

Putting It All Together

Can you see how this method of understanding Scripture works to prevent faulty interpretations? What is happening in the world today, especially in academia, is that people are being taught that language does not have a firm meaning anymore. They are being taught that what they read can potentially mean anything they want it to. As a result, we are seeing strange interpretations of Scripture — especially of Genesis chapters 1–11 — that are leading the Church astray.

Take Hank Hanegraaff, for example. Hanegraaff is popularly known as the "Bible Answer Man" and hosts a radio show by the same name. He is also president of the Christian Research Institute, which publishes the *Christian Research Journal*. In a 2013 article titled "Leviathan, Dragons, and Dinosaurs, Oh My!" Hanegraaff offers his interpretation of the serpent in Genesis 3:

> In short, Eve was not deceived by a talking snake. Rather, Moses used the symbol of a snake to communicate the wiles of the Evil One who deceived Eve through mind-to-mind communication — precisely as he seeks to deceive you and me today.[4]

Does Hanegraaff's interpretation line up with Scripture? Genesis 3:1 explains that a serpent tempted Eve in the garden:

> Now the serpent was more cunning than any beast of the field which the Lord God had made. And he said to the woman, "Has God indeed said, 'You shall not eat of every tree of the garden'?" (Genesis 3:1)

Now, in keeping with the first principle of interpretation, we should look at what the text actually says. In this verse, the text clearly says that there was a serpent that spoke to Eve. What is the context of the passage? Adam and

---

4. Hank Hanegraaff, "Leviathan, Dragons, and Dinosaurs, Oh My!" *Christian Research Journal* 36, no. 2 (2013): 55.

Eve are in the Garden of Eden, before the Fall, and Genesis 3 recounts the entrance of sin and death into the world. All of this is easily understood from the chapter, because God has made His Word understandable for all time.

Furthermore, the Book of Genesis is historical narrative. Genesis 3 gives a straightforward historical account of the temptation by the serpent and Adam and Eve's first sin, which allowed the entrance of death, disease, and suffering into the world. In the New Testament, the Apostle Paul references the serpent, clearly believing it was literal:

> But I fear, lest somehow, as the serpent deceived Eve by his craftiness, so your minds may be corrupted from the simplicity that is in Christ. (2 Corinthians 11:3)

Considering that the context, genre, and history of the passage, not to mention the plain words of the passage, indicate that the serpent was literally in the Garden of Eden, we have to conclude that Hanegraaff's interpretation is incorrect. In fact, it is unclear how, if he were reading Genesis 3 naturally, he could have arrived at the conclusion that the serpent was not there. But this is, sadly, what has happened in many parts of the Church today when it comes to Genesis 1–11.

Now, the irony of Hanegraaff's interpretation is that he writes in his article, "We are to interpret the Word of God just as we interpret other forms of communication — in the most obvious and natural sense."[5] And yet Hanegraaff's interpretation of Genesis 3:1 is anything but natural. It requires us to believe that God presented a scene in the midst of a historical narrative that appears to be historical but is not. It makes God appear to be untrustworthy. Actually, I suggest (and we will see this with many other Christian scholars later on in this book) that Hanegraaff's acceptance of man's ideas concerning an old universe contributes to why he approaches Scripture as he does in Genesis 3.

Taking God at His Word

God communicates through language. When He made the first man, Adam, He had already "programmed" him with a language, so there could be communication. Human language consists of words used in a specific context that relates to the entire reality around us.

---

5. Ibid., p. 11.

Thus, God can reveal things to man, and man can communicate with God, because words have meaning and convey an understandable message. If this were not the case, how could any of us communicate with each other or with God? How could you even know what I am saying through what I write here?

So, does it really matter what a Christian believes about Genesis 1–11? Yes, it does matter! For example, ideas that insert millions of years into, or before, creation undermine the gospel by putting death, bloodshed, disease, thorns, and suffering before sin and the Fall.

Furthermore, it is really a matter of how one approaches the Bible, in principle. It is a matter of authority — is God or man the ultimate authority? If we do not allow the language to speak to us in context, but try to make the text fit ideas outside of Scripture, then ultimately the meaning of any word in any part of the Bible depends on man's interpretation, which can change according to whatever outside ideas are popular.

If one allows evolution and or millions of years to determine our understanding of Scripture, then this can lead to a slippery slope of unbelief through the rest of Scripture. Sadly, this is happening right now as we see an exodus of the coming generations from the Church.[6]

Now, secularists (like Richard Dawkins) proclaim that a person cannot be raised from the dead. Does this mean we should interpret the Resurrection of Christ to reflect this? Sadly, some do just this, saying that the Resurrection simply means that Jesus' teachings live on in His followers. Most conservative Christian scholars would not do this concerning the Resurrection — but they do allow this approach when interpreting Genesis. To me, it is almost like an intellectual schizophrenia. And it has been devastatingly destructive to the Church and culture!

When people accept at face value what Genesis is teaching, they will have no problem accepting and making sense of the rest of the Bible.

Martin Luther once said:

> I have often said that whoever would study Holy Scripture should be sure to see to it that he stays with the simple words as long as he can and by no means departs from them unless an article of faith compels him to understand them differently. For of this we

---

6. Ham and Beemer, *Already Gone.*

must be certain: no clearer speech has been heard on Earth than what God has spoken.[7]

God's people need to realize that the Word of God is something very special. It is not just the words of men. As Paul said in 1 Thessalonians 2:13, "You welcomed it not as the word of men, but as it is in truth, the word of God."

Proverbs 30:5–6 states that "every word of God is pure. . . . Do not add to His words, lest He rebuke you, and you be found a liar." The Bible cannot be treated as just some great literary work. We need to "tremble at his word" (Isaiah 66:5) and not forget:

> All Scripture is given by inspiration of God, and is profitable for doctrine, for reproof, for correction, for instruction in righteousness, that the man of God may be complete, thoroughly equipped for every good work. (2 Timothy 3:16–17)

In the original autographs, every word and letter in the Bible is there because God put it there. Let us listen to God speaking to us through His Word and not arrogantly think we can tell God what He really means!

---

7. Martin Luther as quoted in Ewald M. Plass, *What Martin Luther Says: A Practical In-Home Anthology for the Active Christian* (St. Louis, MO: Concordia Publishing House, 1991), p. 93.

Chapter 5

 The Meaning
of *Yôm*

I have found that many people (including many pastors) will claim the
word for *day* in Genesis 1 does not mean an ordinary day, but when
pressed for when the word *day* does mean an ordinary day, they really do
not know. So why are they making the statement that the word *day* does not
mean an ordinary day in Genesis 1? I suggest that the main reason is because
they have been influenced in some way by the supposed millions of years
proposed by evolutionary scientists, and they are trying to allow for these
long ages somewhere in Genesis 1.

And think about this! If one is trying to fit millions of years into the
Bible, then one cannot insert these years in the genealogies, as that would
destroy them. Really, the only place to attempt this has to be before Adam
— in the six days of creation. According to secularists, the fossil record was
supposedly laid down millions of years before man. Thus, for Christians
who (wrongly, I assert) accept millions of years, they have to somehow fit
them into the Bible before man.

You will find that all the various compromise positions on Genesis have
one thing in common — attempting to fit millions of years into Genesis.
This may result in attempts to interpret the days as long ages, or to put the
millions of years into Genesis 1:1, or to place a supposed gap between Genesis 1:1 and Genesis 1:2 — or allocating Genesis 1 to a non-material account
of origins to allow for these supposed millions of years.

I have found that the majority of Christians who accept millions of years try to maintain that the word for *day* in Genesis 1 does not mean an ordinary day.

Also, when we leave behind the plain meaning of the word *day* in Genesis 1 and replace it with geologic ages of millions of years, the message of the gospel is undermined at its foundation. Long ages in Genesis put death, disease, suffering, and thorns before the Fall — an impossibility if creation was truly "very good" in the beginning. The effort that many Christian academics and church leaders are making to define the days of Creation Week as millions of years is the result of an erroneous approach to Scripture. Rather than allowing Scripture to interpret Scripture and operating on the principles of the historical-grammatical hermeneutic, they reinterpret God's Word on the basis of the fallible beliefs of sinful man. Even if one accepts the days in Genesis 1 as ordinary days, but still attempts to fit millions of years into Genesis (e.g., in a "gap" between the first two verses, or fit the supposed geological ages into Genesis 1:1, and so on), then there is still the insurmountable hurdle of having death, disease, suffering, and thorns before sin — and God calling all this "very good."

The easiest way to understand what the word *day* means in Genesis 1 is to put aside outside influences that may cause you to have a predetermined idea of what the word means. Instead, let the plain meaning of the passage fuel your understanding.

When we take Genesis 1 at face value, it without a doubt tells us that God created the universe, the earth, the sun, moon and stars, plants and animals, and the first two people within six normal-length days. If we are honest about it, we have to admit that we could never get the idea of millions of years from reading this passage.

But, as you will see in the coming chapters, many Christian leaders and scholars do not believe the days of Creation Week were ordinary, approximately 24-hour days. Many of them accept and teach, based on outside influences such as evolutionary ideas, that these days must have been long periods of time — even millions or billions of years.

But before discussing the rampant compromise on the days of creation, I want to explain the meaning of *yôm* in Scripture and how we arrive at the conclusions we do in Genesis 1 that the days of creation were ordinary, approximately 24-hour days. It is incredibly important that believers understand not just the biblical creation view, but also how that interpretation is reached. At Answers in Genesis, we are committed to teaching believers to think critically about claims concerning Scripture. We want to teach solid, biblically based apologetics so that Christians can answer the skeptical questions of our age.

Overview: The Uses of "Day" in Scripture

The Hebrew word for day is *yôm*. Now *yôm* can actually have a number of different meanings. A pastor once said to me, "The word *day* in Hebrew can mean something other than an ordinary day." I said, "Yes, but it can also mean an ordinary day." He responded, "But it can also mean something other than an ordinary day." And what he said is true. But the fact is, the main meaning of the word *yôm* is an ordinary day. He was using the fact that the word *day* can mean something other than an ordinary day as the reason it did not mean an ordinary day in Genesis! Not very sound logic!

A man called me once and said, "Look, I agree with you that evolution is not true, but we don't know what the days of creation were in Genesis 1. We don't know what the word *day* means there, but it doesn't mean an ordinary day." I said, "Can you tell me when the word *day* does mean an ordinary day?" He asked, "What do you mean?" I told him, "Well, if you know it doesn't mean an ordinary day in Genesis 1, you must know when it does mean an ordinary day. I'd like to know why it doesn't mean an ordinary day, and to do that, I need to know when the word *day* does mean an ordinary day so I can see why it doesn't mean an ordinary day in Genesis 1. So can you tell me when the word *day* does mean an ordinary day?" He said, "Huh?"

I find that many people are like that. They are convinced that the word *day* cannot possibly mean a normal-length day in Genesis 1, but they do not have a clue about when it does mean an ordinary day. But you see, many words can have two or more meanings depending upon the context. For instance, the English word *day* can have multiple meanings.

To understand the meaning of *day* in Genesis 1, we need to determine how the Hebrew word for day, *yôm*, is used in the context of Scripture.

- A typical lexicon will illustrate that *yôm* can have a range of meanings: a period of light as contrasted to night, a 24-hour period, time, a specific point of time, or a year. For example, *The Brown Driver Briggs Hebrew and English Lexicon* (*BDB*), which is a classic, well-respected Hebrew-English lexicon, has seven headings and many subheadings for the meaning of *yôm* — but it defines the creation days of Genesis 1 as ordinary days under the heading "day as defined by evening and morning."

- A number and the phrase "evening and morning" are used with each of the six days of creation (Genesis 1:5, 8, 13, 19, 23, 31). This will be discussed more below.
- The word *yôm* occurs in Scripture 2,304 times.[1]
- In Genesis 1:5, *yôm* occurs in context with the word *night*. Outside of Genesis 1, *night* is used with *yôm* 52 times, and each time it means an ordinary day. Why would Genesis 1 be the exception? Even the usage of the word *light* with *yôm* in this passage determines the meaning as an ordinary day.[2]
- The plural of *yôm*, which does not appear in Genesis 1, can be used to communicate a longer time period, such as "in those days" (typically translated as "when"). Adding a number here would be nonsensical. Clearly, in Exodus 20:11, where a number is used with "days," it unambiguously refers to six earth-rotation days.

Understanding *Yôm*: A Three-Pronged Approach

In order to best understand how the word *yôm* is used in Scripture, there are three important aspects of the word that we need to explore. First, we need to look at the normal range of meanings *yôm* has. To do this, it is important to look at many lexicons and the historical uses of the Hebrew word for *day*. You may find the results of this research very surprising! We will also look at the qualifiers that are attached to *yôm* when it refers to a 24-hour day, and we will explore any exceptions to the rule.

Second, we need to understand the context of *yôm* and how that determines meaning. Hebrew is very much a context-based language, so depending on where a word appears and what appears with it, the meaning can change. This is not just true of Hebrew, but of our English language as well. We have words that can mean more than one thing, based on context.

---

1. M. Sæbø, "יוֹם," in G. Johannes Botterweck and Helmer Ringgren, eds., *Theological Dictionary of the Old Testament*, vol. 6, trans. David E. Green (Grand Rapids, MI: Eerdmans, 1990).

2. James Stambaugh, "The Days of Creation: A Semantic Approach" (presented at the Evangelical Theological Society's Far West Region Meeting, Sun Valley, CA, April 26, 1996), p. 16.

Finally, we have to look at the theological understanding of *yôm*. This is part of allowing Scripture to interpret Scripture, which is the basis for the historical-grammatical hermeneutic. When we do not understand something in Scripture, one of our best guides will be other passages that refer to or explain the verse or parts of the verse in question.

What Does Yôm *Mean?*

If we want to find out the range of meanings a Hebrew word such as *yôm* can have, we can turn to Hebrew lexicons. Now, numerous lexicons have been published over the years, and I have found that it is helpful to trace the history of how certain words in Scripture have been treated over time. Often, modern scholars are far more liberal than Bible scholars from one or two hundred years ago.

In the 1800s, a standard Hebrew-English lexicon was Benjamin Davidson's *Analytical Hebrew and Chaldee Lexicon*. Under the entry for *yôm*, the first meaning is "a day." Additionally, Davidson writes that *yôm* could mean "by day, in the day time," "time, duration," or "a definite time."[3] So as far back as the 19th century at least, the standard Hebrew lexicon recognized that *yôm* could mean a 24-hour day, as well as the daylight portion of a day, a duration of time, or a point in time.

Another standard lexicon in the 1800s was *The Hebrew Chaldee Lexicon to the Old Testament Scriptures,* originally written by H.W.F. Gesenius in German. The English translation by Samuel Tregelles offers an almost identical explanation for *yôm*. The entry gives a number of definitions, including "the day," "time," and "a day."[4] Gesenius, like Davidson, understood that *yôm* could have a range of meanings. That fact is reflected throughout Scripture, as *yôm* takes on different definitions based on context.

Based on Genesius's lexicon, *BDB* is another standard lexicon from around the same time period. As I mentioned above, *BDB* has seven headings and many subheadings in the entry for *yôm*. One of the definitions is "day as defined by evening and morning, with references to Genesis 1:5, 8, 13, 19, 23, and 31. The other definitions include "days of any one" (as in

---

3. Benjamin Davidson, *The Analytical Hebrew and Chaldee Lexicon* (1848; repr., Grand Rapids, MI: Zondervan, 1970), s.v. "יום."

4. H.W.F. Gesenius, *Hebrew and Chaldee Lexicon to the Old Testament Scriptures*, trans. Samuel Prideaux Tregelles (1846; repr., Grand Rapids, MI: Wm. B. Eerdmans Publishing Company, 1949), s.v. "יום."

someone's life) and "time."[5] So among scholars in the 1800s, it seems clear that there was general agreement on the range of meanings *yôm* could have, with a 24-hour day being one of the primary definitions.

What about some present-day lexicons? As I said before, many times modern Bible scholars are more liberal in their thinking than early scholars. Jenni and Westermann's *Theological Lexicon of the Old Testament* (*TLOT*), which unlike a typical lexicon explains how a word has been used over the course of time, tells us, "the basic meaning of *yôm* is 'day (from sunrise to sundown)' . . ."[6] *TLOT* continues, "As in most languages, this basic meaning broadens to 'day (of 24 hours)' in the sense of the astronomical and calendrical unit. . . ."[7] Now, *TLOT* takes a compromise position on the creation account in Genesis (I assert because of the influence of millions of years), but in spite of that, it still admits the definition of *yôm* is most broadly "day."

One of the most well-known lexicons today is *The Hebrew and Aramaic Lexicon of the Old Testament* (*HALOT*) by Koehler and Baumgartner (the English translation was published in 2001). Under the entry for *yôm*, *HALOT* provides definitions including, "day, daylight," "day of twenty-four hours," and "period of time."[8] Now, in a lexicon that was published in the midst of many challenges from outside and within the Church to the literal truth of Genesis 1, it would probably be safe to assume that *HALOT* does not consider the appearances of *yôm* in the first chapter of Genesis to be 24-hour days. But actually, it does! Alongside the meaning "day of twenty-four hours," *HALOT* directs readers to Genesis 1:5: "So the evening and the morning were the first day."

Theological Dictionaries. Another source we can turn to for answers to the question of how the word *yôm* is used in Scripture is a theological dictionary. A standard dictionary used in many seminaries is the *Theological Wordbook of the Old Testament* (*TWOT*). The entry for *yôm* in *TWOT* offers a list of definitions as well as further explanation:

5. Francis Brown, S.R. Driver, and Charles Briggs, *The Brown-Driver-Briggs Hebrew and English Lexicon* (1906; repr., Peabody, MA: Hendrickson, 1996), s.v. "יום."

6. Ernst Jenni and Claus Westermann, *Theological Lexicon of the Old Testament*, vol. 2, trans. Mark E. Biddle (Peabody, MA: Hendrickson, 1997), s.v. "יום."

7. Ibid.

8. Ludwig Koehler and Walter Baumgartner, *The Hebrew and Aramaic Lexicon of the Old Testament*, vol. 1 (Boston, MA: Brill, 2001), s.v. "I יום." It is important to note that *HALOT* distinguishes between two different versions of *yôm*, known as *yôm* 1 and *yôm* 2. While *yôm* 1 means day, *yôm* 2 (the same word) means "wind, storm" or "breath." In either case, the meaning is based on context.

Our word is the "most important concept of time in the OT by which a point of time as well as a sphere of time can be expressed." . . . It can denote: 1. the period of light (as contrasted with the period of darkness), 2. the period of twenty-four hours, 3. a general vague "time," 4. a point of time, 5. a year.[9]

According to *TWOT*, the Hebrew word for day clearly indicates a period of time, and the first two definitions relate to the cycle of day and night. Farther into the entry, the writer explains "Time ('days') was created by God (Gen 1). . . ."[10] Exactly! God created time, so why couldn't the days of Creation Week be normal-length days? Despite this, the writer of this *TWOT* entry still takes a compromise view of Genesis, even though it contradicts his own explanation. I suggest the writer has been influenced by outside ideas (such as millions of years), which has resulted in this compromise view.

The *Theological Dictionary of the Old Testament* (*TDOT*), published in 1990, is another well-known dictionary available in many seminaries. Under the entry for *yôm*, the writers explain that *yôm* refers to units of time, specifically a 24-hour day:

> The fixed natural basis of *yôm* is "light." "Day" in the narrow sense refers to the daylight period in contrast to the "night." The relationship of "day" to "night" is essentially that of "light" to "darkness," although night is not totally without light. . . . When longer units are involved, however, we are not dealing with the day as "daylight" but with the calendar day of twenty-four hours, for which Hebrew . . . does not have a special word. This "full day" includes "night". . . . From its outset at creation (Gen. 1:3–5), *yôm* as "full day" had the same beginning as *yôm* in the narrower sense, namely morning. . . .[11]

In other words, in Genesis 1, the days of creation are literal days with a period of daylight and a period of darkness. So another respected theological reference source recognizes that these days seem to be literal days.

---

9. Leonard J. Coppes, "יוֹם," *Theological Wordbook of the Old Testament*, R. Laird Harris, Gleason L. Archer, and Bruce K. Waltke (Chicago, IL: Moody Publishers, 1980).

10. Ibid.

11. M. Sæbø, "יוֹם," G. Johannes Botterweck and Helmer Ringgren, eds., *Theological Dictionary of the Old Testament*, vol. 6, trans. David E. Green (Grand Rapids, MI: Eerdmans, 1990).

Now, there are two more dictionaries worth referencing on this issue that are even more recent. Surely, with all of the compromise on the days of creation happening among Bible scholars, these reference resources will have compromised on Genesis 1 as well. Let's see what they have to say.

The *New International Dictionary of Old Testament Theology & Exegesis* (*NIDOTTE*) tells us that two of the possible meanings of *yôm* are "daylight" and "day (24 hours)."[12] The entry continues:

> As a measurement of time the term (*yôm*) has three principal uses. (a) Its primary meaning is the time of daylight as distinct from the period of darkness, the night. For example, in Gen 1:5 God called the light "day" . . . (b) The term is also used for day in the sense of the complete cycle that includes both daytime and nighttime, e.g. Gen. 1:5: "And there was evening, and there was morning — the first day."[13]

With such an authoritative dictionary as *NIDOTTE* pointing to Genesis 1 as a clear example of *yôm* meaning a 24-hour day, why do so many Bible scholars still insist that the text does not communicate this? After all, the men writing these lexicons and dictionaries are expert Hebraists and scholars — surely they are not mistaken in their understanding of the Hebrew language in the first chapter of the Bible!

The final dictionary I want to examine is *The Dictionary of Classical Hebrew*, published in 1998. Surprisingly, this dictionary also tells readers that *yôm* can refer to a "day, of 24 hours" and points to Genesis 1:5 as an example.[14]

Incredible! Even some of the most respected lexicons and theological dictionaries of our day admit that the days in Genesis 1 were ordinary, normal-length days. So what's the problem then? Why do so many Bible scholars and church leaders refuse to accept the plain reading of the creation account? I remember during a debate with Dr. Walt Kaiser on the *John Ankerberg Show* how he reacted to my pointing out the definitions *BDB* and *HALOT* give for the days in Genesis 1. Dr. Kaiser, who retired in 2006, is distinguished professor of Old Testament and former president of Gordon-Conwell Theological Seminary in South Hamilton, Massachusetts.

---

12. Willem A. VanGemeren, gen. ed., *New International Dictionary of Old Testament Theology & Exegesis*, vol. 2 (Grand Rapids, MI: Zondervan, 1997), s.v. "יוֹם."

13. Ibid.

14. David J.A. Clines, ed., *The Dictionary of Classical Hebrew*, vol. 4 (Sheffield: Sheffield Academic Press, 1998), s.v. "יוֹם I."

Now, I presented these definitions to Dr. Kaiser in the hope that he would see what these Hebraists had to say about the word *yôm* and change his mind about the days of Creation Week. But Dr. Kaiser's response was unfortunate. He said, "My answer is that God had not yet created a 24-hour day, so too bad for Brown-Driver-Briggs and too bad for Koehler and Baumgartner."[15] Sadly, Dr. Kaiser's response is consistent with many compromised Bible scholars and church leaders. They simply do not want to see what God's Word says because of their own presuppositions (and I assert, presuppositions in regard to the supposed millions of years).

While lexicons are incredibly helpful in determining the range of meanings a Hebrew word can have, we also need another piece of information concerning *yôm*. Typically, when *yôm* is used to indicate a 24-hour day, it is accompanied by some combination of morning, evening, and a number. For example, Genesis 1:8 says, "So the **evening** and the **morning** were the **second** day" (emphases mine).

Do you see the pattern? Evening, morning, number, day. That's the easiest way to remember it. These qualifiers are present in each of the instances of Day 6 of Creation Week (except that Genesis 1:5 is worded a bit differently, which will be explained below). In fact, this in the pattern throughout Scripture for the word *yôm* when used in reference to a literal day (one exception will be discussed in the next section).

Literary Devices and Figurative Language. But are there any exceptions to this rule? Actually, there are two verses that follow the pattern, but that do not refer to an ordinary day. I want to focus on just one of them here (Hosea 6:2), but see the footnote for a summary of the other exception.[16] In the Book of Hosea, we find a reference to days combined with numbers (remember, there needs to be a combination of evening, morning, number, day), but the days are not literal days:

> After two days He will revive us;
> On the third day He will raise us up,
> That we may live in His sight. (Hosea 6:2)

---

15. Ken Ham, Jason Lisle, Walt Kaiser, Hugh Ross, interview by John Ankerberg, *The Great Debate on Science and the Bible*, DVD (Hebron, KY: Answers in Genesis, 2006).

16. Zechariah 14:7 does follow the pattern but does not refer to an ordinary day. The verse is apocalyptic and references the future "Day of the Lord," so this language is to be expected.

Now, how do we know these uses of *yôm* are not in reference to literal, 24-hour days? In the historical-grammatical hermeneutic, our goal is to read each passage in its most natural sense. This passage's genre is poetry, which is often filled with figurative language. When we read this verse in Hosea, it becomes clear that three literal days are not what the author had in view.

This literary device is also seen in Proverbs:

> These six things the LORD hates,
> Yes, seven are an abomination to Him. (Proverbs 6:16)

Does the Lord hate only seven things? Of course not. God hates sin in general, and there are many more types of sin than seven. What the author in Proverbs is doing is using a literary device to indicate a much larger concept. The same is true of Hosea 6:2. The author is not trying to communicate that two or three literal days will pass before something happens. No, he is using figurative language to show that the Lord will indeed raise them up at some point, probably in a short amount of time. Since this passage in Hosea is poetic, figurative language is to be expected.

So what is the difference between Hosea 6:2 and the days of creation in Genesis 1? While Hosea 6:2 is poetic, Genesis 1 is not. Dr. Steven Boyd, professor of Old Testament and Hebrew at The Master's College in Santa Clarita, California, has shown definitively that Genesis is historical narrative.[17] In other words, Genesis is intended to be read as literal history! So we can safely assume that *yôm* in Genesis 1 refers to normal-length days.

Meaning Based on Context

As pointed out above, the meaning of *yôm* is determined based on context. Let's apply this to the English word *back*. For example, imagine that you are attending a conference. You might be sitting at the *back* of the room, with your *back* against the *back* of the chair. And you probably came *back* to the conference after being there the night before and now have a sore *back*. What was the meaning of the word *back* in that example? Well, that is a trick question. It had more than one meaning, correct?

The English word *day* is like that. For instance, we could say, "Back in my father's *day*." Does that refer to an ordinary day, or does it refer to a

---

17. Steven W. Boyd, "The Genre of Genesis 1:1–2:3: What Means This Text?" in Terry Mortenson and Thane H. Ury, eds., *Coming to Grips with Genesis: Biblical Authority and the Age of the Earth* (Green Forest, AR: Master Books, 2008), p. 163–192.

period in time? It refers to time, right? What about the statement, "It took ten days to drive across the Australian outback"? That means ten, 24-hour days. What about the phrase, "During the day"? If you go to college during the day, that means basically the daylight portion of a day. These are examples of the word *day* with three different meanings.

In the same way, the Hebrew word *yôm* has a range of meanings. What is interesting is that there are times when *yôm* means time, like "in the day of the Lord." Or "in the time of the judges." Or "in the day that you eat of it you will surely die." All of those uses refer to a period in time, which was one of the options the lexicons above presented as a possible meaning for *yôm*.

What about in Genesis 1? As we learned above, when *yôm* is accompanied by evening, morning, or a number (or a combination of these), then it almost always refers to a literal day. Now, the context of Genesis 1 is the miraculous creation of the universe. There is no reason for this to be a figurative passage — God is literally recounting to us how the universe and everything in it was made.

When we read Genesis 1, we are reading the History Book of the Universe! It is an eyewitness account from the only One who was there. Throughout the chapter, we see the reappearance of the words *morning* and *evening*. In context, these words each denote half of a full day:

> So the evening and the morning were the second day. (Genesis 1:8)

This is the case for all six days of Creation Week. We see evening, morning, number, day. However, Genesis 1:5 provides an interesting exception to the number pattern. Many translations will say there was evening and morning the *first* day. But that is not actually how that verse should be translated.

Abner Chou, associate professor of biblical studies at The Master's College, wrote an article for *Answers* magazine (the family magazine published by our ministry, Answers in Genesis), where he explained how Genesis 1:5 should be translated and why it is helpful to our understanding of *yôm*:

> . . . the Hebrew words in Genesis 1:5 read *one day* and not *first day*. This argues that Moses believed one day is marked by a cycle of morning and evening. . . .[18]

---

18. Abner Chou, "Genesis — The Original Myth Buster," *Answers*, April–June 2013, p. 26–29.

Chou's assertion is reaffirmed in the work of E.A. Speiser, who noted, "In Semitic . . . the normal ordinal series is '*one*, second, third,' etc., not '*first*, second, third,' etc." (emphases Speiser's).[19] And the most authoritative work on the subject also affirms Chou's claim:

> Therefore, by using a most unusual grammatical construction, Genesis 1 is defining what a day is. This is especially needed in this verse [Genesis 1:5], since "day" is used in two senses in this one verse. Its first occurrence means the time during a daily cycle that is illuminated by daylight (as opposed to "night"). The second use means something different, a time period that encompasses both the time of daylight and the time of darkness.[20]

So if Moses, as the inspired author of the Pentateuch, clearly believed that a day meant morning and evening in Genesis 1, why shouldn't we? The normal usage of the word *yôm* allows it, and the context of Genesis 1 demands it. But there is one more aspect to examine that should make very clear how readers are intended to understand *yôm* in the first chapter of Genesis: the theological (Scripture interpreting Scripture) aspect.

What Does Scripture Say about Creation Week?

In order to fully understand the use of *yôm* in the opening chapter of the Bible, we need to examine what other parts of Scripture have to say about it. There is no better interpreter of God's Word than the Word of God itself. In Exodus, we read that God commanded Moses to say to the children of Israel:

> Work shall be done for six days, but the seventh is the Sabbath of rest, holy to the LORD. Whoever does any work on the Sabbath day, he shall surely be put to death. Therefore the children of Israel shall keep the Sabbath, to observe the Sabbath throughout their generations as a perpetual covenant. It is a sign between Me and the children of Israel forever; for in six days the LORD made the heavens and the earth, and on the seventh day He rested and was refreshed. (Exodus 31:15–17)

Here, Moses uses a reference to Creation Week to set up the workweek for the Israelites. Now, if the days of Creation Week were long, indefinite periods of

---

19. *Genesis, The Anchor Bible*, trans. E.A. Speiser (Garden City, NY: Doubleday, 1964), p. 6.

20. Andrew E. Steinmann, "אחד as an Ordinal Number and the Meaning of Genesis 1:5," *Journal of the Evangelical Theological Society* 45, no. 4 (2002): 583.

time, then the reference to the week of creation would set up an incredibly long workweek! But that is not how the days of creation are used in Exodus 31.

"Work shall be done for six days . . . for in six days the Lord made the heavens and the earth." Do you see how similar those statements are? Contextually, it would not make sense if the days in the first statement were 24-hour days and the days in the second statement were millions of years each.

But that is only one instance. Wouldn't it be helpful if Moses had made this sort of a reference to Creation Week more than once? Actually, he did! Moses's clear belief that the days of creation were normal-length days is reaffirmed in Exodus 20:11, in the Fourth Commandment:

> For in six days the LORD made the heavens and the earth, the sea, and all that is in them, and rested the seventh day. Therefore the LORD blessed the Sabbath day and hallowed it.

In Exodus 31 (above), Moses references the Sabbath day: "but the seventh is the Sabbath of rest, holy to the LORD. . . . and on the seventh day He rested and was refreshed." In Exodus 20, Moses writes of the Sabbath once again, explaining that the Lord God Himself blessed the Sabbath and made it holy . . . *after six days of creation.*

Commentators and Scholars. One final place we can turn for help in understanding what *yôm* means in Genesis 1 is the work of commentators and other scholars, such as Hebraists. Of course, humans are prone to error. That is why we are seeing so much compromise in our churches and Christian institutions! However, it is important that we reference the works of scholars who, even if they do not adhere to a literal reading of Genesis 1, still note that the text seems to point to literal 24-hour days of creation.

In *The Anchor Bible*, a well-known translation from the 1960s, E.A. Speiser notes regarding the days of Genesis 1 that "the evening marks the first half of the full day."[21] If the days were not actual days, why would there be mention of an evening portion and a morning portion?

Another scholar, John Skinner, writes emphatically that *yôm* does not refer to long ages:

> The interpretation of םוי as *æon*, a favourite resource of harmonists of science and revelation, is opposed to the plain sense of the passage, and has no warrant in Heb. usage (not even Ps. 90). It

---

21. *Genesis, The Anchor Bible*, trans. E.A. Speiser, p. 6.

is true that the conception of successive creative periods, extending over vast spaces of time, is found in other cosmogonies (De. 55); but it springs in part from views of the world which are foreign to the OT. To introduce that idea here not only destroys the analogy on which the sanction of the Sabbath rests, but misconceives the character of the Priestly Code. If the writer had had æons in his mind, he would hardly have missed the opportunity of stating how many millenniums each embraced.[22]

Now, Skinner holds a compromise view of Genesis, because he denies Mosaic authorship. And yet, even he admits that the creation account simply does not refer to long ages. If it did, why doesn't the text say that?

A final quote comes from the late James Barr, a renowned Hebrew scholar and professor, in a personal letter dated April 23, 1984:

> So far as I know, there is no professor of Hebrew or Old Testament at any world-class university who does not believe that the writer(s) of Genesis 1 through 11 intended to convey to their readers the ideas that (a) creation took place in a series of six days which were the same as the days of 24 hours we now experience; (b) the figures contained in the Genesis genealogies provided by simple addition a chronology from the beginning of the world up to later stages in the biblical story; (c) Noah's flood was understood to be worldwide and extinguished all human and animal life except for those in the ark.[23]

As a Hebraist, Barr is concerned with the meanings of Hebrew words, rather than an agenda related to the Bible and what is often called mainstream "science." So his assessment of the Hebrew text should be given far more weight than that of scholars who readily admit that their goal is to harmonize evolutionary ideas with Scripture.

Conclusion

After looking at the historical uses and views of the meaning of the Hebrew word for *day*, particularly in Genesis 1, it should be clear that the days of

---

22. John Skinner, *A Critical and Exegetical Commentary on Genesis, The International Critical Commentary* (New York: Charles Scribner's Sons, 1917), p. 21.

23. Douglas F. Kelly, *Creation and Change: Genesis 1.1–2.4 in the Light of Changing Scientific Paradigms* (Great Britain: Christian Focus Publications, 1997), p. 50–51.

creation were ordinary days. But what is often so disheartening to me in my ministry is that scholars seem to know what *yôm* means everywhere in Scripture — except Genesis 1.

Why is it in Genesis 1 that there is such a problem? Do we ever hear people say, "Well, I don't know how long Joshua took to march around Jericho — was it a million years? Was it a hundred thousand years?" People seem to know what the word for *day* means there. We certainly do not hear people arguing about the word *day* in the rest of the Old Testament. It is always Genesis 1 that there is a problem.

Why is Genesis 1 the problem? I want to suggest that it is because so many people have been influenced to try to fit ideas from the secular world into the Bible. This book is about the eisegesis problem we face today — the process of man, including professing Christians, reading secular ideas (ideas from outside of Scripture) into God's clear Word. Many Christian academics and church leaders are on perilous ground, denying not just the plain reading of Scripture, but also hundreds of years of scholarship. And they are undermining the authority of the Word — that is the issue!

Readers, this is cause for concern. If Bible scholars and church leaders do not return to the authority of God's Word in the first chapters of Genesis, the entire gospel message is undermined.

If someone claimed there was no bodily Resurrection of Christ — then I am sure most Christians would see that as an attack on the gospel. But when someone reinterprets the days of creation to fit in millions of years, many Christians do not see this as an attack on the gospel, and so they say it does not matter. But it is a much more powerful attack — because it is an attack on the *Word* from which the gospel comes. Satan knows if he can get generations of people to doubt and not believe the Word, then ultimately they will reject the gospel that comes from that Word.

Church attendees, including children and young adults, are being taught that the first 11 chapters of the Bible cannot be trusted. But if that is the case, why should they trust Christ's message of hope? I urge you to call these scholars and leaders — most of whom certainly love the Lord and want to see people come to a knowledge of Christ — back to the authority of God's Word in *every* area.

Chapter 6

 Genesis 1 and
Millions of Years

The *Merriam-Webster's Dictionary* defines eisegesis as "the interpretation of a text (as of the Bible) by reading into it one's own ideas."[1]

When someone reads something into Scripture, that would be an example of eisegesis. For instance, nowhere does the Bible ever speak of millions of years. In Scripture, the Hebrew word for day is *yôm*. It appears throughout Genesis 1 to describe the six days of Creation Week, along with a number and the phrase "evening and morning." I demonstrated in the previous chapter that from the context, according to the rules of Hebrew grammar, this means the days of Creation Week were approximately 24-hour periods — ordinary days.

However, many church leaders and academics today insist the days of Creation Week could be symbolic for millions of years (or somehow the supposed millions of years fit somewhere in Genesis 1). I suggest this is an example of eisegesis. Since the Bible does not mention millions of years, I will show you that the Christian leaders and academics who believe millions of years are represented in Genesis are really bringing a belief from outside of Scripture and reading it into Scripture (resulting in the clear words of Scripture being reinterpreted on the basis of an outside idea). If my assertion is

---

1. Merriam-Webster's Dictionary, s.v. "Eisegesis," http://www.merriam-webster.com/dictionary/eisegesis.

true, then this is a serious issue as it is one that relates to authority — God's Word or man's word.

Sadly, as we have shown conclusively from research,[2] eisegesis has infected much of the Church and many of our Christian colleges and seminaries throughout the world. Some church leaders, especially those who attended seminaries and colleges that have compromised on Genesis with millions of years (and as a consequence so have many church members), have developed a way of thinking that accepts many secular ideas such as millions of years and often even evolution, and they now read these ideas into God's Word. I believe I can document (in this and later chapters) that this is happening and is at epidemic proportions in the worldwide Church. And I do believe the state of our Western culture (gay marriage, abortion — an epidemic of moral relativism) is a reflection of the state of a Church that wittingly or unwittingly has compromised the authority of the Word.

The secular world clearly understands that the Church does not believe God's Word as written, but has accepted evolutionary ideas/millions of years (man's word) as truth and has reinterpreted God's Word to fit. Thus, much of the world does not really have any respect for the Bible and generally does not listen to the message of the gospel that is preached from this book. After all, if some of the Church views parts of the Bible as untrustworthy, why should the secular world listen to the gospel message that comes from the Bible? Even atheist and God hater Bill Maher stated recently, "If it's [the Bible] not 100 percent true, I would say the whole thing [the writings that follow Genesis] falls apart."[3]

In an interview on Revelation TV (United Kingdom), Richard Dawkins was asked by interviewer Richard Condor if there was a particular point when he decided that God did not exist. Dawkins's response actually highlighted the problem with compromise in the Church today:

> Oh well, by far the most important, I suppose, was understanding evolution. I think the evangelical Christians have really sort of got it right in a way, in seeing evolution as the enemy. Whereas the more, what shall we say, sophisticated theologians are quite happy to live

---

2. Ken Ham and Greg Hall, *Already Compromised*, with Britt Beemer (Green Forest, AR: Master Books, 2011).

3. Bill Maher, *Real Time with Bill Maher, HBO*, April 20, 2012.

with evolution. I think they are deluded. I think the evangelicals have got it right in that there really is a deep incompatibility between evolution and Christianity.

I never thought I would say this, but for once, Richard Dawkins and I agree on something. There is indeed a "deep incompatibility" with evolution, millions of years, and God's Word. But Dawkins is not the first evolutionist to recognize the problem with compromise in the Church.

T.H. Huxley (1825–1895), an English biologist and advocate of Darwinian evolution, wrote about the necessity of Genesis to Christian doctrine in his essay "The Lights of the Church and the Light of Science." After quoting Matthew 19:5, where Christ quotes Genesis 2 in relation to marriage, Huxley asks, "If divine authority is not here claimed for the twenty-fourth verse of the second chapter of Genesis, what is the value of language? And again, I ask, if one may play fast and loose with the story of the Fall as a 'type' or 'allegory,' what becomes of the foundation of Pauline theology?"[4]

In other words, if Genesis is not literally true, then were Christ and the Apostle Paul simply wrong in their understanding of Genesis? Huxley continues, quoting 1 Corinthians 15:21–22, where the Apostle Paul writes that in Adam all die but in Christ all live:

> If Adam may be held to be no more real a personage than Prometheus, and if the story of the Fall is merely an instructive "type," comparable to the profound Promethean mythus, what value has Paul's dialectic? While, therefore, every right-minded man must sympathise with the efforts of those theologians, who have not been able altogether to close their ears to the still, small, voice of reason, to escape from the fetters which ecclesiasticism has forged; the melancholy fact remains, that the position they have taken up is hopelessly untenable. It is raked alike by the old-fashioned artillery of the Churches and by the fatal weapons of precision with which the *enfants perdus* [lost children] of the advancing forces of science are armed. They must surrender, or fall back into a more sheltered position.[5]

---

4. T.H. Huxley, "The Lights of the Church and the Light of Science," *Science and Hebrew Tradition* (New York: D. Appleton and Co., 1897), p. 235–236.

5. Ibid.

Did you notice what Huxley says about those who compromise on Genesis with evolutionary ideas? Their position is "hopelessly untenable." This is coming from an evolutionist! You see, the world can recognize inconsistencies in Christians' worldviews — and secularists actually love such compromise, as it helps in their battle to get people to reject the Bible entirely. They see that such compromise is incompatible with the Christian worldview, even though they do not hold the biblical worldview.

Many church members (and particularly their children and subsequent generations) recognize that if the Bible has to be reinterpreted on the basis of man's changing opinions, then the Bible is not absolute truth. When churchgoers, especially young people, are taught to use eisegesis in Genesis, then to be consistent, they will apply this same interpretation method to the rest of the Bible. So why not take secular ideas about marriage (e.g., same-sex marriage) and reinterpret the doctrine of marriage in the Bible — which is happening with coming generations from the Church. Ultimately, they stop taking the Bible seriously, and within a generation or two, people begin to reject the Christian faith and stop attending church. As a result, we see two-thirds of young people walking away from the Church by the time they reach college age.[6]

The Age of the Earth

One of the emphases in this chapter concerns Christians and how they approach the issue of the age of the earth. For those people who want millions of years mixed with Scripture, I have to ask a question: How can there be death, diseases (like brain tumors/cancer), and suffering millions of years before Adam sinned? The reason I ask this is because the idea of millions of years arose in the late 18th and early 19th centuries, as atheists and deists attempted to explain most of the fossil record by natural processes — instead of by the global Flood as recorded in the Bible. Secularists claim that most of the fossil record was laid down millions of years before man. Thus, Christians who accept millions of years are accepting that the fossil record — with its record of death, diseases like cancer seen in fossil bones, animals that ate other animals (bones in their stomachs and so on) and thorns (there are fossil thorns said to be millions of years old) — was laid down millions of years before man appeared on the earth.

---

6. Ken Ham and Britt Beemer, *Already Gone*, with Todd Hillard (Green Forest, AR: Master Books, 2009).

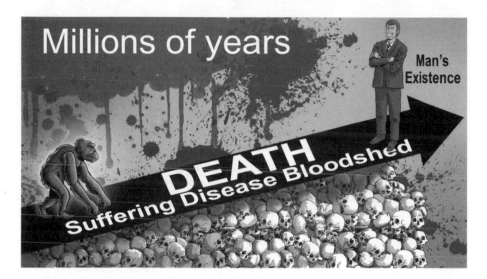

The biblical creationist would look at God's Word and note:

- Genesis 1:31 states that "God saw everything that He had made, and indeed it was very good."

- Genesis 1:29–30 records that animals and humans were vegetarian originally.

- Genesis 3:18 records that thorns came after the Curse.

- Romans 8:22 makes it clear that the whole creation groans because of sin.

- Romans 5:12 states that death was the result of sin.

- 1 Corinthians 15:26 states that death is an "enemy."

The biblical creationist would therefore respond that there could not have been death, carnivory, thorns, disease, and suffering before the Fall. Otherwise, such would contradict God's Word and God would be calling these things "very good"!

Over the years, I have found that in many churches the pastors believe that as long as a Christian does not accept evolution, the age of the earth does not matter. They have the idea that evolution is the problem. But, ultimately, the problem is not evolution — the problem is an authority issue, as I will demonstrate.

When it comes to the issue of origins, evolution is really a symptom, and the supposed millions of years is the disease. (Of course, sin is the ultimate disease — but we are specifically discussing the issue of origins). What undergirds evolutionary thinking is millions of years. Without long ages, evolutionary scientists cannot propose their idea of evolution involving small changes over what is really an incomprehensible amount of time. In fact, historically the idea of millions of years came out of naturalism in the late 1700s and early 1800s. It was popularized before Darwin's ideas about evolution. What's more, when Darwin boarded the HMS *Beagle* and set sail for the Galapagos, he had on board with him books by Sir Charles Lyell, a British lawyer and geologist and a contemporary of Darwin's.

Lyell popularized the idea of millions of years in geological evolution. But if there can be millions of years in geology, why not in biology, too? Thus, Darwin taught that when we see small changes in animals and plants, given enough time, one kind of animal or plant can eventually change into another (e.g., a reptile kind changes into a totally different kind — a bird kind). Time is the issue. Small changes are observed — but the supposed changes for molecules-to-man evolution cannot be observed. But, given millions of years, evolutionists claim this supposedly can happen. Secularists have to have millions of years — it is non-negotiable for their evolutionary beliefs.

The late Dr. Carl Sagan once said, "The secrets of evolution are time and death."[7] Time and death are how life came about. Actually, the Bible does

---

7. Carl Sagan, *Cosmos* (New York: Random House, 1980), p. 4.

not put time and death together. It puts sin and death together, which is a very different scenario.

I want to suggest that this idea of millions/billions of years is actually the pagan religion of the age, intended to explain life without God. It is the foundational aspect of the whole evolutionary process. Without long ages, there cannot be evolution. That is why the secular world will mock anyone who does not believe in millions of years. They cannot allow someone to even question their long ages — they have to have such, regardless of what arguments can be used against this belief.

Sadly, many Christian academics and church leaders have accepted the idea of millions of years and added it to the Bible. In many cases, they do not understand the difference between operational and historical science and have left it to evolutionary scientists to determine some or all of our origins. And I also believe they are often intimidated by the secular world, which accuses them of being anti-intellectual, anti-science, or anti-academic if they do not accept millions of years. Many succumb to this intimidation (some because of academic pride, I believe).

I assert that this addition of millions of years to the Bible has been a major factor in the undermining of biblical authority in the Church today. It has also been one of the reasons that two-thirds of young people in America walk away from the Church by the time they reach college age (and our research and experience suggests this phenomenon permeates the Church in the Western world). When America's Research Group performed the research for our book *Already Gone* (2009), one of the things they found was that the age of the earth had great bearing on whether young people developed doubts about God's Word.

There really is no doubt that the majority of Christian leaders in numerous churches across America would teach that Christians can accept millions of years and/or that the age of the earth does not matter. In fact, there are many different positions in Christendom on the age of the earth.

The reason there are so many different positions on Genesis — whether it is the gap theory, the day-age view, progressive creation, theistic evolution, Adam as a metaphor for Israel, cosmic temple view, the framework hypothesis, historic creation, and so on — is because of man's attempts at fitting millions of years into the Bible. Every single one of these positions undermines the authority of the Word of God, based on one common factor: how to fit millions of years into Genesis.

Think about it: where can you try to force millions of years to fit in the Bible? Not in the genealogies, as that would destroy the history in the Bible. In fact, the secular view of the fossil record requires that the millions of years come before man. According to secular scientists, the fossil record was laid down millions of years before man evolved. So when Christians then take millions of years and try to fit them in the Bible, to fit with the belief from the secularists they have accepted, they inevitably have to add the supposed long ages before man — before the creation of Adam and Eve — within the six days of Creation Week.

I would suggest that much of the Church today is very guilty of adding to the Word of God, particularly concerning the issue of origins in Genesis. Two important passages of Scripture to meditate on when dealing with the problem of eisegesis remind us of whose word matters most:

> Stop regarding man, whose breath of life is in his nostrils; for why should he be esteemed? (Isaiah 2:22, NASB)

> Trust in the LORD with all your heart, and lean not on your own understanding; in all your ways acknowledge Him, and He shall direct your paths. (Proverbs 3:5–6)

Scripture is clear — trust in the Lord, not man! And yet, we have many Christian academics, pastors, and other leaders saying, "Well, because of these outside ideas of evolution and millions of years, we need to reinterpret parts of Genesis." When I first began speaking on the origins issues in the late 70s, I made the statement that if leaders in the Church continue to try to add evolution and/or millions of years into Genesis, eventually people in the Church will end up rejecting Genesis as history. And what do we observe happening today? Sadly, there is an increasing number of Christian academics who now reject a literal Adam and Eve, and a literal Fall! They are appealing to man's historical science, rather than to God's historical science (God's Word). This is not adherence to Scripture; it is adherence to man's secular ideas. At its root, it is an authority issue. Increasingly, people in the Church are making man the authority over God's Word. And this is at epidemic proportions in the Church throughout the world. It is nothing more than the Genesis 3 attack when Satan was able to get Adam and Eve to doubt the Word of God ("Did God really say. . . ?"). And we are warned in 2 Corinthians 11:3 that Satan will use the same method on us — and he is, with great success!

But I fear, lest somehow, as the serpent deceived Eve by his craftiness, so your minds may be corrupted from the simplicity that is in Christ. (2 Corinthians 11:3)

Does the Universe Have the Appearance of Age?

People have come to me and said, "Why couldn't God have created the universe with the appearance of age?" Why would we want that? Some believe it would account for why the universe looks old. But I have to ask, have we ever seen a *young* universe? Do we know what an old one looks like compared to a young one? How do we know it looks old? The reason anyone says the universe "looks old" is because they have already been influenced by secular scientists about millions and billions of years.

Those millions and billions of years never existed, and the universe does not look old. God did not create with the appearance of age. No, He created everything mature. What about Adam? Didn't God create Adam with the appearance of age? No, He created Adam mature, fully functioning, and perfect. Now if we were to take Adam, who was created mature and fully functioning (including reproductive maturity) to a doctor today and have him dissected, the doctor would say, "What happened? This doesn't make sense. It doesn't fit. Why?" It would not make sense because Adam was created perfect, unlike us who are suffering the effects of sin.

What people mean by the "appearance of age" is really just a universe that is decaying because of sin. It is not decaying because of millions of years. God did not create with the appearance of age; He created a mature universe. And because of Adam's sin, and subsequently all of our sin, we see the universe falling apart. When people refer to the appearance of age, they are assuming the dating methods work. Philosophically, they have a problem. The dating methods do not work. Again, these people are being influenced from outside of Scripture — that is why they even ask this question.

Let's consider a number of the positions taken in the Church that attempt to fit millions of years (and even evolution) into Genesis.

The Gap Theory

The first major attempt to harmonize the biblical account of creation with the idea of vast ages in our modern era of history (beginning in the 1800s) was known as the "gap theory." Proponents of this view claim that a huge gap of time (perhaps several billion years) exists between Genesis 1:1 and Genesis 1:2:

> In the beginning God created the heavens and the earth. [Supposed "gap" would be here.] The earth was without form, and void; and darkness was on the face of the deep. And the Spirit of God was hovering over the face of the waters.

There are different versions of the gap theory, but the most popular version is the "ruin-and-reconstruction" idea, which claims that during the supposed gap between verses one and two of Genesis 1, Satan supposedly ruled the earth and led a rebellion against God. As a result, God destroyed this original creation with a flood called Lucifer's flood. Gap theorists believe that Genesis 1:2 describes the conditions of the world following this supposed flood. The *Scofield Reference Bible* explains that this original creation is where fossils and dinosaurs came from, millions of years ago:

> Relegate fossils to the primitive creation, and no conflict of science with the Genesis cosmogony remains.[8]

After the "ruin" of the original creation, this version of the gap theory states that God recreated everything in six days. So proponents of "ruin and reconstruction" usually believe in a literal six-day creation — but it is a recreation, after the supposed long ages (millions of years).

The idea of the ruin-reconstruction gap theory seems to have come from a Scottish Presbyterian minister by the name of Thomas Chalmers, who began to preach this idea in 1804. Chalmers was a leader of the Free Church of Scotland movement. The gap theory enjoyed a great deal of acceptance in the Church. By that time, the idea of millions of years was becoming popular in the United Kingdom. Gap theorists often argue that the word translated as "was" in most English versions of Genesis 1:2 should actually be translated "became" as in "the Earth became formless and void." However, based on the context, this does not really make sense. The gap theory also has a number of hermeneutical (interpretive) problems.

Now, I typically write and speak about Hebrew grammar with great fear and trepidation. I am not a Hebrew scholar; I am a communicator and teacher. However, I do consult with Hebrew experts concerning these

---

8. C.I. Scofield, ed., *Scofield Reference Bible* (New York: Oxford University Press, 1945), p. 4.

matters. Now we have to ask: Does the Hebrew grammar allow for a gap between Genesis 1:1 and 1:2? No! According to Hebrew scholars, time cannot be inserted between Genesis 1:1 and Genesis 1:2 because verse 2 does not follow verse 1 in time.

Verse 2 uses a Hebrew grammatical device called a "*waw*-disjunctive." This is where a sentence begins with the Hebrew word for "and" (*waw* ו) followed by a noun such as the "earth" (*erets* ארץ). A *waw*-disjunctive indicates that the sentence is describing the previous one — it does not follow in time. In other words, verse 2 is describing the conditions of the earth when it was first created — "without form and void." Hebrew grammar does not allow for the insertion of vast periods of time between Genesis 1:1 and 1:2.

I had someone ask me once, "Why would God create an earth like that? Why would He create it in a chaotic state?" Actually, God did not create the earth in a chaotic state — He created it "without form and void." The land surface had not risen yet; that happened on Day 3. There was no life on earth either. Verse 2 is really an apt description of the earth God first created, covered in water, without form, and devoid of life.

Second, Exodus 20:11 clearly teaches that everything was created in the span of six days — this is the basis for our workweek:

> For in six days the LORD made the heavens and the earth [referencing verse one of Genesis 1], the sea, and all that is in them, and rested the seventh day. Therefore the LORD blessed the Sabbath day and hallowed it. (Exodus 20:11)

Under the principle of Scripture interpreting Scripture, this passage clearly does not allow for vast periods of time between any of the days of creation — contrary to the teachings of gap theorists.

The last issue is that most versions of the gap theory put death, thorns, carnivory, disease (like cancer), and suffering (as observed in the fossil record) long before Adam's sin. Of course, that really means that God would have considered such things to be "very good" — which is not consistent with His character.

Sadly, there have been a couple of well-known study Bibles that have pushed the gap theory in their study notes and commentaries on Genesis. I mentioned the *Scofield Reference Bible* earlier. Between Genesis 1:1 and 1:2, the Scofield Bible notes, "Earth made waste and empty by judgment."[9] This does not appear in the actual text of Genesis, but it has been added in to the Scofield Bible.

Another study Bible that promotes the gap theory is the Newberry Bible. In Genesis 1, the Newberry Bible contains a marginal note indicating that Ussher's date of 4004 B.C. for the creation begins at verse 2.[10] What was happening in verse 1? We can assume some form of the "ruin-and-recon-struction" view. There is even a large space between verses 1 and 2 on the page of this Bible — likely representing a supposed "gap."

Dake's Annotated Reference Bible has even more to say about the gap theory. The notes in this study Bible indicate that man's historical science must be mixed with Scripture:

> When men finally agree on the age of the earth, then place the many years (over the historical 6,000) between Genesis 1:1 and 1:2, there will be no conflict between the Book of Genesis and science.[11]

The problem with this assertion is that there is no conflict between observa-tional science and the Bible — only between man's historical science (man's beliefs about the past) and the Bible. But rather than trust God's Word on creation, Dake appeals to man's belief in millions of years and claims that the Bible says nothing about the age of the earth:

> We cannot say how old the earth is because we do not know WHEN the beginning was. God's creation of the heavens and the earth in the beginning could have been millions and billions of years ago. If geologists can prove the age of the earth to be what they claim, we have no scriptural authority to disagree. They cannot con-tradict the Bible, for it does not reveal any time element in connec-tion with the earth's original creation. This much is certain, accord-ing to Scripture, that the earth is more than 6,000 years old, and there were inhabitants on the earth before the days of Adam. The earth was cursed and flooded, as in Gen. 1:2 because of sin before the 6 days of re-creation in 1:3–2:25. Lucifer was already a fallen

9. Ibid., p. 3.

10. Thomas Newberry, *The Holy Bible* (London, England: Hodder and Stoughton, 1895), p. 1.

11. Finis Jennings Dake, *Dake's Annotated Reference Bible* (Lawrenceville, GA: Dake Bible Sales, 1963), p. 51.

creature when he came into Adam's Eden, having already ruled the earth, rebelled and caused the first flood.[12]

Actually, we *can* say with authority that the earth is approximately 6,000 years old, based on the six literal days of creation (which I assert were ordinary days, as discussed in the previous chapter) and the genealogical records provided in the Old Testament. Of course, the Bible does not say exactly what the age of the earth is — if it did, it would be out of date the next year! (Remember, the written Word was complete about 2,000 years ago.) But God's Word gives specific details about the history from the beginning that allows us to calculate the approximate date of creation.

Genesis 1:1 tells us that the earth was created on Day 1 of Creation Week: "In the beginning God created the heavens and the earth." We know that Adam was created on Day 6, so we can begin our calculation there, leaving five days before Adam. When we add up the dates from Adam to Abraham, using the genealogies in Genesis 5 and 11, we arrive at about 2,000 years. Most scholars agree that Abraham lived around 2,000 B.C. Then from Abraham to the present day, we arrive at about 4,000 years. So in total, from Day 1 of Creation Week until now, only around 6,000 years have passed.

We may not enjoy reading all the "begats" in biblical genealogies, but they hold some very important clues about the age of the earth!

Now, Dake's study Bible includes an explanation of the supposed "original" creation as though it is fact — yet it is not actually found in the text:

> The ante-chaotic age — from the original creation (1:1) to chaos (1:2), during which time Lucifer ruled the earth in perfection, before he fell and caused the earth to be made chaotic and flooded. This age took in all the period of the dateless past, the original creations, Lucifer's reign in perfection, the period of rebellion by Lucifer and pre-Adamites, the actual war between heaven and earth, culminating in the defeat of Lucifer and his armies as they invaded heaven and the chaotic period on earth after the defeat of Lucifer's kingdom. These periods were of unknown length and could be called the Eternal Past.[13]

---

12. Ibid., p. 53.
13. Ibid., p. 58.

That last line is especially problematic — "periods" of "unknown length." This sort of eisegesis allows for the squeezing of millions of years between the first two verses of Genesis 1. The line of reasoning that gap theorists take here violates the first principle of the historical-grammatical hermeneutic, which is to observe the text. Genesis 1 says nothing about long ages, so it is unreasonable to assert that not only were there long ages but also a series of events that are pure speculation.

The first major publication that popularized the gap theory was *Earth's Earliest Ages* by G.H. Pember (1837–1910), an English theologian. In his book, Pember essentially contradicts himself. He starts by saying that we must start with Scripture (and we say "Amen" to that) — but he then proceeds to add millions of years between Genesis 1:1 and 1:2:

> Let him but believe that the Bible is the infallible word of the great Creator, and that all men are, and ever have been, prone to error, and he will readily see that to discover the truth of any doctrine he must first strive to divest himself of preconceived notions, of all that he has ever heard about it, and of all feeling either for or against it. And then, with prayer for the Spirit's aid, let him examine every portion of Scripture which bears upon it, noting the simple and obvious teaching of each, and observing how the various texts interpret and corroborate one another. So will he by God's help arrive at the truth.[14]

According to Pember's method outlined above, readers of the Bible should look for "the simple and obvious teaching of each" portion of Scripture. Readers must carefully observe the text, so as not to commit eisegesis. But then Pember, not much farther into the book, commits this very error:

> . . . but there is no hint of the time which elapsed between creation and this ruin. Age after age may have rolled away, and it was probably during their course that the strata of the earth's crust were gradually developed. Hence we see that geological attacks upon the Scriptures are altogether wide of the mark, are a mere beating of the air. There is room for any length of time between the first and second verses of the Bible. And again; since we have no inspired account of the geological formations, we are at liberty to believe that they were

---

14. G.H. Pember, *Earth's Earliest Ages* (Glasgow: Pickering & Inglis, Printers and Publishers, 1900), p. 9.

developed just in the order in which we find them. The whole process took place in preadamite times, in connection, perhaps, with another race of beings, and, consequently, does not at present concern us.[15]

What Pember has done here is lifted man's historical science above the Word of God. Because man's evolutionary geology claimed in his time that long ages led to the rock layers and fossil record, Pember writes that "any length of time" could fit between the first two verses of Genesis 1. I have detailed this because I believe many of our Christian leaders today (including even many conservative ones) are committing the same type of error as Pember — but they do not seem to see it, even as Pember did not see the error he was committing (even though he spoke against it!).

What's more, Pember joins others in claiming there were "preadamites." Where in Scripture are these so-called pre-adamites? We cannot find them in the Bible, because they are not mentioned. There was no such thing. According to 1 Corinthians 15:45, the first man was Adam. There are no pre-adamites.

More recently than Pember, Arthur Custance (1910–1985), a Canadian anthropologist and professing Christian, wrote *Without Form and Void*, in which he also promoted the gap theory. He claimed that Genesis 1:2 has a different meaning than we usually understand:

> By and large, therefore, I suggest that the rendering, "But the earth *had become* a ruin and a desolation," is a rendering which does *more* justice to the original. . . . It is, after all, quite conceivable that some catastrophe *did* occur prior to the appearance of Man for which we do not yet have the kind of geological evidence we would like. Only twenty years ago uniformitarianism reigned supreme — but recently the Theory of Continental Drift has shaken this long established doctrine to its foundations. There could be other surprises yet in store for us.[16]

This is a common idea among gap theorists. Genesis 1:2 clearly says, "The earth was without form, and void." But Custance and other gap theorists argue that the word *was* should actually be translated "became" or "had

---

15. Ibid., p. 28.

16. Arthur C. Custance, *Without Form and Void: A Study of the Meaning of Genesis 1:2* (Ontario, Canada: Doorway Publications, 1970), p. 116.

become." So the verse would read, "The earth *became* without form, and void," or "*had become* without form, void." Now, I do not want to deal with the technical aspects of Hebrew. Suffice it to say, no major English translation adopts the gap theorists' view of Genesis 1:2. The word really is *was*. Genesis 1:2 is simply a description of the earth as explained earlier — it was without form, and void.

The reason gap theorists insist on an alternate translation for Genesis 1:2 is because they not only want to fit long ages into Genesis, but they also hold to the belief that Lucifer was judged at that point. Because of Lucifer's judgment, they claim, the earth became without form, and void. They often refer to Jeremiah 4:23, which states, "I beheld the earth, and indeed it was without form, and void; and the heavens, they had no light." Now, the context of this passage is a judgment on the Israelites because of their sin, and it contains the same Hebrew phrase used in Genesis 1:2. They read that and decide that there must have been a judgment in Genesis 1 as well. But that is not a good hermeneutic — Jeremiah is not interpreting the meaning of Genesis 1:2. We cannot use a subsequent use and application of that phrase to establish a prior meaning.

For example, consider Winston Churchill. Churchill, when talking about the Battle of Britain pilots, made the comment that this was their finest hour. Because that is such a famous statement, people will sometimes use it in reference to other situations. For instance, someone might say about a hockey team that has just won a game, "Wow, this was their finest hour," thinking back to the time that Churchill made that statement about the Battle of Britain. This does not mean that Churchill was referring to a hockey game or a soccer game when he first said that in reference to the Battle of Britain. Not at all. We take the phrase he used and then use it in a different way, known as a literary allusion, but it does not mean we then go back and reinterpret what Churchill meant or was referring to. We have exactly the same situation with Jeremiah and Genesis. The way the phrase is used in Jeremiah cannot be used to determine the meaning in Genesis. The prophet took the phrase from Genesis and applied it in a particular way as an allusion to what happened in Genesis 1, because the earth originally was without form and void — it did not have life. Jeremiah is saying, "Look what's happened now. God's judging the land because of your sin. The land is like it was originally before God added form, life." Jeremiah is alluding back to that — using a literary allusion.

Not long ago, I spoke in a conference in Nashville. Afterward, someone said, "My pastor is teaching me the gap theory, and he uses Genesis 1:28 where it says to be fruitful, multiply, and replenish the earth, which means refill the earth." I replied, "Your pastor needs to teach you correctly. If you go back and look at the Hebrew word that's translated 'replenish' in the King James, you'll find in other translations they don't use the word *replenish*. There's a reason for that. The Hebrew word translated 'replenish' means fill or fill up, or fulfill. It doesn't mean refill."

Stacia McKeever, one of our staff members at Answers in Genesis, wrote an article on the translation of the word *replenish*, available on our website. She explains what the word really means:

> The word *replenish* in the King James Version was used in the seventeenth century (when the King James Version was translated) to simply mean "fill." It expressed such ideas as to stock, fill, supply, or inhabit. Replenish is related to the word *replete*; being replete with happiness is being full with happiness.[17]

Furthermore, according to the *Oxford English Dictionary*, the first recorded uses of the word *replenish* to mean "to fill again" occurred as early as 1612, one year after the King James Version of the Bible was published.[18] It was used in a poetic sense.

But Genesis 1:28 is not poetry. The point is that the English word *replenish* has changed meanings over the centuries so that today it generally means "to fill again." But it did not mean that when the King James Version was first translated. As far as we know, at that time it meant "to fill," which is exactly what the Hebrew word (translated *replenish* in the King James) means if you look it up in any Hebrew dictionary.

I remember the day I had lunch with the late Adrian Rogers — a great Christian leader and powerful Bible expositor. He and his wife, and his associate pastor at the time and his wife, took me out for a meal. I will never forget it. We sat down at the restaurant, and Dr. Rogers said to me, "I've always believed the gap theory." I thought, *Oh dear, what do I do now?* He said, "Tell me, why is the gap theory wrong?"

"Do you really want me to tell you what I believe?"

---

17. Stacia McKeever, "Replenish or Fill?" Answers in Genesis, http://www.answersingenesis.org/articles/2008/12/22/contradictions-full-of-meaning.

18. *Oxford English Dictionary*, s.v. "Replenish."

"Yes, I want you to tell me." He was such a grandfatherly man. I loved Dr. Rogers. So I started writing down all these sorts of arguments on a napkin — I wish I had kept that napkin. At the end of that, he looked at me and said, "I need to give up the gap theory." It was an incredible conversation. I was so moved by his humble spirit. But, sadly, there are many Christian leaders who would not be prepared to say something like that about the gap theory or any other compromise position because they are long-held, cherished views.

I want to suggest that ultimately, the reason pastors argue for the gap theory and these odd translations and definitions is not because they are trying to make an argument from Scripture. I believe they have been influenced by sources outside of Scripture, particularly secular scientists' conclusion that the universe is billions of years old. And that is what is destroying the Church in America. We are letting man be the authority over the Word of God, and we are incorporating man's ideas into the Word of God.

A Self-Defeating Argument

Over the years, I have spoken on the gap theory numerous times. But it really hit me one day how inconsistent the gap theory is. It is logically inconsistent. Think about it. The gap theory actually explains away the very thing it is supposed to be accommodating.

What do I mean by that? Well, why would gap theorists choose to place a gap in between Genesis 1:1 and 1:2? Ultimately because they want to fit millions of years into Genesis. And where did the millions of years come from? The idea came from man's belief that the fossils were laid down slowly over long ages before man appeared on the earth. So, in essence, the gap theorist says, "I'll accept the millions of years developed by those who claim the layers of fossils were laid down slowly over long ages, and place all this in a gap between Genesis 1:1 and 1:2, and then explain it away with a catastrophe called Lucifer's flood." And right there, he has just done away with the reason he wanted millions of years in the first place. If a catastrophe produced the fossils — then the reason for the millions of years in the first place has been destroyed! What an incredible inconsistency.

The gap theorist explains the fossil record with a catastrophe, but the idea of millions of years comes from the belief that most of the fossil layers were formed over slow processes, not a catastrophe. The gap theory actually fails to accommodate secular geology because secularists do not recognize a global Flood of any kind to explain the fossil record. I often say to people, if you want to explain the fossils with a flood, why on earth try to do it with a flood that the Bible does not even talk about? Why not do it with one the Bible does talk about, specifically the Flood of Noah's day?

The gap theory also eliminates the evidence for the global Flood. The global Flood of Noah's day is the only one found in the Bible. Gap theorists generally advocate a local flood for this event. Why? Arthur Custance, a gap theorist, wrote that the Flood was local:

> . . . a strict adherence to the *literal* wording of chapters 6 to 8 of Genesis leaves us with little alternative than to view the Flood as universal insofar as mankind was concerned since the human race was reduced to eight souls only, but local insofar as man was at that time still confined to a comparatively small geographical area.[19]

Here's the point: in the 1800s, there were a number of church leaders who started to talk about a local flood rather than a global one. Why? Because if there had been a global Flood, it would have ripped up all the fossils that gap theorists believe were already there from a supposed flood between Genesis 1:1 and 1:2 and would have re-deposited them. What's more, because evolutionists believe the fossils came by slow processes over millions of years, there cannot have been a global Flood. Therefore, gap theorists postulate a local flood. Getting confused?

The reason the gap theorists argue for a local flood is because they are influenced from outside of Scripture. In fact, I think the summary from *Dake's Annotated Reference Bible* above sums up what they are really doing: "When men finally agree on the age of the earth, then place the many years (over the historical 6,000) between Genesis 1:1 and 1:2, there will be no conflict between the Book of Genesis and science."

The gap theorists (like all others who compromise Genesis with millions of years) have confused operational and historical science, and have appealed to man's word over God's. There is no doubt that gap theorists have started outside of Scripture.

---

19. Arthur C. Custance, *The Flood: Local or Global?* vol. 9, The Doorway Papers (Grand Rapids, MI: Zondervan, 1979), p. 7.

Historic Creation

The historic creation view, which is really a modified gap theory, was popularized by John Sailhamer, professor of Old Testament Studies at Golden Gate Baptist University in Brea, California, and author of *Genesis Unbound*. This view has become very popular among some Christian leaders and academics.

Many proponents of the historic creation view believe that God created the heavens and the earth over an indefinite period of time in Genesis 1:1. Then in Genesis 1:2 and following, proponents claim, God prepared the uninhabitable land for man in six days. Sailhamer explains this view further:

> In the first act, God created the universe we see around us today, consisting of the earth, the sun, the moon, the stars, and all the plants and animals that now inhabit (or formerly inhabited) the earth. The biblical record of that act of creation is recounted in Genesis 1:1 — "In the beginning, God created the heavens and the earth." Since the Hebrew word translated "beginning" refers to an indefinite period of time, we cannot say for certain when God created the world or how long He took to create it. This period could have spanned as much as several billion years. . . .[20]

There it is, the real motive: accepting billions of years and attempting to fit this into the text of Scripture. Whenever I read what scholars are writing about a particular position they hold on Genesis, I look for the motivation. What I find is that all of what I would call compromise positions have one thing in common — attempting to fit millions of years into the Bible. If you read what these scholars write, ultimately you will find a statement that clearly shows this is really their motivation.

Sailhamer proposes his idea in order to squeeze long ages into the text. Now, the obvious question is, what does Dr. Sailhamer do with the description of creation in the rest of Genesis 1, if everything in the universe was created in the first verse? He has an answer for that, too:

> The second act of God recounted in Genesis 1 and 2 deals with a much more limited scope and period of time. Beginning with Genesis 1:2, the biblical narrative recounts God's preparation of a

---

20. John Sailhamer, *Genesis Unbound* (Sisters, OR: Multnomah Books, 1996), p. 14.

land for the man and woman He was to create. . . . According to Genesis 1, God prepared the land within a period of a six-day work week.[21]

Sailhamer's ideas, of course, are not found in the text of Genesis. In fact, we might look at his proposition and think, "No one in his right mind would believe this — it's not even in the Bible!" Sadly, the influence of academics like Sailhamer has filtered into the teachings of well-known pastors today.

Mark Driscoll, pastor of Mars Hill Church in Seattle, Washington, holds the historic creation view and describes it in an article:

> In this view, Genesis 1:1 records the making of all of creation by God out of nothing (or *ex nihilo*) through a merism of "heavens and earth," which means the sky above and land below, or the totality of creation. Since the word used for "beginning" in Genesis 1:1 is *reshit* in Hebrew, which means an indefinite period of time, it is likely that all of creation was completed over an extended period of time (anywhere from days to billions of years). Then Genesis 1:2 begins the description of God preparing the uninhabitable land for the creation of mankind. The preparation of the uncultivated land for and creation of Adam and Eve occurred in six literal twenty-four hour days. This view leaves open the possibility of both an old earth and six literal days of creation.[22]

The historic creation view, as Driscoll clearly says, is simply an attempt to harmonize millions of years with the literal account of creation in Genesis. What's more, the word *reshit* does not mean "an indefinite period of time," as Driscoll claims. It means "beginning, chief," or "first."[23] By itself, the word does not explain how long ago the beginning was, but that information is provided in Scripture. The beginning started the first day, and God created everything in six days and rested for one. As we discussed earlier, based on the genealogies given in Scripture, and accepting the six literal days of creation, we can determine that this took place about 6,000 years ago.

---

21. Ibid., p. 14.
22. Mark Driscoll, "Answers to Common Questions about Creation," The Resurgence, http://theresurgence.com/2006/07/03/answers-to-common-questions-about-creation.
23. Francis Brown, Samuel Rolles Driver, and Charles Augustus Briggs, *Enhanced Brown-Driver-Briggs Hebrew and English Lexicon*, electronic ed. (Oak Harbor, WA: Logos Research Systems, 2000), 912.1.

Another prominent evangelical pastor who holds the historic creation view is Matt Chandler, lead pastor of The Village Church in Dallas, Texas — a church with a congregation of over 10,000 people. While Chandler is undoubtedly a gifted teacher, his recent book reveals that he has some very problematic views on Genesis:

> If I had to label myself, I would tend to be more of what's called a "historic creationist." Following from the work of scholars like John Sailhamer — whose book *Genesis Unbound* is brilliant — historic creationists point out that the phrase "in the beginning" in Genesis 1:1 contains the Hebrew word *reshit*, which does not mean a determined piece of time but rather represents the early stages of an unknowable period of time. So in Sailhamer's historic creationism view, "in the beginning God created" refers to a time sometime before the seven days next covered began. . . . However, historic creationists absolutely believe that after you get past verses 1 and 2, we are seeing literal twenty-four-hour days, as God grooms a section of land that was uninhabitable. . . . In my estimation, then, historic creation solves a lot of the tension Christians feel in the Genesis creation account.[24]

The influence of academics like Dr. Sailhamer could not be clearer — Chandler even refers to Sailhamer's book as "brilliant." But I always have to ask, what is the real motivation here? What drives Chandler to accept a view that cannot be shown from Scripture? While he clearly rejects evolution, Chandler claims that some aspects of man's historical science should be mixed with Scripture:

> The historic creationism view, however, is biblical and historically faithful and leaves room for the proper accommodation of science. "In the beginning," Genesis 1:1 reads. We don't know how long that beginning was. Could it have been billions of years? Maybe.[25]

Keep in mind that when these Christian scholars use the word *science* in such statements, most of the time they are referring to man's historical science

---

24. Matt Chandler, *The Explicit Gospel*, with Jared Wilson (Wheaton, IL: Crossway, 2012), p. 96–97.

25. Ibid., p. 101.

(i.e., beliefs about the age of the earth or sometimes even evolution), not observational science.

But why accept long ages and not evolution? The foundation of evolution is millions and billions of years, so what makes the acceptance of one and not the other a "proper accommodation of science"? Secularists would not accept that. What I find is that many of these Christian scholars will say that Adam was made from dust and Eve from his side, just as Scripture clearly states in Genesis 3. They will use Scripture to say you cannot add evolution to the Bible as the idea of evolution does not come from the Bible. But they seem to miss the obvious point that millions of years is not found in Scripture, and in fact, as outlined before, Scripture contradicts millions of years! They are really accepting geological evolution and astronomical evolution (billions of years) but not biological evolution — *but none* of these ideas are found in Scripture. I claim they are committing eisegesis (something they would not do elsewhere in Scripture) for the sake of fitting millions of years into the Bible.

The Day-Age View

Other positions, such as the day-age view, move past the supposed gap between Genesis 1:1 and 1:2, and attempt to insert millions of years and evolution directly into the days of creation, beginning with Genesis 1:3–5:

> Then God said, "Let there be light"; and there was light. And God saw the light, that it was good; and God divided the light from the darkness. God called the light Day, and the darkness He called Night. So the evening and the morning were the first day.

The whole issue here involves the length of the days of creation. Among many of the churches, seminaries, and colleges across America and around the world, the majority of our Christian leaders and the majority of Christians say, "We don't know how long the days of creation were. Maybe they were millions of years. We really don't know or can't know." I want to suggest that the main reason they say that has nothing to do with Scripture and everything to do with — again — trying to force man's historical science into Scripture.

The day-age view is one such attempt to force long ages into the Bible. Those who promote this view claim that each of the days of creation was an extremely long period of time. In support of this view, some even quote from the Book of Psalms and 2 Peter:

> For a thousand years in Your sight are like yesterday when it is past, and like a watch in the night. (Psalm 90:4)

> But, beloved, do not forget this one thing, that with the Lord one day is as a thousand years, and a thousand years as one day. (2 Peter 3:8)

They claim the verses say that "one day is as a thousand years," so therefore they can claim the length of a day in Scripture can vary greatly.

Many people have come to me and said, "The Bible says a day is like a thousand years." And then they cite 2 Peter 3:8 as proof. The first thing I typically respond with is, "Read the rest of the verse. It also says a thousand years is like a day. That cancels the other out."

What's more, those who promote this view actually misquote the Bible. What does 2 Peter 3 really tell us? It does not say a day is like a thousand years. It says that *with the Lord* one day is as a thousand years. What is the context of 2 Peter 3? "Where is the promise of His coming?" This is dealing with the topic of the Second Coming.

The point in this part of the passage is that God is outside of time. Natural processes and time do not limit God. To God, a day is like a thousand years and a thousand years is like a day because He is the great I Am. He exists in eternity. He is outside of time. We are the ones who are bound by time, because we were created in time.

The main problem with citing these verses is that they do not even refer to the days of creation. We cannot cite a New Testament passage to determine the meaning of an Old Testament word. The meaning of a Hebrew word depends on the rules of Hebrew grammar — not a phrase written in Greek in the New Testament! These verses in 2 Peter are really teaching that God is not limited by time, and that he is longsuffering, "not willing that any should perish but that all should come to repentance" (2 Peter 3:9).

The day-age view was made popular after George Stanley Faber, a respected Anglican bishop, began teaching it in 1823. Ever since, this view has been altered bit by bit to accommodate man's changing beliefs about origins. Some day-age theorists believe in theistic evolution; others believe in "progressive creation" (these ideas will be discussed in subsequent chapters).

The day-age view is based on the assumption that because the Hebrew word for "day" can mean "time" in general in some contexts, then it is appropriate to interpret it to mean "time" in general in Genesis 1. However, it is clear that the context of Genesis 1 (as I will demonstrate) does not allow for this interpretation.

Incidentally, people who promote the day-age view by claiming a day is like a thousand years have another problem! Six thousand years is not going to help much when they really want millions of years to fit into the Bible! Psalm 90:4 says a thousand years is like "a watch in the night." What does the day-age theorist do with that? Is he going to limit a day to four hours or three hours depending on which watch?

But those who quote 2 Peter 3 to attempt to allow for long ages are inconsistent in another way. They do not quote 2 Peter 3 when talking about any other days (over 2,000 instances) in the Old Testament! For instance, what about Jonah? Would they say they think Jonah was in that great fish for 3,000 years? After all, a day is like a thousand years, right? Of course not! It is always the days of creation so many Christians want to relegate to long ages or unknown lengths. Why?

I believe that people who hold that the days of creation in Genesis 1 are not literal days are ultimately caving to the pressure of the world to somehow fit man's historical science — man's beliefs about the past — into the Bible.

Framework Hypothesis

The framework hypothesis was developed in 1924 by Arie Noordtzij.[26] About 30 years later, Meredith Kline popularized the view in the United States while N.H. Ridderbos did the same in Europe. Currently, it is one of the most popular views of Genesis 1 being taught in our seminaries to future Church leaders and academics. But even though the framework hypothesis is popular in academia, people in our churches have not heard this view fully explained, though they have heard of some of its claims.

Now, the framework hypothesis is really just an attempt to show that Genesis 1 is something other than historical narrative. Proponents of this idea claim that the first chapter of Genesis is not to be taken as literal history. They

26. For a fuller explanation of the framework hypothesis, see Tim Chaffey and Bob Mc-Cabe, "Framework Hypothesis," in *How Do We Know the Bible Is True?* Vol. 1, Ken Ham and Bodie Hodge, gen. eds. (Green Forest, AR: Master Books, 2011), p. 189–199.

make the claim that Genesis 1 simply reveals that God created everything and that He made man in His own image, but that it gives us no information about how or when He did this.

All framework hypothesis advocates agree with the two triads of "days" argument. They claim that the two triads of "days" is a type of parallelism where the topics of days 1–3 are parallel with those of days 4–6. Mark Futato writes, "Days 1 and 4 are two different perspectives on the same creative work."[27] In other words, days 1 and 4 are just two different ways of stating the same event, as are days 2 and 5, and days 3 and 6.

	Formation of the World		Filling of the World
Day	(Items Created)	Day	(Items Created)
1	darkness, light	4	heavenly light-bearers
2	heavens, water	5	birds of the air, water animals
3	seas, land, vegetation	6	land animals, man, provision of food

There are a variety of problems with the framework hypothesis. First, the idea that Genesis 1 is poetic and not historical is inconsistent with the fact that Genesis 1 is written as a historical narrative. Hebrew scholar Stephen Boyd has clearly shown that Genesis 1 is written as historical narrative rather than poetry.[28]

Second, the above chart is inconsistent with the text of Genesis 1:1–2:3. Water was not created on the second day, but the first (Genesis 1:2). Another problem with this chart is that the "heavenly light-bearers" of Day 4 were placed in the "heavens" of Day 2 (Genesis 1:14). This is problematic if the framework hypothesis proponent believes Days 1 and 4 are the same event viewed from different perspectives, because the placement of the light-bearers occurred prior to the creation of the heavens described in Day 2, according to their chart. How could the stars be placed in something that did not exist yet?

Finally, the order of events is crucial. The framework hypothesis argues that the days of Creation Week are not chronological, but theological. But, besides denying the historical trustworthiness of God's Word, this claim fails because if we rearrange the chronology, then it totally breaks down.

27. Mark D. Futato, "Because It Had Rained: A Study of Gen 2:5–7 with Implications for Gen 2:4–25 and Gen 1:1–2:3," *Westminster Theological Journal* 60 (Spring 1998): 16.

28. Boyd's research is described in Don DeYoung, *Thousands . . . Not Billions* (Green Forest, AR: Master Books, 2005), p. 158–70.

What Are Some Other Christian Leaders Saying?

This book is about the decline of the Church's view of Genesis 1–11, which has led to a catastrophic decline in believing in the absolute authority of the Word of God in the Church. Many Christian academics and church leaders have abandoned a literal understanding of Genesis, or have compromised part of Genesis, in their attempts to fit various aspects man's historical science (beliefs) into the Bible. I want to show you what they are saying, in their own words, about how they believe one should understand various aspects of Genesis 1. Now many of these scholars are godly people who have a sincere burden to preach God's Word and see people saved for eternity. However, I also believe they are in error on this issue — wittingly or unwittingly committing eisegesis and thus really undermining the authority they are really preaching from. You will probably recognize some of their names. When I quote from them or challenge what they state about Genesis, I am not questioning their Christian commitment. In fact, for a number of these scholars I have great respect and often read and use aspects of what they have written. But sadly, when it comes to Genesis, I see major problems!

Now, I often speak on the issue of Christian colleges and seminaries, and how students are being led astray by the rampant compromise in them. In 2011, the book *Already Compromised* (co-authored by myself with Greg Hall) was published.[29] In it, we included the results of surveys conducted by America's Research Group on what is being taught in our Christian colleges and seminaries. Compromise with man's historical science is rampant in our church and Christian institutions. Let me give some examples.

Greg Boyd, senior pastor of Woodland Hills Church in St. Paul, Minnesota, explains in one interview that it was in college when he gave up his belief in a literal Genesis:

> So I was taught that if Adam and Eve weren't literal and if Genesis 1 wasn't literal, then the whole Bible was a book of lies. It took one semester of college for my faith to be destroyed, going into it with that kind of mindset.[30]

---

29. Ken Ham and Greg Hall, *Already Compromised*, with Britt Beemer (Green Forest, AR: Master Books, 2011).

30. Greg Boyd, "Dangers of an Ultra-Literal Perspective with Greg Boyd," BioLogos, http://biologos.org/resources/multimedia/greg-boyd-on-the-dangers-of-an-ultra-literal-perspective.

The college Boyd attended likely was not teaching a literal Genesis if he went in with those beliefs and left believing something completely different. Boyd now pastors a church and is a promoter of open theism, the false belief that God does not know the future. But what does Boyd teach his congregation about the opening chapters of Genesis?

> And more often than not, it's the young-earth creationists who are very passionate that we hold to a literal interpretation of Genesis 1. And if you let go of that, then the Bible is the book of lies, or the Christian faith comes crumbling down, or people are going to turn into atheists, or whatever. They really are convinced of that. The trouble with that is that whenever the church has leveraged — to hold that view is to, among other things, you have to declare war on the vast majority of the scientists who deal with paleontology and geology and all the other sciences that are predicated on evolutionary theory. If that really is the center of the faith, then we have to do that. But if it's not, all other things being equal, it makes more sense to allow that to have some variety of interpretations so we don't require a person to reject 98% of the scientists who are out there in order to become a Christian.[31]

We at Answers in Genesis have made it clear many times before that a person's view of origins is *not* a salvation issue, but it is an authority issue and a gospel issue. A belief in evolution and/or millions of years *does* undermine the authority of the Word of God and the foundation of the gospel message (because then death is not a result of sin).

Sadly, Boyd has accepted man's ideas on origins and allowed them to influence his view of biblical authority. And he is not the only one.

William Lane Craig, a professor at the Talbot School of Theology at Biola University, is a professing Christian and a well-known philosopher. Craig, in my opinion, has an extremely low view of biblical creation, recently referring to young-earth creationism as an "embarrassment." He holds to an old earth, as he explained when asked in an interview how old the earth is:

---

31. Greg Boyd, "Free For All Q&A — Were Dinosaurs Created Before Man" Woodland Hills (YouTube channel), http://www.youtube.com/watch?v=XCVhsWiE6Xg&playnext=1&list=PLCE0355A3DA883558&feature=results_main.

The best estimates today are around 13.7 billion years or so. . . .
I don't think [a 6,000-year-old earth] is plausible. The arguments
I give are right in line with mainstream science. I'm not bucking
up against mainstream science in presenting these arguments. I'm
going with the flow of what contemporary cosmology and astrophysics supports. . . . There isn't any biblical account of the age of
the earth. There's nothing in Genesis or elsewhere in the Bible that
says how old the universe is.[32]

Man's historical science wins once again as a prominent Christian academic
takes what the secular world believes and adds it to Scripture. Craig is one of
the Christian professors teaching the next generation of pastors and seminary
professors, yet he obviously does not want to stand for God's Word in the
face of criticism from the world. While it may seem scholarly to accept what
he calls "mainstream science" (i.e., millions of years and evolutionary ideas
— man's historical science), Dr. Craig, contrary to what he himself believes,
is undermining the authority of God's Word and exalting man's fallible word.

Now, Craig correctly explains in a question and answer session that the
origins debate has much to do with how one views the genre of Genesis. But
even as a great scholar, he seems to miss that Genesis (including Genesis 1) is
historical narrative; we can read it and trust that it is an eyewitness account
from the Creator of the universe. But Craig says the Genesis account of
origins is open to many interpretations, and he does not seem to believe
there are correct and incorrect interpretations (but he is adamant that those
who believe in a young universe are wrong): "Among educated Christians,
it's always been known that Genesis is open to a very wide range of different
interpretations that are quite consistent with different theories of evolutionary biology."[33]

These men are not alone in their compromise views of Genesis. There
are many in the Church who are leaving behind a historical understanding
of Genesis 1 in favor of views that incorporate long ages, in order to accommodate man's current historical science (millions of years belief).

---

32. William Lane Craig, interview by Michael Coren, "William Lane Craig is not
a creationist," YouTube, http://www.youtube.com/watch?v=y7WNzoiUAe8&safety_
mode=true&persist_safety_mode=1.

33. William Lane Craig, "Does Evolution Disprove Christianity?" YouTube, http://www.
youtube.com/watch?v=XdVBfIWE6sg&feature=related&safety_mode=true&persist_safe-
ty_mode=1.

It's Not a Secondary Issue!

One time, a minister was interviewing me on radio. He said, "Look, you agree that there are different understandings of eschatology, right? Premillennial, Amillennial, and Postmillennial. There are many different views of eschatology."

"Yes," I said. He went on, "And you can have different views of baptism — immersion, sprinkling, and different views in regard to speaking in tongues, and a number of other issues." Once again, I said, "Yes." He continued, "So we can have different views on Genesis then. Same thing." At this point, I replied, "No, it's not."

Really, when talking about eschatology, baptism, tongues, and so on, and all the different views on them, for the most part, believers are starting from Scripture and trying to understand the issue. But the reason we have so many different views of Genesis is mostly because people are starting outside of Scripture with the secular views of our day and adding them to Scripture. This is absolutely undermining the authority of the Word of God. It is eisegesis in response to man's historical science.

Some Christians think that as long as they do not believe in evolution, then it does not matter what we believe about the age of the earth and universe. But it does matter because it matters what God's Word clearly states.

Now, we will discuss more on compromise positions in the next chapter. But I want to suggest to you that what we need to be doing is rejecting the whole reason that all of these different compromise positions exist: that is, Christian leaders adopting the old-age view of the universe, and attempting to incorporate millions of years into the Bible.

As I will demonstrate from their own words, those who compromise the Bible by and large admit that if you take Genesis as written, beginning with Genesis 1, then Scripture teaches God created in six literal days about six thousand years ago. But many Christian leaders reject this. Why? It really comes down to the fact they are influenced by man's ideas outside of Scripture and try to inject these into Scripture.

Yes — it is a major authority issue of our day.

Chapter 7

 # Genesis and Evolutionary Ideas

While attempting to add millions of years to the Bible is the primary area of compromise for many Christian leaders, many have also attempted to mix some form of Darwinian evolution with Scripture. More and more, we are seeing the rise of evolution-friendly understandings of God's Word, especially in the Book of Genesis, no matter how much they contradict the plain meaning of Scripture.

It is hard to forget statements made by Dr. Bruce Waltke, a well-known Old Testament scholar and commentator on Genesis, who in an interview answered the question, "Why Must the Church Come to Accept Evolution?"

> I think that if the data is overwhelming in favor — favor — of evolution, to deny that reality will make us a cult. Some odd group that's not really interacting with the real world.[1]

I remember the first time I watched this shocking interview (which was taken down soon after it was posted online); I could not believe a Christian academic would make such a claim. But you see, Waltke's words highlight the problem that is evident in the Church and among Christian college faculty

---

1. Bruce Waltke, "Why Must the Church Come to Accept Evolution," BioLogos, http://biologos.org/resources/bruce-waltke-why-must-the-church-accept-evolution (no longer available).

today: some in the Church fear that they will be looked down on if they do not accept evolutionary ideas, and they will be characterized as people who "deny" science, as anti-intellectuals and anti-academics, as people who do not want their children to be successful in this technologically advanced society.

What's more, it is not unusual for many of these compromising Christian academics to try to convince us that they have a much deeper understanding of how Scripture and science work together — and that evolutionary ideas really are what God intended to communicate to His people! Sadly, a belief in millions of years opens the door for a belief in evolutionary ideas, because evolution is founded on long ages. It is not surprising when Christian leaders who compromise on the age of the earth eventually come to accept some form of theistic evolution as well.

Today, theistic evolution, which claims that God used evolution as a means of bringing about creation, is promoted primarily by the organization BioLogos. The people at BioLogos usually refer to their brand of theistic evolution as evolutionary creation. The BioLogos website explains its stance on evolution as follows:

> We believe that God created the universe, the earth, and all life over billions of years. . . . We believe that the diversity and inter-relation of all life on earth are best explained by the God-ordained process of evolution with common descent. Thus, evolution is not in opposition to God, but a means by which God providentially achieves his purposes. Therefore, we reject ideologies that claim that evolution is a purposeless process or that evolution replaces God.[2]

Now, what the academics at BioLogos do not recognize in their statement is that evolution was an idea developed specifically to explain the world *without God*. It is based on naturalism. So the idea that evolutionary processes do not replace God is preposterous. They directly contradict biblical teaching and were intended to replace God when they were developed.

Another position that has been widely promoted is progressive creation. This is really a form of old-earth creationism, but I have included it in this chapter on Genesis and evolutionary ideas because progressive creationists typically reject biological evolution (though they really accept a modified form of this), but accept astronomical and geological evolution.

---

2. "What We Believe," BioLogos, http://biologos.org/about.

Hugh Ross and his organization Reasons to Believe have heavily promoted progressive creation. On the Reasons to Believe website, the organization's ideas about the authority of Scripture on creation are explained as follows:

> We believe that the physical universe, the realm of nature, is the visible creation of God. It declares God's existence and gives a trustworthy revelation of God's character and purpose. In Scripture, God declares that through His creation all humanity recognizes His existence, power, glory, and wisdom. An honest study of nature — its physical, biological, and social aspects — can prove useful in a person's search for truth. Properly understood, God's Word (Scripture) and God's world (nature), as two revelations (one verbal, one physical) from the same God, will never contradict each other.[3]

Now, here's the problem with the view that the "book of nature" (as some refer to it) is deemed equivalent to the Bible: while the world around us does give us a general revelation of God's existence (Romans 1), we still need a worldview firmly rooted in God's Word to make sense of the world. Romans 1 does not in any way imply that nature gives us an account of origins — only that if one does not believe in God, then they are without excuse. Nature itself does not support evolutionary ideas, unless it is read with evolutionary assumptions to force such an explanation on nature. Also, nature is cursed — because of sin. Ross often refers to nature as the "67th book of the Bible," putting it on the same plane as the special revelation of the 66 books! The 66 books are not cursed — nature is! This is important to understand, because what is called "nature" exhibits the results of the Curse, such as death, suffering, and disease! The only way to understand nature (Ross's supposed 67th book) is to look at it through the 66 books! Now, the ideas that Reasons to Believe promotes do contradict Scripture in many ways, which will be discussed below.

Theistic Evolution

Supporters of theistic evolution believe that God used evolution over long ages to create the universe. The idea of theistic evolution is really an attack on the Bible's account of the creation of Adam. If we take Genesis in a

---

3. "Creation," Reasons to Believe, http://www.reasons.org/about/our-mission.

straightforward way, as written, then Adam was made from the dust of the earth, and he was made in the image of God (just as all of us are) — and Eve was created from Adam's side. But theistic evolution teaches that instead, Adam and Eve simply evolved from ape-like creatures.

Sadly, many liberal Christian academics and Christian leaders accept this evolutionary view of Adam and Eve, and see no problem with incorporating such evolutionary ideas into the Bible, and reinterpreting the history to try to make it fit. So what are some of the problems with theistic evolution? The overarching issue is that theistic evolution is inconsistent with the character of God. It makes Him responsible for millions of years of death, disease, and suffering.

When God had finished His work of creation, He called it all "very good" (Genesis 1:31). But a world full of death, disease, and suffering can hardly be called "very good."

Consider the Words of Jesus:

> Now behold, one came and said to Him, "Good Teacher, what good thing shall I do that I may have eternal life?" So He said to him, "Why do you call Me good? No one is good but One, that is, God." (Matthew 19:16–17)

Only God's attributes can determine the definition of "good" — and such a definition does not fit with suffering, death, disease, and bloodshed. As is obvious from Scripture, a "very good" creation was marred by sin, and thus death (described as an "enemy") entered a once-perfect world. Now it is a fallen, groaning world because of sin (Romans 8:22) — not a "very good" world as originally described before man's rebellion.

As with day-age and gap theories, theistic evolution is not supported by Scripture and does not fit with the Bible's account of Creation, the Fall, or the redemption available in Christ.

Genesis 1 tells us that God created the universe out of nothing (Colossians 1:16–18 confirms this — all things were created by and for Jesus Christ). It was the first recorded miracle! What's more, Scripture states that He completed His creation in just six days (as discussed in the previous chapter), and rested on the seventh. But theistic evolution denies the plain words of Scripture on creation. This view does not accept that God created in six, 24-hour days, and does not accept the order in which God created as recorded in Genesis 1. Really, theistic evolution attempts to rewrite all of Genesis 1 and 2!

According to Genesis 3, Adam chose to rebel against God when he ate from the one tree God told him not to eat from. Because of Adam's sin, all of mankind is fallen. Sin entered the world, and with it came death, disease, suffering, and thorns. Until that point, everything in creation was "very good." There was no death — even all the animals were vegetarian. Since Adam's sin, however, the Apostle Paul tells us in Romans that all of creation has been affected:

> For the creation was subjected to futility, not willingly, but because of Him who subjected it in hope; because the creation itself also will be delivered from the bondage of corruption into the glorious liberty of the children of God. For we know that the whole creation groans and labors with birth pangs together until now. (Romans 8:20–22)

When Adam sinned, God placed a Curse on creation — but He had already planned to redeem sinful man and deliver creation from the corruption. First Peter 1:20 tells us Christ "was foreordained before the foundation of the world, but was manifest in these last times for you." The Curse was a very real consequence of a very real problem: man's rebellion against God. How does a belief in evolution undermine this reality? Well, it claims that God *used* death and suffering to accomplish His purposes, and yet the Scripture calls death an enemy — the "last enemy" (1 Corinthians 15:26). How can God be good if He acts in a way that is inconsistent with His character? He cannot be, which leaves theistic evolution with some major problems.

Lastly, we know that God carried out His plan of redemption by sending His Son, Jesus Christ, to live a sinless life, die a criminal's death on the Cross, and to rise again three days later. All of this, for our sin. The Apostle Paul writes, " 'The first man Adam became a living being.' The last Adam became a life-giving spirit" (1 Corinthians 15:45). Here, Paul refers to Christ as "the last Adam," a clear indication that he believed Adam to have been a real man whose sin led to the Fall of all mankind. This is the very foundation of the message of redemption!

Theistic evolution, however, undermines this message. How? The acceptance of evolution will ultimately very likely lead to a denial of the historicity of Adam and of the Fall. What's more, what inevitably happens when we begin to reject the miracle of creation is that we start to reject other miracles too. A rejection of the Resurrection may not be far behind the acceptance of evolutionary ideas. After all, there is no scientific explanation for a dead man coming to life again. It had to be a miracle — just like creation. If one accepts ideas based on naturalism to reinterpret Genesis, then why not be consistent and reinterpret the Resurrection and Virgin Birth to fit with ideas based on naturalism!

I would submit that the acceptance of evolutionary ideas is not just a compromise — it undermines the very message of the gospel of Jesus Christ. Sadly, many Christian leaders and academics do not see this danger, and they continue to push these ideas to their audiences.

BioLogos: Encouraging Compromise in the Church

Since its founding in 2007, BioLogos has been trying to convince Christian leaders that evolutionary ideas and millions of years are compatible with Genesis. Dr. Francis Collins, the director of the National Institutes of Health (NIH) and a leader of the Human Genome Project, started BioLogos with the intent of encouraging a discussion of how "science" and faith interact. Of course, when the word *science* is used in such a context, it is usually referring to man's historical science (e.g., man's beliefs about millions of years, evolution, and so on).

The premise that "science" and Christianity are in conflict is not really a legitimate one. Evolutionary ideas and Christianity are and should be in conflict; molecules-to-man evolution is an attempt to explain the world without God. But Dr. Collins does not see it that way. In a 2009 interview with Dan Harris of ABC News, Dr. Collins explained his view of God's Word and nature:

> I like the idea that God gave us two books. He gave us the book of God's Words — the Bible — which I read every day and which I trust to give me great truth, but which in many ways has parts that I don't entirely understand. But that other book God gave us, the book of God's works — nature, which science allows us to uncover — is also an opportunity to learn about the nature of God, to worship, if you will.[4]

---

4. Francis Collins, interview by Dan Harris, "Can Christianity and Science Coexist?" ABCNews, http://www.youtube.com/watch?v=M5sMva2ydoU&feature=related.

On that basis, BioLogos actively encourages pastors to engage their congregations on evolutionary ideas. In 2012, in cooperation with Point Loma Nazarene University in San Diego, California, BioLogos hosted a workshop for science teachers, specifically teachers from Christian schools. While the workshop's description notes that "course faculty will respect the wide range of views" on creation, it lays out clearly the bias of the faculty: "BioLogos and Point Loma Nazarene University biology faculty hold the view that God created all of life through a gradual process over time."[5]

The authority of Scripture is what's at stake here. These are faculty members at a Christian university and a Christian organization. Likely, they would all affirm the inspiration of Scripture — but they choose not to believe God's Word is inerrant in Genesis chapters 1–11. Dr. Collins makes it very clear where he stands on the trustworthiness of Scripture's account of creation:

> We interpret [Genesis] as explicit these days. It is not a textbook of science! It would not have suited God's purposes to lecture to His children about radioactive decay and such things as DNA. What God was trying to teach us through those words is the nature of God and the nature of humans. And that comes through loud and clear.

Now, I would not say that Genesis is a "textbook of science" either. But it is a book of history (God's historical science). One could even say it is a textbook of historical science. And when the all-knowing, all-powerful Creator of the universe gives us a historical account of how He made the world, we should listen, instead of telling Him, "I know you said you made the world in six days, but clearly what you really mean is millions of years. I know you said you formed man from the dust of the earth, but obviously you really meant that you guided man's evolution over hundreds of thousands of years, from single-celled organism to ape-like creature to man."

Sadly, however, BioLogos does not seem to be interested in listening to what the God of creation has to say about how it happened. In fact, in January 2013 they announced a new president: Dr. Deborah Haarsma, formerly professor and chair in the department of physics and astronomy at Calvin College (a Christian college) in Grand Rapids, Michigan.

---

5. BioLogos, "Summer Workshops for Teachers," http://biologos.org/events/summer-workshops-for-teachers.

Dr. Haarsma, while at Calvin College, actively encouraged church leaders to "engage" their congregations on evolutionary ideas. She serves as a co-director of The Ministry Theorem, a Calvin Seminary program that promotes resources from people such as Francis Collins and William Dembski, both of whom do not hold a literal view of Genesis 1–11.

What does Dr. Haarsma, a professing Christian and former Christian college professor, believe about Genesis? Well, Dr. Haarsma claims that Genesis 1 does not tell us how the universe was created:

> [Genesis 1] is a message of how God interacts with His creation and of our role in creation. It's several key theological messages. But it is not a message about the how and the when of creation. God didn't bother to teach the ancient Hebrews that the world was actually round. He didn't bother to teach them that it was actually atmosphere in the sky instead of a solid sky dome. He let them keep believing that. He accommodated the message to where they were at. And I find that so comforting to us today that God is willing to accommodate His message to our limited understanding. We don't have to have a perfect scientific understanding of the world to get God's message for us. And for that reason, I don't think we need to draw from Genesis 1 a chronology of how God created, a timeline of specific physical events, but rather these very important theological views.[6]

Dr. Haarsma's thesis, that Genesis is not about "the how and the when of creation," flies in the face of the plain words of Genesis 1–11. If Genesis 1 is not about how God created, and if we cannot figure a rough estimate for the age of the earth from the detailed genealogies in Genesis 5 and 11, then what exactly can we trust in the first 11 chapters of the Bible? And who gets to make that decision? Unfortunately, BioLogos has chosen a president who denies the authority of Scripture when it comes to Genesis — which fits the beliefs of the entire organization.

Progressive Creation

Progressive creation is one of the more popular of the compromise views in the Church today. What's more, most progressive creationists are also day-

---

6. Deborah Haarsma, "How does Genesis contrast, as a story of origins, with those of surrounding cultures at the time?" Test of Faith (YouTube channel), http://www.youtube.com/watch?v=Y0rmW-LYI9s&list=PL92A0F470C382EC08&index=9&feature=plpp_video.

age supporters: they believe that each of the creation days was a long period of time. I mentioned earlier that most progressive creationists do not accept biological evolution per se. Instead, progressive creationists believe that God created in stages over many millions of years (but such a progression does follow that of biological evolution).

They believe that God created certain animals millions of years ago and then they died out. Then God created more animals that died out. Eventually, He got around to making humans. How exactly is the position of a progressive creationist any better than that of a theistic evolutionist? Well, it's really not.

Just like theistic evolutionists, progressive creationists believe in millions of years of disease, death, suffering, and thorns before Adam's sin. Really, progressive creationism undermines the gospel message for the same reasons that theistic evolution does. It makes the redemption offered by Christ meaningless when it implies that death and suffering are "very good" creations of God. Really, such views blame God for death (and the groaning of this world), instead of our sin!

A more detailed look at the beliefs of progressive creationists also reveals that they accept geological and astronomical evolution, even if they do not accept biological evolution (although in essence I suggest they really do). Progressive creation teaches that the so-called big bang actually happened and has been proven by scientific inquiry and observation. But is there evidence for the big-bang idea in Scripture? No, so really the big bang has become the lens through which progressive creationists such as Dr. Hugh Ross interpret Genesis.

Dr. Ross once stated at a Dallas Theological Seminary chapel service that life would not even be possible on earth without billions of years:

> It only works in a cosmos of a hundred-billion trillion stars that's precisely sixteen-billion-years old. This is the narrow window of time in which life is possible.[7]

At that same chapel service, Dr. Ross went on to do some "editing" of the Bible:

> Therefore it allows me to make an interesting paraphrase of John 3:16, if you'll permit — For God so loved the human race that he

---

7. Dallas Theological Seminary chapel service, September 13, 1996.

went to the expense of building a hundred-billion trillion-stars and carefully shaped and crafted them for sixteen-billion years so that at this brief moment in time we could all have a nice place to live.[8]

Talk about eisegesis! Really, Dr. Ross's statements are a shining example of how evolutionary ideas (astronomical, geological, anthropological, and biological) are read into Scripture. This is a gross misrepresentation of the Word of God, and Dr. Ross will be held to account one day for this sort of misleading idea.

In another lecture, Dr. Ross made another claim about life, saying, "Life is only possible when the universe is between 12 and 17 billion years."[9] What is the problem with Ross's ideas? They ignore the fact that God, who is all-powerful, is entirely capable of creating a fully functioning, mature universe right from the very beginning. Ross instead lifts up man's ideas as the key to understanding the creation of the universe, rather than the account of God Himself. His motivation for his views on Genesis and origins is driven by his acceptance of secular beliefs about origins that have their basis in naturalism.

In light of the view that life is only possible with billions of years, how do progressive creationists handle the six days of creation? Reasons to Believe actually has a chart available online that details their most up-to-date view of the Creation Week.[10] Day One, according to the chart, was 1.5 billion years long, Day 2 was 1 billion years, and Day 3 was just over 1.25 billion years. This is no different than the day-age view, except that progressive creationists need these long ages in order to make their view of the order of creation (based on the secular evolutionist belief) fit the Scriptures.

As their name indicates, progressive creationists believe God "progressively" created species on earth over billions of years (basically in the same order as proposed by evolutionists). Rather than one kind evolving into another, however, progressive creationists hold that God simply created new species to replace extinct ones, starting with single-celled organisms and culminating in the creation of Adam and Eve. Thus it is very similar to the theistic evolution view — except that instead of God guiding evolution, God supposedly steps in to create new species over millions of years

---

8. Ibid.

9. Toccoa Falls Christian College, Staley Lecture Series, March 1997.

10. Reasons to Believe, "Genesis 1 Creation Days," http://www.reasons.org/files/articles/creation_timeline_chart_color_201107.pdf.

in the same basic order as evolutionists propose. It is just another attempt to fit man's ideas of millions of years into God's Word. It is nothing but eisegesis.

They accept what the evolutionists say about the order of the development of life on earth — even though it directly contradicts what the creation account in Genesis says. You see, evolutionary scientists claim that the first life forms were marine organisms, while the Bible states that God created land plants first (on Day 3). Reptiles are supposed to have come before birds according to evolutionists, while Genesis states that birds came first. Evolutionists believe that land mammals came before whales, but the Bible teaches that God created whales first.

Now, it is common to hear people say that there is a "conflict" between the Bible and "science." But the real conflict is between evolutionary ideas about the past, and the Bible's account of history (a battle between man's historical science and God's historical science) — and the above contradictions are just another confirmation of that. Evolution, as far as the secularists are concerned, was truly a solution for them to explain life without God.

How does Dr. Ross justify his giving man's word more credence than God's? Through the argument that nature is the supposed "67th book" of the Bible! Of course, what he really means by nature is evolutionary ideas — man's attempts to explain life without God (man's fallible interpretation of the evidence of the present in an attempt to supposedly explain origins). Dr. Ross explains:

> Not everyone has been exposed to the sixty-six books of the Bible, but everyone on planet Earth has been exposed to the sixty-seventh book — the book that God has written upon the heavens for everyone to read.
>
> And the Bible tells us it's impossible for God to lie, so the record of nature must be just as perfect, and reliable and truthful as the sixty-six books of the Bible that is part of the Word of God. . . . And so when astronomers tell us [Ross uses the example of scientists attempting to measure distances in space and goes on to say that] it's part of the truth that God has revealed to us. It actually encompasses part of the Word of God.[11]

---

11. Toccoa Falls College, Staley Lecture Series, March 1997.

Now, Dr. Ross is correct in saying that God cannot lie — but creation "groans and labors with birth pangs" because of the effects of sin (Romans 8:22). It is not possible for man, who is fallen, to say that his fallible interpretation of the evidence in relation to the past is as perfect as God's infallible Word that gives us a historical account of origins. God is perfect; man is not. Romans 1 makes it clear that if people do not believe in God they are without excuse, because it is so evident from the creation around us. But nowhere does Romans 1 even imply that nature gives us an account of origins! Fallible humans who reject God's Word in Genesis attempt to give their story about origins to explain the creation.

Part of the suffering creation endures because of sin is carnivorous activity among animals. But Dr. Ross is so convinced that the universe is billions of years old, and that death and suffering were present long before the Fall, that he argues that carnivorous activity actually *benefits* creation:

> In a previous *Today's New Reason to Believe* post, I described how new research proves that the carnivorous activity of sperm whales brings great benefit, not only to their prey, but literally to all species of ocean life. They even play a crucial role in helping resolve our global warming problems.[12]

To counter the argument that death before the Fall would mean that God calls suffering and death "very good," Dr. Ross simply says that creation was very good, but not perfect. His eisegesis problem is so great, he resorts to arguing that God's idea of "very good" includes pain, suffering, and death! So where does Dr. Ross find biblical evidence for this? He turns to Job and Psalms:

> In Genesis 1 God tells us that he created two kinds of large-bodied mammals: animals easy for humans to tame and animals difficult to tame. God made both kinds of creatures before he created Adam and Eve. . . . Contrasted with herbivores, carnivores make for poor agricultural service but are easy to housebreak and train, eager to entertain, and capable of forming deep emotional bonds with their owners. (The two most popular and beloved animal companions in the United States, cats and dogs, are carnivores.) In both Psalms and

---

12. Hugh Ross, "Thank God for Carnivores," Reasons to Believe, http://www.reasons.org/articles/thank-god-for-carnivores.

Job, God declares that he shows his love and care for predators by providing them with prey. Clearly, the Bible identifies carnivorous activity as one component of God's good creation.[13]

The Bible "clearly" identifies this? Dr. Ross has appealed to two passages about the post-Fall world (in Job and Psalms) to make an argument about the pre-Fall state. Really, Dr. Ross should have turned to the beginning of Scripture to understand the origin of death. And besides, the passages on Job and Psalms were not written as a historical account of cosmology — but Genesis was!

In Genesis 2, we learn that death is a punishment:

> And the Lord God commanded the man, saying, "Of every tree of the garden you may freely eat; but of the tree of the knowledge of good and evil you shall not eat, for in the day that you eat of it you shall surely die." (Genesis 2:16–17)

Sin, God tells Adam, is punishable by death. So if death and bloodshed (of living creatures — creatures with a *nephesh* or life spirit) in any form was present before God declared that creation was "very good," then death too would be "very good" and not a punishment. Some people have tried to argue that this passage does not refer to animals, and they are right. But we could argue it also is only directed to Adam — and yet Eve also died because of Adam's rebellion . . . and so do we, because of sin. The relationship of sin and death affects the whole of creation. By the way, Ross argues that plants "died" before sin. But plants do not have a *nephesh*! Plants are not "alive" in the same way *nephesh* creatures are.

What's more, Dr. Ross could have referred to Genesis 3:21, where I believe it is obvious that the first recorded animal death takes place. If animals had been dying for millions of years prior, wouldn't it have been mentioned in Scripture? Not once does God tell Adam and Eve that He has given them animal meat for food in the Garden of Eden. It was not until after the Flood (Genesis 9:3) that God gave the animals to man for food — and this in no way makes death a "good" thing either.

The progressive creationism of Hugh Ross and Reasons to Believe suffers from a host of biblical problems — the above are just a few! Their encouragement to believers to accept man's ideas as "just as perfect" as God's

---

13. Ibid.

Word is leading believers — Christian leaders, academics, and many in the Church — astray. And as generations of people influenced by such views doubt and ultimately disbelieve Scripture, we see generations now walking away from the Church.[14] Sadly, the compromise does not end here.

Christian Leaders Appealing to . . . Man's Ideas?

Because of the influence of theistic evolution and progressive creation, many Christian academics and church leaders have accepted such compromise positions on Genesis. As a result, even more compromised views of Genesis have been gaining prominence, all on the basis that they allow for the integration of so-called "science" (i.e., evolutionary ideas) and the Bible.

Cosmic Temple View and the Ancient Near East

One such position is the cosmic temple inauguration view, and it was put forth by Dr. John Walton, professor of Old Testament at Wheaton College in Wheaton, Illinois. (He was a professor at Moody Bible Institute for about 20 years). Dr. Walton, in his book *The Lost World of Genesis One,* is a clear example of a Christian appealing not to God's Word for answers about our origins, but instead to man's ideas:

> In my book I've tried to show that the account in Genesis 1 is not intended to be an account of material origins. If that's so, the Bible has no narrative of material origins. And if that's so, then we don't have to defend the Bible's narrative of material origins against a scientific narrative, because the Bible doesn't offer one. In that case, we can say, well, if the Bible doesn't offer us a narrative, we can look to science for the narrative.[15]

In defense of his idea, Dr. Walton draws on ancient Near Eastern mythologies because he believes that they help today's people understand how the original readers of Genesis thought. Now, it can be very helpful to examine the history and culture of the original audience for biblical texts. Walton's point in doing this, however, is to make the case for why Genesis 1–2 cannot be read as history:

---

14. Ken Ham and Britt Beemer, *Already Gone.*

15. John Walton, "John Walton on Defending the Authority of Scripture," BioLogos, http://www.youtube.com/watch?v=72qbEeRP-Ys&feature=related.

The problem is, we cannot translate their cosmology to our cosmology, nor should we. If we accept Genesis 1 as ancient cosmology, then we need to interpret it as ancient cosmology rather than translate it into modern cosmology. If we try to turn it into modern cosmology, we are making the text say something it never said.[16]

So what does Dr. Walton do with the statements in Genesis 1 about God creating? The chapter clearly states that is what God was doing. Well, in a reference resource on Genesis, Walton explains away these references by drawing on — you guessed it — ancient Near Eastern literature:

> **In the beginning (1:1).** Whereas we may be inclined to ask, "The beginning of what?" information from the Bible and the ancient Near East leads us in another direction. In the Old Testament "beginning" . . . refers to a preliminary period of time rather than the first in a series of events. . . . If creation is the act of bringing something into existence, we must ask what constituted existence in the ancient world. . . . Those definitions, however, are culturally determined.[17]

Rather than dealing directly with the plain words of Genesis 1, Dr. Walton questions the meanings of words and sheds doubt on the reliability of God's account of creation. While it may be true that the definitions of words are determined based on context, God is the author of language. Isn't He able to give man a timeless account that can be understood by all generations and translated effectively? Of course He can, and He did — the Bible. (Whatever happened to the doctrine of perspicuity?)

If Genesis 1 is not a literal account of creation, then what is it? In *The Lost World of Genesis One*, Walton claims that the creation account in Genesis does not teach a physical creation, but rather a "nonfunctional" earth being made "functional." Similar to the framework hypothesis, Walton splits the six days of creation into two parts: the first three days for God to make the heavens and earth functional, and the second three days for God to create "functionaries" such as the sun, moon, and stars.

---

16. John H. Walton, *The Lost World of Genesis One: Ancient Cosmology and the Origins Debate* (Downers Grove, IL: InterVarsity Press, 2009), p. 17.

17. John Walton, *Genesis, Zondervan Illustrated Bible Backgrounds Commentary* (Grand Rapids, MI: Zondervan, 2013), p. 10–11.

God's purpose in making the cosmos "functional," according to the cosmic temple inauguration view, is that He is "building" Himself a temple. Walton explains that the seven days of Genesis 1 are not days of creation, but days of inauguration:

> In summary, we have suggested that the seven days are not given as the period of time over which the material cosmos came into existence, but the period of time devoted to the inauguration of the functions of the cosmic temple, and perhaps also its annual reenactment. . . . Genesis 1 focuses on the creation of the (cosmic) temple, not the material phase of preparation.[18]

Unsurprisingly, some of Dr. Walton's argument seems to be driven by a desire to harmonize what modern secular scientists say about origins (i.e., evolution/millions of years) with what Genesis teaches. If Genesis 1–2 is not a literal account of creation, but instead a time of God making "functional" His "cosmic temple," then millions of years/evolutionary ideas can be mixed with Genesis. And indeed, Walton writes, "If Genesis 1 does not require a young earth and if divine fiat does not preclude a long process, then Genesis 1 offers no objections to biological evolution. Biological evolution is capable of giving us insight into God's creative work."[19] Once again, I assert that the real motivation for his view on Genesis is not to take the text as it should be taken, but to fit man's fallible belief about millions of years into Scripture.

The cosmic temple inauguration view leaves the historical aspects of the creation account in Genesis behind in favor of an interpretation that allows evolution/millions of years to be mixed with Scripture. The view does not allow God, the One who was there at the beginning, to be the Creator; instead, it relegates Him to the role of making an already existent cosmos "functional."

More Christian Leaders on the Historical Value of Genesis One

To illustrate how rampant compromise in the Church has become when it comes to evolutionary ideas and millions of years, I wanted to include statements from various Christian academics and church leaders. Now, many of the academics and church leaders who have compromised on Genesis can

---

18. Walton, *The Lost World of Genesis One: Ancient Cosmology and the Origins Debate*, p. 92.
19. Ibid., p. 138.

still be (and many are) influential for the gospel — and love the Lord — but they are inconsistent in how they treat various parts of the Bible. And what is evident as you read these, as you see what these people have to say in their own words, is that they are picking and choosing which parts of the Bible they are willing to trust and which parts they feel cannot be trusted based on man's fallible ideas. Not all of these leaders necessarily hold to all aspects of evolution (biological, anthropological, astronomical, and geological), but they have all denied the historical value of Genesis 1 in some way.

Joel Hunter, senior pastor of Northland, A Church Distributed, in Longwood, Florida, explains his view of creation, specifically that it does not matter how God created, just that He did:

> I would say the vast majority of our people sitting in those pews, who are very uncomfortable with, "Look, it was six, 24-hour days, and if you think anything else, then you don't believe in Scripture." These are science teachers, these are scientists, these are bright businessmen and businesswomen, and people who have been thinking. And they just say, "Wait a minute, God is God. God could choose any way He wants to create the world, and it doesn't make it any less marvelous. In fact, it makes it more marvelous, because He would be so intricate in its creation."[20]

What a faulty view of the Scriptures! It absolutely matters how God created, because His Word tells us how He did it — "For He spoke, and it was done" (Psalm 33:9). If that is not how it actually happened (and is recorded in detail in Genesis 1 and 2), then why would God give us an account of creation?

Another prominent church leader, Tim Keller, pastor of Redeemer Presbyterian Church in Manhattan, made a blatantly offensive statement about those who read Genesis 1 and 2 as historical narrative:

> You actually have this choice before you. You can either believe that Genesis 1 and 2 contradict each other, and that we can't trust the Bible. That somebody wrote Genesis 2 and somebody wrote Genesis 1, and some idiotic editor slapped them together. And they totally contradict each other, and that's the way the Bible is — it's

20. Joel Hunter, "Danger of Preaching on Genesis with Joel Hunter," BioLogos, http://biologos.org/resources/multimedia/joel-hunter-on-the-danger-of-preaching-on-genesis.

just this compendium, right? Or you can believe that Genesis 2 is historical reportage, and Genesis 1 is a poem.[21]

So Keller presents us with a choice: we can either believe the Bible had an "idiotic editor," or we can believe that God did not mean what He said in Genesis 1. This is a sad, sad statement from a man who preaches to thousands of people each week, who has authored a number of books, and who is held in high regard in the Christian community — and no doubt has seen many people saved under his ministry. He misses the obvious — that Genesis 1 is an overview of creation in chronological order, and most of Genesis 2 is a detailed account of the sixth day of creation (particularly in regard to the creation of Adam and Eve). One has to ask about his motivation for such a view. I suggest it is really because of the influence of secular views on the origins issue.[22]

J.P. Moreland, distinguished professor of philosophy at the Talbot School of Theology at Biola University, also highly regarded among many Christians, explained how he views evolution and long ages during a presentation at Rick Warren's Saddleback Church:

> Are there areas of difficulty? Yes, there are. There's evidence for the theory of evolution, and it's hard to square some parts of this theory of evolution with the early chapters of Genesis. Again, there's evidence for an old universe. I happen to favor an old universe, but for those who hold to a recent universe and the days of Genesis are six, 24-hour days of creation, that's a problem. Again, we haven't found a lot of archaeological evidence yet for a universal flood of Noah.[23]

Moreland, like so many other evangelicals, has confused evidence (and, specifically, interpretation of evidence) with worldview. Remember the issue of starting points? The evidence that is available to us is the *same* — it is our starting point that makes the difference. The evidence does not fit with the evolutionary worldview, but it makes sense when examined from the biblical perspective.

---

21. Tim Keller, "Q&A: How Do Genesis 1 and 2 Relate?" YouTube, https://www.youtube.com/watch?v=2L3kj5SLmjI.

22. For more information on Keller's position, see his paper, "Creation, Evolution, and Christian Laypeople," BioLogos, http://biologos.org/uploads/projects/Keller_white_paper.pdf.

23. J.P. Moreland, presentation at Apologetics Weekend, Saddleback Church, September, 5, 2009; available online at http://www.youtube.com/watch?v=vB04xWfxHKA.

Really, there are not "areas of difficulty" for biblical creationists, because we have an inerrant account of Creation, the Fall, and the Flood. Moreland's assertion is based on an acceptance of evolutionary historical science, specifically long ages, and not on the inspired Word of God. That is why he sees "areas of difficulty."

William Lane Craig, research professor of philosophy at the same school as Moreland, explains that his own view of origins is "somewhat agnostic . . . somewhere between progressive creationism and theistic evolution. Any of those would be acceptable in my understanding of the evidence."[24] Like Moreland, Craig places a high amount of importance on the supposed evidence for evolution and millions of years, rather than looking at the evidence through the lens of biblical authority.

So how does Craig reconcile some of the problems posed by theistic evolution and progressive creation, such as animal death before the Fall?

> What the Scripture says is that God looked at the creation He had made and it was "very good." But the idea that there was no animal death or suffering prior to the Fall is, I think, a young creationist myth that isn't in the text at all.[25]

Myth — that is Dr. Craig's assumedly researched answer to the problem of death before the Fall in the compromise views of progressive creation and theistic evolution. You see, Dr. Craig is not even dealing with the issue; instead, he attacks biblical creationists.

Over at Westmont College (a Christian college) in Santa Barbara, California, two more professors have made very public compromises on Genesis. Dr. Jeffrey Schloss, professor of biology, said in an interview with BioLogos that the evidence for evolution is "overwhelming":

> So evolution in terms of just genetic change over time — that's not even an idea, that's just a brute observation. We see it. Evolution in the sense of whether that genetic change over time has resulted in the diversity of species we see now, which is the proposition of

---

24. William Lane Craig, "William Lane Craig's View on Creation and Evolution," YouTube, http://www.youtube.com/watch?v=cSc92EDm5gU&feature=related&safety_mode=true&persist_safety_mode=1.
25. Craig, "On Young Earth Creationism and Animal Death," YouTube, http://www.youtube.com/watch?v=0xhqvulqoj4&safety_mode=true&persist_safety_mode=1.

common descent, that is an idea, that's an interpretation. But the evidence for the truth of that interpretation is overwhelming.[26]

Dr. Schloss is right in one sense — we do see genetic change over time, specifically genetic change in *pre-existing* genetic information. Many times as creatures reproduce, they lose genetic material (or genetic material is re-distributed, and there are different combinations of already existing genetic material), but they do not haphazardly gain new genetic information. What we have *never* observed is a process that would allow the types of changes necessary for molecules-to-man evolution. We have never observed one kind changing into another kind (e.g., the dog kind evolving into a totally different kind of animal). The supposed evidence for evolution is not "overwhelming." In fact, the evidence (which biblical creationists and evolutionary scientists share) is the same evidence, and when properly interpreted, confirms the Bible's account of origins, not the evolutionary belief.

Finally, Tremper Longman III is professor of biblical studies at Westmont College and was co-editor with Peter Enns of the *Dictionary of the Old Testament: Wisdom, Poetry, and Writings*. Now, Enns's ideas, most of which fly in the face of the history in Genesis, will be dealt with in a later chapter. But Dr. Longman, like so many of the scholars and church leaders in this chapter, does not have a high view of Genesis 1–11.

Longman clearly places evolutionary ideas above God's Word in the following explanation:

> A lot of people stumble with the creation account in the Old Testament, because they've been conditioned to think that it presents a view of creation that's so much at odds with modern scientific ideas about creation, and there are those out there that say the Bible teaches a six day, 24-hour creation followed by a 24-hour period of rest — a seven-day creation week. In other words, they interpret the text in a highly literalistic way and that seems so much at odds with what scientists are discovering. But this is an imposition of a modern reading on the scriptural text. The biblical text is not disputing Darwin. . . .[27]

---

26. Jeffrey Schloss, "Evolution: What We Know and What We Don't," BioLogos, http://biologos.org/blog/evolution-what-we-know-and-what-we-don't.

27. Tremper Longman III, "Tremper Longman III — On the Creation Account — Part 4," YouTube, http://www.youtube.com/watch?v=KysKaOAl2MA&lr=1.

Dr. Longman is correct — Genesis is not *directly* disputing Darwin's ideas, because Darwin was not around and his evolutionary ideas were not in existence when Genesis was written. But God's account of creation is no less accurate just because many scientists today have been influenced by evolutionary thinking.

What's more, there are many things that God's Word does not directly dispute, but we still understand to be incorrect because of the clear teaching of the Scriptures. For example, the Bible does not directly say, "Abortion is wrong." But it does say that all human beings are made in God's image (Genesis 1:26–27). Scripture affirms that God "covered me in my mother's womb" and that "I am fearfully and wonderfully made" (Psalm 139:13–14). Based on just these two references, we can say with certainty that the murder of an unborn baby is the murder of a human being made in the image of God. But modern secular scientists' evolutionary view of human beings would have us believe that an unborn baby is not truly human until much later in its development in the womb — or even not until his birth. Should we apply Longman's logic with the creation account in Genesis to the issue of abortion? Absolutely not! Evolutionary ideas cannot be allowed to usurp the clear teaching of God's Word.

Evolutionary Ideas and God's Word — They Don't Mix!

But it is not just the Bible's account of origins that is in conflict with man's ideas — but the Bible's account of what will happen in the future is also in conflict with what man proposes.

Now, the so-called big-bang model teaches a concept of creation that is completely opposite of Scripture's account. According to this view, the universe came into existence billions of years ago. The big bang eventually led to the slow origin of the earth and solar system.

The big-bang idea claims the sun came before the earth, and the earth began as a molten, fiery rock. But Genesis 1 clearly describes that the earth was created before the sun, and it was covered with liquid water (Genesis 1:2–9, 16):

> In the beginning God created the heavens and the earth. The earth was without form, and void; and darkness was on the face of the deep. And the Spirit of God was hovering over the face of the waters. (Genesis 1:1–2)

Evolutionary thinking also claims that the end of the universe will be accompanied by heat death. The sun will burn out and everything will freeze. But what does God's Word say about the end of the universe?

> But the day of the Lord will come as a thief in the night, in which the heavens will pass away with a great noise, and the elements will melt with fervent heat; both the earth and the works that are in it will be burned up. (2 Peter 3:10)

Rather than a heat death, the Bible tells us that the earth one day will be destroyed by fire. What more needs to be said about the fact that the Scriptures clearly teach against these ideas of man in his attempts to explain the universe without God?

It is important to note, too, that the term "big bang" was coined by Sir Fred Hoyle in 1949. However, Hoyle was not the man who proposed the idea. Georges Lemaître, a Belgian physicist and Roman Catholic priest, first suggested in 1927 that the universe expanded, and in 1931 proposed that at one time all matter in the universe was concentrated into a single point. While Hoyle actually advocated a competing idea known as the steady state model, Lemaître's big bang idea became more widely accepted as time went on.

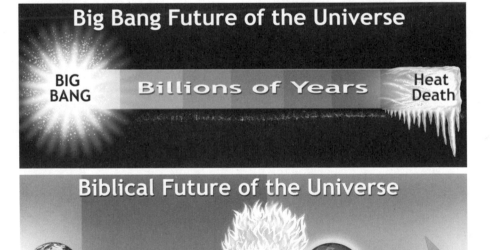

You see, the big bang idea comes out of an attempt to explain the world based on the laws of time and nature — basically, naturalism. Lemaître kept what he called his religious beliefs and what he called his "science" clearly separated, saying that his big bang idea left the materialist free to deny God's existence. Of course, the big bang is not operational science (i.e., testable, observable, or repeatable) but historical science (i.e., assumptions about the unobservable past). The big bang and evolutionary ideas in general are really a religion that is used to explain away God. So how can Christians possibly justify mixing these ideas with the Word of God?

Church, this is cause for concern. The many quotes listed here are just a fraction of the claims being made by Christian leaders and scholars about evolution, millions of years, and Scripture. Many of these people love the Lord and share the same mission as every Christian — to share the gospel and make disciples of every nation. But their inconsistent beliefs about Genesis undermine not just the authority of the Bible, but also the very message of the gospel that they seek to share — because they are undermining the Word from which the gospel comes. And they are in essence blaming God for death — instead of blaming our sin.

Christian scholars, academics, pastors, and church leaders, I urge you, for the sake of your students, congregations, and the gospel, to stand firmly on the authority of God's Word in *every* area, and not to be taken captive by secular man's fallible, evolutionary/millions of years thinking.

The following diagrams really sum up what is happening.

Conservative Theologians and Academics

Genesis 1-11   Genesis 12 - Revelation 22

Many Christian leaders (including many conservative ones) take the same basic view of evolution and or millions of years as does atheist Richard Dawkins, and call that "science." They then reinterpret Genesis to fit man's belief about origins into Scripture. This is eisegesis.

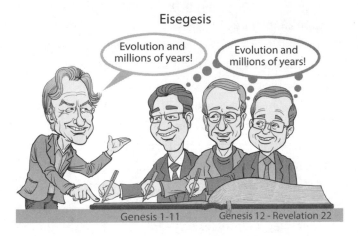

But then the same Christian leaders will use Scripture concerning the Resurrection and the Virgin Birth to tell Richard Dawkins he is wrong not to believe in the Resurrection or the Virgin Birth. This is exegesis.

These Christian leaders are being totally inconsistent. They use one hermeneutical principle for Genesis 1–11 (eisegesis), but a totally different one for the rest of the Bible (exegesis). Most would never perform such eisegesis that they use in Genesis on the rest of Scripture. Why can't they see this gross inconsistency? Academic peer pressure? Academic pride? We all need to examine our hearts in regard to how we approach the Word of God.

Chapter 8

 # Was There a Global Flood?

The idea that most of the fossil record was laid down before man came out of naturalism, as man attempted to explain the fossil layers without God's revelation concerning a global Flood. But if most of the fossil record was the result of this global catastrophe of Noah's day, then this has great bearing on discussions concerning the age of the earth.

The most catastrophic event in history was the global Flood of Noah's day. In fact, the Flood is the key to understanding where many of the rock layers and much of the fossil record came from. It also explains much of our changing climate, weather patterns, and a host of other changes the earth has undergone.

But many Christian scholars and leaders do not see the relevance of the Flood, particularly whether it was global or local. After all, they say, a belief in a global Flood is not necessary to a person's salvation. Instead, they gloss over the issue of the Flood and tell people, "Love Jesus! We don't know if what the Bible says about the Flood is actually true — it probably isn't. But trust Jesus!"

And really, aren't rocks and earth's history the domain of geologists, because the Bible is not a science textbook? That way, if the secular geologists say there was never a global Flood, then that settles it! Christian leaders and academics who hold to millions of years and evolutionary ideas will often agree with secular geologists and claim that there was not a global Flood.

But this is a crucial question! What's at stake, ultimately, is the authority of *all* of God's Word. You see, if the text of Scripture in Genesis 6–8 teaches that the Flood was global and we reject that teaching, then we undermine the reliability and authority of other parts of Scripture. Either God's Word is trustworthy and authoritative in all that it affirms, or it is not.

BioLogos: The Flood Is a "Fascinating Story"

The theistic evolution group BioLogos, unsurprisingly, endorses a local flood. Of course, because the people at BioLogos hold to an old earth and evolutionary ideas, they have to explain the fossil record and the rock layers through evolutionary means. If most of the fossil record was a result of Noah's Flood, then the supposed millions of years of earth history evaporates!

But what's even more disturbing about the position of BioLogos is the way they refer to the historical account on their website as a "fascinating story." Now, I have argued before that it is incredibly important that we treat the historical accounts in the Bible as literal history. As I explain in my book *Already Gone*, our research showed that students who regularly attended Sunday school were likely *not* to believe that all the accounts in the Bible are true and accurate.[1]

I would suggest that the doubt these students have about the accuracy of Scripture is because many church leaders treat the accounts in Scripture as just "stories" (the word *story* means "fiction" to many today), and some leaders do not even believe the accounts themselves! Sadly, this sort of compromise is all too common in today's Sunday school programs.

What BioLogos presents however is not simply a treatment of the account of the global Flood as a "story," but it also attempts to make a scientific argument for why the Flood is impossible. At the same time, BioLogos attacks the position of those who hold to the inerrancy and authority of God's Word, and thus promotes a local flood rather than a global one (as the Scripture clearly teaches):

> The Genesis Flood of Genesis 6–9 tells a fascinating story. Sometimes referred to as Noah and the Ark, it is a common fundamentalist claim that the biblical flood must have been a worldwide one, or else Scripture as a whole is undermined. From this point of view,

---

1. Ken Ham and Britt Beemer, *Already Gone*, with Todd Hillard (Green Forest, AR: Master Books, 2009), p. 38–39.

the flood is often used in an attempt to account for the geologic column, which is otherwise seen as evidence of a very old Earth. However, a balanced interpretation of Scripture does not force the reader to believe that the Flood was a worldwide phenomenon. The scientific and historical evidence summarized below supports the idea that the flood was indeed catastrophic, but that it was local, recent and limited in scope.[2]

Really, what BioLogos is saying is that those who hold to a literal, historical view of Genesis do not have a "balanced interpretation" of Scripture. So if taking God at His Word is not "balanced," then what is? Clearly, for BioLogos this means an understanding that includes evolutionary/millions of years ideas, resulting in a local flood. The point of the Flood narrative then becomes simply a "story" to teach some sort of theological truths, as they explain:

> Beyond its place in history, the Genesis Flood is also a part of the greater narrative of the Bible. It highlights theological points concerning human depravity, faith, obedience, divine judgment, grace and mercy.[3]

There is no doubt that we can learn all these things from the Flood narrative; indeed, God often uses the accounts of Scripture to teach more than just history. But that does not negate the fact that Genesis 6–9 is still historically accurate.

The root problem is that those Christians who believe in evolution and millions of years just cannot allow for a global Flood. To do so would destroy the fundamental nature of what they believe. If there were a global Flood, then that would mean that the belief in a fossil record of millions of years, and in theistic evolution is untenable. A global Flood producing most of the fossil record would eliminate the supposed millions of years of history before man. The fossil record is used by the secularists as a supposed record of biological evolution over millions of years. There are many Christians, like many of those at Biologos, who then take the secular view of evolution and attempt to add God to it, adopting the position of theistic evolution.

---

2. "How Should We Interpret the Genesis Flood Account?" BioLogos, http://biologos.org/questions/genesis-flood.

3. Ibid.

What's more, a global Flood would show that God does not break His promises. Not only did God promise to save Noah and his family from the coming judgment of the Flood, He also promised never to flood the world again. There are still local floods, of course, but there has never been anything on the scale of the global Flood since Noah's day. The Bible teaches us in 2 Peter 3 that there will be another global judgment — but by fire next time.

More Questions Than Answers

Another popular claim among those who hold to an old earth is that the Flood was not global, it was "universal." What people mean by this term is that the Flood only affected the area of the earth where there was a population of humans. They believe that Noah and his family were saved from what is a local flood under another name.

When people try to explain to me that God only sent a universal flood, my question for them is, "Why couldn't Noah and his family just leave the region? They had plenty of time to move. Why go through all the trouble of building an Ark when they could just go to a place where the 'universal flood' would not affect them?"

Of course, there is no good answer to my question, because the idea of a universal flood does not make sense to begin with. If the Flood were confined to a single region or area, how can the description given in Genesis 7:19 be true? "And the waters prevailed exceedingly on the earth, and all the high hills under the whole heaven were covered."

Genesis says that *all* the high hills under the *whole heaven* were covered. That statement would be blatantly false if the Flood were not a global event. Sadly, however, there are many Christian leaders who do not see it that way.

For instance, Hank Hanegraaff, popularly known as the Bible Answer Man, holds to an old earth and alludes to a belief in a universal flood. In his book *The Creation Answer Book*, he answers the question, "Does Genesis confirm the reality of a global Flood?" His answer does not demonstrate any support for the reality of the global Flood Genesis describes. Instead, Hanegraaff waffles, indicating that we should turn to evolutionary "science" (in other words, man's historical science) for the answer to the question:

> Furthermore, the biblical text is not designed to communicate whether the Flood was global with respect to the earth or universal

with respect to humanity. That debate is ultimately settled by a proper "reading" of the book of nature. . . . Finally, since civilization was largely confined to the Fertile Crescent, we need not automatically presume that the floodwaters covered the globe.[4]

Based on Hanegraaff's beliefs regarding the age of the earth, where he says that "an earth measured in billions of years is no threat to a biblical view of creation," it is very likely he subscribes to a universal (local) flood.[5]

Sadly, Hanegraaff does not hold to a young earth (which is what is really driving his interpretation of the Flood). He writes in other parts of his book that "the age of the earth is at least hundreds of times older than the age presumed by young-earth creationists."[6] He writes that "independent empirical evidence all converge on a limited range of dates for the origin of the universe, a date somewhere between 10 and 20 billion years ago."[7]

The compromises only continue from there, with a denial of literal days of creation and the acceptance of death prior to the Fall (Hanegraaff's view on this will be discussed in a later chapter). The troubling part about all of this is that Hanegraaff is the host of a popular radio show and fashions himself as knowing what the Bible teaches on these topics. He is influential — and he is using his influence to lead people astray, whether he realizes it or not. Hanegraaff's *The Creation Answer Book* really leaves believers with more questions than answers — and thus leads to people doubting (and ultimately disbelieving) the Word of God. This is all part of today's Genesis 3 ("Did God really say. . . ?") attack on God's Word.

Progressive Creation and a Local Flood

Progressive creationism (as discussed previously) is the position on Genesis that teaches that the universe is billions of years old and that God "progressively" created species that died out, created more that died out, and so on, leading to the fossil record we have today. In keeping with their acceptance of millions of years and astronomical and geological evolution, progressive creationists also deny a global Flood. Again, the driving reason for this interpretation of the Flood is the acceptance of the supposed millions of years.

---

4. Hank Hanegraaff, *The Creation Answer Book* (Nashville, TN: Thomas Nelson, 2012), p. 86–87.

5. Ibid., p. 141.

6. Ibid., p. 101.

7. Ibid., p. 103.

Typically, progressive creationists believe that the Flood of Noah's day was a local flood, limited to the Mesopotamian region. Progressive creationists erroneously believe that the rock layers and fossils found around the world are the result of billions of years of earth history, rather than from the biblical Flood. However, progressive creationists will call the Flood a "worldwide" or "universal" flood. But by worldwide or universal, they do not mean global (in the sense of the entire earth being covered by water) — but only part of the globe, or universal as far as the population is concerned. One has to understand how people define terms to really understand what they mean!

Dr. Hugh Ross and Reasons to Believe promote a local flood, adhering specifically to what he calls a universal flood, like Hanegraaff described above. Dr. Ross explains in an article on the Reasons to Believe website, "Based on the meaning of the word *universal*, 'encompassing all members of a category or group,' in this case 'all humanity,' our position can best be described as the universal flood view."[8]

Now, the word *universal* can be very deceptive to some people. Dr. Ross often says that he believes in a "universal" or "worldwide" flood. For example, in another article on the Reasons to Believe site, Dr. Ross writes, "In both its linguistic and historical context, world in the Genesis passages refers not to the entire planet but rather to the 'world' of people. So the Flood could have been worldwide without being global."[9] Dr. Ross does not believe that the Flood covered the whole earth. He argues that the text of Genesis 7 does not really say that the Flood covered the whole earth.

But is that what Genesis 7 says? Read it for yourself:

> And the waters prevailed exceedingly on the earth, and all the high hills under the whole heaven were covered. The waters prevailed fifteen cubits upward, and the mountains were covered. And all flesh died that moved on the earth: birds and cattle and beasts and every creeping thing that creeps on the earth, and every man. All in whose nostrils was the breath of the spirit of life, all that was on the dry land, died. So He destroyed all living things which were on the face of the ground: both man and cattle, creeping thing and bird of the

---

8. Hugh Ross, "Exploring the Extent of the Flood: Part One," Reasons to Believe, http://www.reasons.org/articles/exploring-the-extent-of-the-flood-part-one.

9. Ross, "Exploring What the Bible Says: The Extent of the Flood: Part Two," Reasons to Believe, http://www.reasons.org/articles/exploring-the-extent-of-the-flood-what-the-bible-says-part-two.

air. They were destroyed from the earth. Only Noah and those who were with him in the ark remained alive. (Genesis 7:19–23)

Genesis plainly states that *all* the high hills under heaven were covered — this would not be possible if the Flood were local. What's more, *all* livings things on the earth were destroyed. This was a global, catastrophic event, not a small flood affecting only a small part of the earth. There is ample evidence for the Flood, but in his book, *The Genesis Question*, Ross states:

> Most skeptics (and even non-skeptics) assume that a Flood of such immense proportions would leave behind substantial evidence, a deposit that geologists today should be able to find.[10]

You see, if there really was a global Flood, we would expect to find billions of dead things buried in rock layers laid down by water all over the earth — and that is exactly what we do find. It is not the evidence that is lacking, but Dr. Ross's starting point that is wrong. He has accepted man's fallible historical science instead of God's infallible historical science (the revelation in Scripture).

Now, Dr. Ross recognizes in his book that there are massive sedimentary layers laid down by water all over the earth, full of dead things, and he continues by stating:

> The assumption that clear evidence "should" remain must be challenged. The Flood, though massive, lasted but one year and ten days. A flood of such brief duration typically does not leave a deposit substantial enough to be positively identified thousands of years later.[11]

Of course, how could Dr. Ross know this is "typical" when he has never experienced such a flood of that duration? In the face of clear evidence for a global, catastrophic Flood, what does Dr. Ross do? Basically, he just waves it away, saying there is no way an event we have never witnessed could do that, even though we have seen many local catastrophes cause massive erosion and deposition (e.g., the Mount St. Helens eruption in 1980).

Furthermore, in Genesis 9, God promised that He would never again send a flood to destroy all flesh and cover the earth — the rainbow was the sign of that promise:

---

10. Hugh Ross, *The Genesis Question: Scientific Advances and the Accuracy of Genesis* (Colorado Springs, CO: NavPress, 2001), p. 159.
11. Ibid.

I set My rainbow in the cloud, and it shall be for the sign of the covenant between Me and the earth. It shall be, when I bring a cloud over the earth, that the rainbow shall be seen in the cloud; and I will remember My covenant which is between Me and you and every living creature of all flesh; the waters shall never again become a flood to destroy all flesh. The rainbow shall be in the cloud, and I will look on it to remember the everlasting covenant between God and every living creature of all flesh that is on the earth. (Genesis 9:13–16)

There have been many floods since Noah's day, but never a global one. To believe in a local flood, then, is to say that God broke His promise.

The Flood was a major event in earth's history. Those who believe in millions of years, including Dr. Ross, ardently reject that this global event ever occurred. By doing so, they (whether Christian or non-Christian) are proclaiming that the words of Genesis 6–9 cannot be taken as written. (This is especially disturbing coming from Christians.) If that is so, should anyone believe the rest of Genesis — or the rest of the Bible for that matter — as written? As I keep insisting — the age of the earth is an authority issue. Is God the ultimate authority — or fallible man?

The Flood and Ancient Near Eastern Mythology

Peter Enns, former senior fellow with BioLogos, argues that the Flood should not be understood as a global event in light of ancient Near Eastern literature:

It is virtually certain that one or more local floods in Meso-potamia — perhaps around 3000 B.C. according to some scholars — provide the historical basis for all the flood stories that come from that area. But the geological record, at least as interpreted by mainstream scientists, discounts any notion of a "worldwide" flood that killed *every single creature on earth, save a few* (Genesis 6:7; 7:21–23), a few thousand years ago [emphasis Enns's].[12]

The views Peter Enns puts forth will be discussed in a later chapter, but he holds to evolutionary ideas, like the rest of the people at BioLogos. So by

---

12. Peter Enns, "Gilgamesh, Atrahasis, and the Flood, Part 3," BioLogos, http://biologos.org/blog/gilgamesh-atrahasis-and-the-flood-part-3.

necessity, he cannot believe in a global Flood — his *a priori* acceptance of millions of years will not allow it. Regardless of what Scripture states, Enns, like so many Christian academics, has accepted man's fallible historical science and uses that to reinterpret God's infallible historical science. But since when should Christians give more credence to fallible "mainstream scientists" than they do to God's Word? The geological record, when read in light of the Bible's account of the Flood (and the fact that death, disease, thorns, and suffering came after sin), actually makes more sense than it does from an evolutionary perspective. The geological evolutionary view presents a host of problems that must be dealt with (and that cannot be satisfactorily answered apart from the Bible). Many of these problems are dealt with in articles on the Answers in Genesis website, AnswersInGenesis.org.

How do these Christian academics use the ancient Near Eastern view to reject the plain reading of the biblical account? Enns, like Hanegraaff and Ross, argues for a type of universal flood:

> Of course, for the ancient writer of Genesis, the world was a much smaller, flatter place. Perhaps what he and other ancient writers wrote reflects how they *perceived* the world. The "earth" was what they saw when they walked outside — a vast stretch of flat land with mountains off in the distance. When a devastating flood came and swept away everything in its path, it seemed like "the whole earth" to the ancient writer. If you think about it, one should actually *expect* ancient writers to use "worldwide" language given their state of knowledge.[13]

There is value in understanding how an ancient culture understood certain things and how they used language. This sort of knowledge can be very helpful in better understanding Scripture. However, such study should not be used to explain away what Scripture clearly says. Such a dismissal attributes Scripture to that of just the level of fallible man — instead of it being the inspired Word of God for all people for all time (2 Timothy 3:16). God's Word is not the fumbling attempts of fallible man to write down an understanding of the Word; it is the very God-breathed Word, as God inspired those He chose to write it down so we would have His infallible revelation to us.

---

13. Ibid.

It is not the purpose of this book to deal with the perspicuity of Scripture, but this doctrine that many greats have written about and adhered to (including the great reformer Martin Luther) seems to be lost on many of these modern scholars. I remind them of verses like these:

> The statutes of the LORD are right, rejoicing the heart; the commandment of the LORD is pure, enlightening the eyes. (Psalm 19:8)

> And so we have the prophetic word confirmed, which you do well to heed as a light that shines in a dark place, until the day dawns and the morning star rises in your hearts. (2 Peter 1:19)

> Your word is a lamp to my feet and a light to my path. (Psalm 119:105)

What is clear in Genesis 6–9 is that there was a Flood that covered the *whole world*. The description in Genesis does not lead to any other conclusions. Moreover, if the Bible is truly inspired by God, who cannot lie, how could it be possible that Scripture means something less than it says? That would be a lie. If the Flood was anything less than worldwide or global (i.e., covered the whole earth), then what the Bible says is untrue and cannot be trusted. Enns, however, holds fast to the ancient Near Eastern interpretation, claiming that a plain reading of the Flood account is a "modern imposition":

> To interpret the Genesis flood as a complete global catastrophe is a modern imposition onto an ancient story. Ancients simply did not think of the earth in that way. This is where "Flood Geology" gets off on the wrong foot. Apart from the well-documented scientific problems with this approach, it expects a worldview that Genesis is not prepared to deliver.[14]

Once again, Enns has demonstrated in his own words that he places more authority on man's fallible ideas than on the Word of God. Really, there are not scientific problems with a global Flood — the evidence fits the best from the global Flood perspective. But there are plenty of scientific and theological problems with the local flood perspective. Genesis cannot deliver the *evolutionary* worldview, which is exactly where the local flood idea originates.

---

14. Ibid.

It is directly contradictory to the biblical worldview, which includes a catastrophic global Flood.

Enns and others are actually imposing their fallible views from outside of Scripture onto God's revelation!

The Case for a Global Flood

The researchers at BioLogos, Hugh Ross, Hank Hanegraaff, and many other progressive creationists, theistic evolutionists, and other compromisers recognize that they cannot believe in a global Flood and millions of years at the same time. So they have accepted the millions-of-years time frame of the secular world and rejected God's clear revelation in Scripture. This is an attack on the authority of the Word of God. Ultimately, it is an attack on the gospel, for the gospel comes from this same Word. Also, to accept millions of years is to blame God for death, disease, suffering, and thorns — instead of blaming our sin in Adam.

It is obvious that if there was a global Flood; this catastrophic event would have eroded billions of tons of sediments and then would have deposited them all over the world.[15] And that is exactly what we find. Dr. Andrew Snelling (PhD in geology from Sydney University, Australia — currently Director of Research at Answers in Genesis) has outlined six geological evidences for a global Flood: 1. fossils of sea creatures high above sea level due to the ocean waters having flooded over the continents; 2. rapid burial of plants and animals; 3. rapidly deposited sediment layers spread across vast areas; 4. sediment transported long distances; 5. rapid or no erosion between strata; and 6. many strata laid down in rapid succession.[16] These evidences all make sense when examined through the biblical worldview.

Think about it: if you accept a real global Flood, then you destroy evolution's millions of years of history, as supposedly recorded in the fossils found in the layers of rock. If most of the fossil layers were laid down during the year of the catastrophic Flood, then the supposed millions of years of evolutionary history before man is eliminated. Those who claim God used evolution to form life have no foundation — except that of God's revelation,

---

15. As a comparison, just look at what happened with the small, local catastrophe of the 1980 eruption of Mount St. Helens and the almost immediate formation of massive sedimentary deposits.

16. Andrew Snelling, "Geologic Evidences for the Genesis Flood," Answers in Genesis, http://www.answersingenesis.org/articles/am/v2/n4/geologic-evidences-part-one.

which details how God created the universe, including life on earth in six literal days of creation approximately 6,000 years ago.

To summarize, those who continue to hold to a local flood have questions left to answer. For instance, if the Flood was local, why did Noah have to build an Ark? He could have walked to the other side of the mountains and missed it. If the Flood was local, why did God send the animals to the Ark so they could escape death? There would have been other animals to reproduce that kind if these particular ones had died. If the Flood was local, why was the Ark big enough to hold all the different kinds of vertebrate land animals? If only Mesopotamian animals were aboard, the Ark could have been much smaller. If the Flood was local, why would birds have been sent on board? These could simply have winged across to a nearby mountain range. If the Flood was local, how could the waters rise to fifteen cubits (eight meters) above the mountains (Genesis 7:20)? Water seeks its own level. It could not rise to cover the local mountains while leaving the rest of the world untouched. If the Flood was local, people who did not happen to be living in the vicinity would not be affected by it. They would have escaped God's judgment on sin. If this had happened, what did Christ mean when He likened the coming judgment of all men to the judgment of "all" men in the days of Noah (Matthew 24:37–39)? A partial judgment in Noah's day means a partial judgment to come. If the Flood was local, God would have repeatedly broken His promise never to send such a flood again.

How sad that the very evidence of the judgment of the Flood is being used by secularists and many Christians to indoctrinate generations in evolutionary ideas — thus creating doubt and ultimately unbelief in the Word of God.

At Answers in Genesis and the Creation Museum, we teach the truth concerning the global Flood of Noah's day. At the same time, we also teach the lesson symbolized by the Ark, which God told Noah to build to save Noah, his family, and representatives of all the land-animal kinds from the destroying effects of the Flood.

Just as Noah and his family had to go through a doorway into the Ark to be saved, so each of us needs to go through a doorway to be saved: Jesus Christ, the Son of God, is our Ark of salvation.

> I am the door. If anyone enters by Me, he will be saved, and will
> go in and out and find pasture." (John 10:9)

Chapter 9

The Necessity of a Historical Adam

Back in 1987 when my first major book, *The Lie: Evolution*, was published, I was warning the Church that if Christian leaders (pastors, Bible college and seminary professors, Christian college professors, and so on) continued with the rampant compromise with millions of years and Genesis — then it would eventually lead to increasing numbers of Christian leaders giving up a literal Adam, literal Eve, and a literal Fall. We are now seeing that happen.

The attacks on the historicity of the creation account in Genesis have certainly been common for many years now, but the latest challenges have been increasingly related to whether Adam and Eve are historical figures. Like the Flood of Noah's day and the length of time for creation, there are church leaders and Bible scholars who will say that this also is another secondary issue — that it does not really matter what we believe about Adam and Eve.

The battle over whether Adam and Eve were historical figures (just like the battle over the age of the earth) really comes down to a battle over the authority, inspiration, infallibility, and inerrancy of the Bible. Can we truly trust what the Bible says about the first humans? Secularists respond with a resounding "no," followed by a growing part of the Church that is once again influenced by the secularists' account of origins and is denying the Bible's creation account in Genesis in favor of evolutionary ideas.

But what we believe about Adam does matter. Now, it's important to note that our belief about a historical Adam, just like the global Flood or the creation account, is not a salvation issue. The Christian leaders and academics who do not hold to the Bible's account of the historical Adam can still be saved and are still able to be influential for Christ — in spite of the clear inconsistency in their belief system. Salvation is conditioned upon faith in Christ. So people can be totally inconsistent on certain matters but can still be saved if they are born again as the Bible defines. Of course, only God truly knows the heart of each person on this matter.

So, what are the implications of denying a historical Adam? The Apostle Paul explains that it was "through one man sin entered the world, and death through sin, and thus death spread to all men, because all sinned" (Romans 5:12). That one man was Adam, whose act of rebellion against God — eating from the tree of the knowledge of good and evil — led to the Fall of all mankind. But if there was no literal Adam, then we have to ask the question: where did death and sin come from?

Now, theistic evolutionists, progressive creationists, and other old-earth creationists all hold to death (and disease and thorns — because these are evidenced in the fossil record they accept was laid down millions of years before man) before the Fall. But the origin of sin, death, and disease is a problem that, without the account of a perfect creation marred by sin, those holding these compromised positions have a hard time dealing with. Some

old-earth positions accept a literal Adam and a literal Fall — but they still have the problem of death, disease, and thorns before sin!

But for those who do reject a literal Adam and a literal Fall, I assert that this makes Christ's death and Resurrection completely unnecessary. The Apostle Paul affirms this fact in 1 Corinthians 15:22 when he writes, "For as in Adam all die, even so in Christ all shall be made alive." Later in the same chapter, Paul refers to Christ as "the last Adam" (1 Corinthians 15:45). If all have not actually died (experienced spiritual and eventual physical death) in the first Adam, then it is not actually necessary for Christ to make us alive as the last Adam. According to a view without the Fall, we should already be alive, apart from Christ. But this does not sound like the gospel message — in fact, this is not at all what the gospel teaches.

The Uncertain Sound of the Christian Community

In June 2011, the magazine *Christianity Today* published a cover story titled "The Search for the Historical Adam." The author, Richard Ostling, catalogued the various movements in the Christian community concerning the historicity of Adam and Eve, drawing on the work and statements of Christian scientists and Bible scholars. The article's byline reads, "The center of the evolution debate has shifted from asking whether we came from earlier animals to whether we could have come from one man and one woman."[1]

Ostling's conclusion was clear: a belief in a literal Adam and Eve, or at least in those two as the progenitors of the entire human race, is becoming less common among Christian academics and church leaders. Why such a decline? In short, evolutionary ideas (beliefs from outside of Scripture) are influencing their thinking.

And although Ostling certainly did not defend biblical creation in the *Christianity Today* article, he outlined quite correctly just how much is at stake by giving up biblical authority in favor of the evolutionary worldview:

> The potential is certainly there: the emerging science could be seen to challenge not only what Genesis records about the creation of humanity but the species's unique status as bearing the "image of God," Christian doctrine on original sin and the Fall, the genealogy of Jesus

---

1. Richard N. Ostling, "The Search for the Historical Adam," *Christianity Today*, June 2011, p. 23.

in the Gospel of Luke, and, perhaps most significantly, Paul's teaching that links the historical Adam with redemption through Christ.[2]

This should be enough to push any Christian to defend Scripture's account in Genesis as true history. And yet, compromised academics and church leaders seem able to live with such inconsistency, viewing humanity as descended from animals on the one hand, while on the other claiming that we are in the image of God.

There are a variety of views on the historical Adam that stray from the plain reading of Scripture, many of which will be explored below. If you are reading this chapter as a Christian who is skeptical of the existence of Adam and Eve or of the historical accuracy of the Bible's account of human origins, I urge you to consider carefully the implications of such a viewpoint on the rest of the gospel message. Holding to a literal Genesis is not necessary for salvation, but it is necessary to maintain a consistent view of the *whole* of Scripture. And although it may not be a salvation issue as such, it is certainly an authority issue — and a gospel issue.

Adam and Eve . . . A "Primal Pair"?

A common claim, especially among theistic evolutionists, is that Adam and Eve were not the first couple. Rather, they claim Adam and Eve were a couple of early hominids that were specially selected by God to be in relationship with Him. What many theistic evolutionists imagine is that as ape-like creatures slowly evolved into modern-day humans, at some point, God selected out a couple or a group to be in His image.

This compromise position is really a compromise in itself. The evolutionary view does not allow for a first couple. Rather, it proposes that ape-like creatures evolved over long ages into modern-day humans, in multiple parts of the world. For theistic evolutionists and others who accept the evolutionary story of humanity's origins, the allowance for some sort of "primal pair" (as some of these Bible scholars refer to Adam and Eve) does not fit with the supposed evolution of humanity they are accepting and is driving them to this compromise.

Compromised Christians in the United Kingdom

I have pointed to the United Kingdom many times as an example of where America is quickly headed spiritually. Church attendance in the United

_____
2. Ibid., p. 24.

Kingdom is incredibly low, and compromised views of Scripture are very prevalent there — even in the remnant of conservative churches.

Dr. John Lennox, professor of mathematics at the University of Oxford (England), wrote a book titled *Seven Days That Divide the World* (Zondervan, 2011). Dr. Lennox is highly respected as an evangelical in the United Kingdom. There is no doubt he preaches the gospel and also is orthodox in his teaching of the Word of God (except when it comes to Genesis). Because he is obviously an active Christian with a very amenable disposition, he has a position of considerable influence on the conservative church in the United Kingdom, in Eastern and Western Europe, and increasingly in the United States. I co-authored a critique of his book to help people understand his compromise on God's Word.[3]

Dr. Lennox is a much-admired Christian professor in the United Kingdom, but sadly his book paints biblical creationists in a bad light. My co-author and I found it very interesting that Dr. Lennox referenced only one creationist article (from 1999) in his book, despite the breadth of current materials available. Answers in Genesis alone has published numerous books and articles written by experts in their fields. But Dr. Lennox instead chose to reference secularists and Christians who have compromised on Genesis. Not one of the well-known and respected biblical creationist researchers and writers (many with PhDs from respected secular universities) was referenced.

There is no doubt that Dr. Lennox is prepared to allow for God to use the evolutionary process in the creation of human beings. We suggest that Dr. Lennox has one hermeneutic (method of interpreting Scripture) for Genesis 1–11 but a different one for the rest of Scripture. There is no doubt that Dr. Lennox would not use his hermeneutical approach (taking ideas from outside the Bible to reinterpret the Genesis account of creation) when dealing with the Virgin Birth or the Resurrection.

In his book, one of Dr. Lennox's first attacks on biblical creation is to redefine what it means to read the Bible "literally." He writes, "When we are dealing with a text that was produced in a culture distant from our own both in time and in geography, what we think the natural reading is may not have been the natural meaning for those to whom the text was originally

---

3. Ken Ham and Steve Golden, "John Lennox and a Sad Divide," Answers in Genesis, http://www.answersingenesis.org/articles/2012/10/19/john-lennox-seven-days-book-review.

addressed."[4] Biblical creationists who believe the Genesis account of six literal days of creation are reading the Bible "literalistically," according to Lennox.

Dr. Lennox preaches the gospel and no doubt people have been led to Christ through his teaching of God's Word. However, that does not discount the fact that his teaching on Genesis and his compromise with evolution and millions of years undermines the authority of the Word of God in spite of his sincere intentions to the contrary.

Such collective compromise by numerous Christian leaders has been a major contributing factor to the demise of the Church in our Western world. In England, research indicates about two-thirds of young people do not believe in God, and church attendance plummeted from around 60 percent to about 5 percent of the population. Even though the gospel is preached in places, the big picture is one of a Church that has been devastated, leading to an almost spiritually dead culture in England.

This should be a warning to America. Where England is today is where America will be tomorrow — for the same reasons. Increasing numbers of Christian academics take positions similar to that of Dr. Lennox.

N.T. Wright, professor of New Testament and early Christianity at University of St. Andrews in Scotland, explains in an interview with BioLogos that he believes it is important that something like what Genesis 3 describes actually happened. However, he is not so sure Genesis is historically accurate on the origin of human beings:

> I do think it matters that something like a primal pair getting it wrong did happen, but that doesn't mean I'm saying that therefore Genesis is kind of positivist, literal, clunky history over against myth. Far from it. I think for instance that the six days of Genesis — I'm with John Walton from Wheaton College on this — I think the six days of Genesis would be interpreted in terms of this is how you describe how people make a temple or a tabernacle.[5]

Wright's ideas here are typical of what many Christian academics and leaders are promoting. They do not see the need for a historical Genesis, but they are unwilling to go as far as eliminating Adam and Eve entirely. And

---

4. John Lennox, *Seven Days That Divide the World* (Grand Rapids, MI: Zondervan, 2011), p. 22–23.

5. N.T. Wright, "Adam and Eve with N.T. Wright," BioLogos, http://biologos.org/resources/multimedia/nt-wright-on-adam-and-eve.

one result of this is the view that Adam and Eve were chosen out of many to be the first couple.

Another professor and professing Christian in the United Kingdom, Dr. Denis Alexander, is also the director of the Faraday Institute for Science and Religion at St. Edmund's College in Cambridge, England. In an interview with the organization Test of Faith, which has developed curricula for teaching children theistic evolution, Dr. Alexander asserts that Adam and Eve were "neo-lithic farmers" chosen by God:

> I take [Genesis] in a more historical sense, actually, myself. And so I would see Adam and Eve not as the first human beings on the earth. I think there were plenty of human beings around in the kind of neo-lithic times that Genesis describes for us. But if we go to the Genesis text, it certainly appears that they were farmers, there were other people around at the time — because if you remember, after Cain had killed Abel, he was a fugitive on the earth. And he said to God, "I'm afraid. I'm going to be a fugitive in the earth, and I'm afraid of people killing me." . . . So it looks as if the Genesis text is telling us about things going on in neo-lithic times, maybe six to eight thousand years ago and so forth. So one of the understandings would be that Adam and Eve were actually neo-lithic farmers that God chose to come into fellowship with Himself, and to understand what fellowship with God was all about. . . . And it was those people, that couple, actually, who then fell from God's grace.[6]

Dr. Alexander is speaking out of both sides of his mouth in this quote. On the one hand, he claims he takes Genesis as historical, but on the other, he says that he does not believe Adam and Eve were the first humans. How does that latter claim fit with the historical narrative of Genesis, which says that the first humans were indeed Adam and Eve? By "historical manner," Dr. Alexander is really trying to leave room for evolutionary ideas about human origins. It is the typical maneuverings of these compromisers to somehow fit evolution and/or millions of years into the Bible but still maintain the essence of the Christian message.

---

6. Denis Alexander, "Who Were Adam and Eve?" YouTube, http://www.youtube.com/watch?v=EbgMgOKF9u8&list=PL9EC74CB9413E14C1&index=12&feature=plpp_video.

His appeal to where Cain got his wife is an age-old argument that we have answered numerous times.[7] Many secularists, and now some Christians, have claimed that for Cain to find a wife, there must have been other people on the earth who were not descendants of Adam and Eve. But Genesis is very clear that Eve was the first woman ("And Adam called his wife's name Eve, because she was the mother of all living," Genesis 3:20). So where *did* Cain find his wife?

In Genesis 5:4 we read, "After he begot Seth, the days of Adam were eight hundred years; and he had sons and daughters." Over the course of their lives, Adam and Eve had many male and female children. Scripture does not tell us how many exactly, but considering their long lifespans (Adam lived for 930 years — Genesis 5:5), it seems logical to think that there were many. Remember, Adam and Eve were commanded to "be fruitful and multiply" (Genesis 1:28).

So if we work purely from Scripture, we can determine that when there was only one generation, brothers and sisters would have had to marry each other. We are not told when Cain married or many of the details of other marriages and children, but we can say for certain that Cain's wife was either his sister or a close relative. Dr. Alexander's assertion that Genesis is actually dealing with "neo-lithic farmers" does not respect the historical nature of Genesis; rather, it is an intentional meshing of evolutionary ideas with Scripture. For a detailed answer to Cain's wife, I suggest you read the article referenced above.

A final example of the ideas being promoted in the United Kingdom comes from Alister McGrath. McGrath is professor of theology, ministry, and education at King's College London and head of the school's Centre for Theology, Religion, and Culture. Not long ago, McGrath also interviewed with Test of Faith on the issue of Adam and Eve. His answer was, sadly, not supportive of a literal interpretation of Genesis:

> Certainly one of the most important questions concerning the origins of life is what are the status of Adam and Eve? Are these real, historical figures who lived, say, 6,000 years ago? Or are they metaphorical representations? And again, it's a very interesting question, because certainly the whole theory of evolution and indeed our knowledge of cosmology, I think, would shift those time frames back

---

7. See Ken Ham, "Cain's Wife — Who Was She?" in *The New Answers Book 1*, Ken Ham, gen. ed. (Green Forest, AR: Master Books, 2006), p. 64–76.

a very long way. But certainly one can say something like this: There are those who will say that Adam and Eve in some way designate specific historical figures. I can understand why people say that. I think it makes quite a lot of sense. But for me it makes even more sense to say that in some way Adam and Eve are stereotypical figures and in some way they encapsulate the human race as a whole. . . .[8]

McGrath's idea shares the same feature as Wright's and Alexander's — he is unwilling to admit that the text of Genesis is historical because of the evolutionary ideas he has accepted. So while McGrath can see why a biblical creationist would insist that Adam was historical, he somehow has come to the conclusion that it makes more sense that Adam was not — that the figures in Genesis are representations of the whole human race. These ideas may sound unbelievable and shocking, especially since they are coming from professing Christians, but they are not unique to the United Kingdom.

Compromise Among U.S. Christian Leaders

Challenging the historicity of Adam and Eve is becoming more and more common in the United States, particularly among Christian academics. Now, as with the age of the earth and the length of Creation Week, the historicity of Adam is not a salvation issue. But it is an authority issue and a gospel issue. While the scholars and church leaders in this chapter may deny some part of the Genesis account of human origins, that does not speak to their salvation or their influence for the gospel. For instance, Dr. John Lennox in the United Kingdom does not hold to a literal Genesis, but he is extremely influential in the Christian community there. It is the same for scholars here in America. That being said, what we believe about Adam and Eve still has a huge impact on our understanding of the rest of Scripture, if we are being consistent.

As we learned in the chapter on hermeneutics, a proper hermeneutic observes the text of Scripture very closely. Genesis states clearly that Adam was formed from the dust of the ground on Day 6 of Creation Week. If we are working solely from Scripture (i.e., maintaining a consistent historical-grammatical hermeneutic), then that is the only conclusion we can come to.

---

8. Alister McGrath, "What Are We to Make of Adam and Eve?" YouTube, http://www.youtube.com/watch?v=yL5su0zmpKM&list=PLF4C6C2C69DA9BCD3&index=12&feature=plpp_video.

But not all Bible scholars agree. Tremper Longman III, a professor of biblical studies at Westmont College in Santa Barbara, California, explains his view on the historicity of Adam and Eve:

> A lot of people believe that Genesis 1 and 2 sort of insists on the idea that there is one literal, historical Adam. And they might go and say that literal, historical Adam was created by a special act of God and not a result of, say, an evolutionary process. There are a lot of difficult questions associated with it, but I think you could only insist on the idea that there's one historical Adam if you read Genesis 1 in a very highly literalistic way, rather than understanding that it is using ancient Near Eastern concepts to express how God did create the first human beings. I just personally don't think that Genesis 1 and 2 prohibits the idea that there is a[n] evolutionary process.[9]

The question is, *why* do biblical creationists "insist" on a historical Adam, created by a special act of God? Because that is exactly what the text says occurred. But Longman, like Peter Enns and others, subscribes to the ancient Near Eastern view of Scripture, insisting that the ancient Israelites would not have understood the text to mean what it says.

Because Longman discounts the notion of a literal reading of Genesis 3, he is able to fit an evolutionary worldview into the text. If Genesis is not meant to be understood as historical narrative, then what is the problem with inserting long ages, evolution, and any number of fallible ideas into the text?

Longman continues, explaining that he is not really sure what to think of the idea of a historical Adam:

> Whether there's sort of one moment when God says, "This is the first human being," and it is one individual. Or whether *Adam* stands for mankind — after all, the Hebrew word *Adam* does mean "mankind" — that's a different question. And one that, at least, I haven't completely resolved in my own thinking yet. There's still open questions.

9. Tremper Longman III, "Is There a Historical Adam — Part 12," YouTube, http://www.youtube.com/watch?v=I8Pk1vXL1WE.

Really, based on the text of Genesis, there are no "open questions" concerning whether Adam was a single individual and the first human or whether he simply represented many humans. There are no open questions about whether God created by a miraculous act or whether he used evolutionary means. Scripture is incredibly clear on these points: God created by speaking in six, normal-length days, and Adam was the first man. And yet, academics like Longman are teaching our students that they cannot trust the plain meaning of Scripture because there are still "open questions" that are fueled by the evolutionary worldview.

Longman is certainly not alone in his view. Daniel Harrell, senior pastor of Colonial Church in Edina, Minnesota, is willing to admit that there was a historical Adam and Eve, and even that it is important to the authority of Scripture that they were real people. However, he stops short of accepting that they were the first humans:

> I guess I appreciate how, for many conservative Christians, a historical Adam and Eve is very, very important. I think one of the things that have been discussed here is how, in Corinthians and Romans, Paul's referent back to Adam and Eve is almost necessary as a historical figure given the way that he is describing them. Something that has been helpful to me is that I don't think that a historical Adam and Eve is problematic from a Biblical historical context. I think Adam and Eve as the first humans is what the problem is. You could say, and I think we've had some pastors say, that God does this special creation thing of Adam and Eve in the context of the evolutionary epic. God could do that, and that's fine.[10]

It may be helpful to Harrell to believe that Adam and Eve were not in fact the first humans — but it cannot be because he is concerned about the authority of Scripture on this issue. Harrell continues and presents his own idea of how to handle the Bible's account of the first humans versus the evolutionary story:

> You could also say that God specially selects Adam and Eve for this covenant relationship, much as He did for Abraham in the biblical epic, so that Adam and Eve become representative of the

---

10. Daniel Harrell, "A Pastor Deals with Adam and Eve," BioLogos, http://biologos.org/resources/multimedia/daniel-harrell-a-pastor-deals-with-adam-and-eve.

kind of relationship then that God intends to have with all people. And this is a point of possible convergence that allows those that are very worried about an historical Adam and Eve to breathe easier, and those who are very concerned about integrity with DNA findings and evolutionary science to also breathe easier.[11]

Harrell's solution may help theistic evolutionists to "breathe easier" about the inclusion of their fallible ideas in the biblical account, but it shows little regard for the view of biblical creationists and the authority of Scripture. Either Genesis is correct in its account of human origins or it is not — Harrell cannot have it both ways. This sort of compromise from a church leader should be startling to Christians. It does nothing to defend the authority of God's Word, and at its worst, it undermines the message of the gospel of Christ. Christianity does not need points of "convergence" with mainstream secular ideas of origins. Christians, rather, should be sharing the truth of God's Word, of the gospel, and calling fellow believers to make the Bible their foundation in every area — yes, even in how they approach science — both observational and historical science.

BioLogos and a Historical Adam

As such vocal representatives of the evolutionary creationism (i.e., theistic evolution) view, we would expect BioLogos to have a firm position on the historicity of Adam. Surprisingly, that is one issue that the organization has officially avoided taking a position on (at least according to their website), though based on their researchers' papers and even their position statement below, it is easy to guess what the majority of those at BioLogos believe. Their official answer to the question, "Were Adam and Eve Historical Figures?" is as follows:

> Genetic evidence shows that humans descended from a group of several thousand individuals who lived about 150,000 years ago. This conflicts with the traditional view that all humans descended from a single pair who lived about 10,000 years ago. While Genesis 2–3 speaks of the pair Adam and Eve, Genesis 4 refers to a larger population of humans interacting with Cain. One option is to view Adam and Eve as a historical pair living among many 10,000 years

---

11. Ibid.

ago, chosen to represent the rest of humanity before God. Another option is to view Genesis 2–4 as an allegory in which Adam and Eve symbolize the large group of ancestors who lived 150,000 years ago. Yet another option is to view Genesis 2–4 as an "everyman" story, a parable of each person's individual rejection of God. **BioLogos does not take a particular view and encourages scholarly work on these questions.** [emphasis mine][12]

Right away, readers know what the academics at BioLogos put their trust in when it comes to creation — and it is not the Word of God. In fact, the special creation of a single couple as the beginning of the human race seems to be dismissed out of hand here. Instead, multiple compromise positions are presented, followed by the statement that BioLogos does not have a particular view. But they do: BioLogos rejects the Genesis account of human origins as literal history — as it is written.

Dr. Francis Collins, a theistic evolutionist and the founder and former president of BioLogos, offered his own view on the historicity of Adam in his book *The Language of God* (New York: Free Press, 2006). Ostling recounts in *Christianity Today* that Collins "reported scientific indications that anatomically modern humans emerged from primate ancestors perhaps 100,000 years ago — long before the apparent Genesis time frame — and originated with a population that numbered something like 10,000, not two individuals."[13] Now, Dr. Collins's view is not surprising, since he holds to evolutionary ideas and must then try to fit them into Scripture. But in his more recent book, co-authored with Dr. Karl Giberson, former vice-president of BioLogos (and a former professor at Eastern Nazarene College, a Christian university), his claims about the Bible are even more disturbing. Collins and Giberson argue in *The Language of Science and Faith* that Genesis provides no answers regarding the origin of humans:

> We make no claim that the description provided here is how God created us. Neither science nor the Bible answers that question. The Genesis account says little about how God created. Adam was created from dust and God's breath; Eve was created from Adam's rib. . . .

12. "Were Adam and Eve Historical Figures?" BioLogos, http://biologos.org/questions/evolution-and-the-fall.

13. Ostling, "The Search for the Historical Adam," p. 23–24.

None of these "explanations" can possibly be actual descriptions. . . . Based on what we know today about both science and the ancient world of the Hebrews, it is simply not reasonable to try to turn the brief comments in Genesis into a biologically accurate description of how humans originated.[14]

This is not the first time Dr. Giberson has attempted to offer what he considers a better explanation than what the Bible gives regarding origins. One of his other books, *Seven Glorious Days: A Scientist Retells the Creation Story*, is his attempt at editing Scripture to fit with evolutionary ideas. And now, without any support, Collins and Giberson proclaim that the Bible's explanation for how Adam and Eve were created is not satisfactory. They conclude that literal readings of Genesis, "unfortunately, do not fit the evidence."[15]

And that leads us back to the question this book is centered on: If the Bible is not trustworthy in its first 11 chapters, how can we trust the rest of it?

Collins and Giberson are no longer with BioLogos, but the newest president of the organization, Dr. Deborah Haarsma, does not seem to support the biblical view of Adam and Eve either. In an article series on the historical Adam, Haarsma writes, "Biologist Dennis Venema has told us of the genetic evidence that humans share a common ancestor with animals, and that the first humans numbered in the thousands. . . . this genetic evidence is being confirmed repeatedly as more studies are done."[16] Venema also appeared on National Public Radio for a story on the historical Adam and Eve, in which he explained that our descent from a single couple goes against all the genetic evidence collected today.[17] It is clear in the interview that he has based his view on evolutionary understandings of the data.

Once again, members of BioLogos are ultimately placing their faith in man's fallible word, rather than God's infallible Word. Their conclusions are made based on what evolutionists have to say about human origins, at the cost of the clarity and sufficiency of Scripture.

---

14. Francis Collins and Karl Giberson, *The Language of Science and Faith* (Downers Grove, IL: InterVarsity, 2011), p. 206.

15. Ibid., p. 208.

16. Deborah Haarsma, "Historical Adam: Moving Ahead in Faith, Not Fear," Think Christian, http://thinkchristian.net/historical-adam-moving-ahead-in-faith-not-fear/.

17. Dennis Venema, interview by Barbara Bradley Hagerty, "Evangelicals Question the Existence of Adam and Eve," National Public Radio, http://www.npr.org/2011/08/09/138957812/evangelicals-question-the-existence-of-adam-and-eve.

Animal Amnesia?

Dr. William Dembski, research professor of science and culture at Southern Evangelical Seminary in Matthews, North Carolina, suggested a rather unique form of compromise on the Genesis account of creation. He proposes a theodicy, to attempt to come up with a way to incorporate millions of years and evolutionary ideas into Scripture by suggesting the possibility that humanity suffers from a form of amnesia about its supposedly evolutionary origins.

Dr. Dembski puts forth his idea in his book *The End of Christianity*. For the theistic evolutionists reading his book, Dembski attempts to demonstrate how such a view of Genesis would be compatible with evolution and millions of years:

> For the theodicy I am proposing to be compatible with evolution, God must not merely introduce existing human-like beings from outside the Garden. In addition, when they enter the Garden, God must transform their consciousness so that they become rational moral agents made in God's image. . . .[18]

This sounds very much like the views of some of the other scholars I have mentioned previously, who claim Adam and Eve were a "primal pair" specially selected by God. But here, Dr. Dembski goes further, claiming that Adam and Eve (or whoever he believes the earliest humans were) would have been "human-like" creatures. We can only assume he means an ape-man and ape-woman of some sort, who were not endowed with the image of God until God gave it to them, making them "fully human."[19]

Why would Dr. Dembski propose such a bizarre idea about Adam and Eve? And why would he be so willing to capitulate to theistic evolutionists and others who hold to evolutionary ideas and long ages? The answer is that Dr. Dembski is not convinced of the Bible's claims about creation himself:

> The young-earth solution to reconciling the order of creation with natural history makes good exegetical and theological sense. Indeed, the overwhelming consensus of theologians up through the Reformation held to this view. I myself would adopt it in a heartbeat except

---

18. William Dembski, *The End of Christianity: Finding a Good God in an Evil World* (Nashville, TN: B&H Publishing, 2009), p. 159.

19. Ibid., p. 158.

that nature seems to present such a strong evidence against it. I'm hardly alone in my reluctance to accept young-earth creationism.[20]

Now, like so many academics today, Dr. Dembski is willing to say that on the surface the Bible's account in Genesis makes sense as it is written, but man's interpretation of evidence outside of the Bible must be used to reinterpret aspects of the creation account. But note that if one takes God's Word as authoritative (". . . makes good exegetical and theological sense . . ."), then it is obvious the earth is young. But the word *except* tells us that disagreement is coming — "*except* that nature seems to present such a strong evidence against it" (emphasis added).

So what does Dembski mean by stating that "nature seems to present such a strong evidence against it?" He further states:

> A young earth seems to be required to maintain a traditional understanding of the Fall. And yet a young earth clashes sharply with mainstream science. [21]

In an article, he writes:

> Dating methods, in my view, provide strong evidence for rejecting this face-value chronological reading of Genesis 4–11.[22]

It really comes down to the fact that Dembski accepts the fallible secular dating methods (based on numerous fallible assumptions) and uses their results to trump the Word of God! That is the problem with the Church — accepting man's words over God's words. Yes, it is a battle over authority. Who is the ultimate authority — God or man?

After establishing his position regarding biblical creation and ideas outside of Scripture, Dr. Dembski offers a more detailed explanation of his idea:

> Any evils humans experience outside the Garden before God breathes into them the breath of life would be experienced as natural evils in the same way that other animals experience them. The pain would be real, but it would not be experienced as divine justice in response to willful rebellion. Moreover, once God breathes

---

20. Ibid., p. 55.
21. Ibid., p. 77.
22. William Dembski, *Christian Theodicy in Light of Genesis and Modern Science*, 49. This essay was later expanded into Dembski's book and is no longer available on the web.

the breath of life into them, we may assume that the first humans experienced an amnesia of their former animal life: Operating on a higher plane of consciousness once infused with the breath of life, they would transcend the lower plane of animal consciousness on which they had previously operated — though, after the Fall, they might be tempted to resort to that lower consciousness.[23]

Let's consider this statement and Dr. Dembski's statement quoted above about "human-like beings" in the Garden of Eden. Could God have introduced "human-like beings" into the garden? On the one hand, Dembski seems to believe the garden was perfect, but his belief in billions of years prevents such a view. Death and suffering would have existed in the world with animals eating each other and so on. What I understand Dembski to be saying is that because God is infinite and knew man would fall, He created a world in which there would be billions of years of death and suffering — so that when God gave Adam and Eve souls and they were then made in the image of God, they would fall (sin) in a perfect garden and then see the effects of their sin in the death and suffering outside the garden (which chronologically existed before sin but is actually a result of their sin, as God knew they would fall)!

Dr. Dembski's interpretation proposes that God judged the world with millions of years of animal death, disease, extinction, and other natural evil — and this judgment was because of man's sin, which occurred *after* all this natural evil. What kind of judge would punish a man with prison resulting in great suffering for his family *before* he committed a crime? Dembski's theodicy turns God into a grossly unjust Judge. But as Genesis 18:25 says, "Shall not the Judge of all the earth do right?"

Dr. Dembski explains this concept by arguing for two types of time: *chronos* and *kairos*. Dembski writes that while young-earth creationists read the text in its plainest sense (i.e., literal 24-hour days), "in our current mental environment, informed as it is by modern astrophysics and geology, the scientific community as a whole regards young-earth creationism as scientifically untenable."[24] Because evolutionary history does not fit with the Genesis account of creation, Dembski proposes an alternative understanding of the concept of time in Genesis: God's time and man's time.

---

23. Dembski, *The End of Christianity*, p. 154–155.
24. Ibid., p. 126.

Hank Hanegraaff, who shares Dembski's position, explains these two types of time in his *The Creation Answer Book*. Hanegraaff first claims that he "cannot abide animal death prior to the fall as consistent with a 'very good' creation."[25] And yet, just a short while later, following after Dembski's book, Hanegraaff uses the idea of two allegedly different types of time (God's time and man's time) to argue in favor of death before the Fall! He writes, "There is little difficulty conceiving of a transcendent God who predestines natural evil to precede the fall even though the fall is the necessary cause of the evils that precede it."[26] In other words, God supposedly created a fallen, sin-cursed world because He knew Adam would sin millions of years later. The effects of the Curse preceded the Fall itself, in Dembski's and Hanegraaff's interpretations.

But does any of this fit with what the Bible plainly says? In thinking about whether Adam and Eve were "human-like beings," let's consider this passage of Scripture:

> And the LORD God formed man of the dust of the ground, and breathed into his nostrils the breath of life; and man became a living being. (Genesis 2:7)

Note the order here: God made man from dust, added the divine breath, and this caused Adam to become a living being. The Hebrew words translated "living being" are the same Hebrew words used to describe sea creatures, birds, and land animals in Genesis 1:21, 24, 30 and Genesis 9:10. So the Bible is absolutely clear: God did *not* make some human-like living being and then later added the divine breath or divine image to make it become man. The Scriptures teach man plus divine breath equals living being, *not* living being plus divine breath equals man. Paul affirms the literal truth of Genesis 2:7 when he says in 1 Corinthians 15:45 that "the first man Adam was made a living soul" (KJV). This is further confirmed by the judgment of God in Genesis 3:19. Adam was made from dust, and when he died, he returned to dust — he did not return to a human-like or ape-like being!

Upon creating Adam, Scripture explains that God placed him in the garden:

---

25. Hank Hanegraaff, *The Creation Answer Book* (Nashville, TN: Thomas Nelson, 2012), p. 105.

26. Ibid., p. 128.

Then the LORD God took the man and put him in the garden of Eden to tend and keep it. (Genesis 2:15)

And the LORD God said, "It is not good that man should be alone; I will make him a helper comparable to him." (Genesis 2:18)

And Adam said: "This is now bone of my bones and flesh of my flesh; she shall be called Woman, because she was taken out of Man." (Genesis 2:23)

Note that Eve was made *from* Adam (by supernatural surgery, not by any natural process) after Adam was *in* the garden. Eve did not come into the garden as some "human-like being" to be transformed by God into a full human being.

The Apostle Paul affirms Eve's origin in the infallible Scriptures:

For as woman came from man . . . (1 Corinthians 11:12)

For man is not from woman, but woman from man. (1 Corinthians 11:8)

For Adam was formed first, then Eve. (1 Timothy 2:13)

These passages all quote from Genesis 2:23 and Genesis 2:24 as literal history — so the literal history from Genesis is that the woman was made *from* Adam after he was already *in* the garden.

Also in the garden, God made the animals and brought certain land animals to Adam for him to name and to show that he was alone. Obviously, these animals were not aggressive, so God had to have non-aggressive animals in the garden. But outside the garden, according to Dembski, there was a world that was "red in tooth and claw," as the poet Tennyson stated. But Genesis 1:30 states that all the animals were plant eaters originally. It is unclear how Dembski handles this, but perhaps he would suggest this was applicable only to the animals in the garden.

Clearly, Dr. Dembski's proposed ideas concerning the accounts of creation and the Fall do not square with the Bible. But he, like many other Bible scholars and church leaders, has bowed to the pressure to integrate evolution and millions of years into Scripture. No wonder we see generations of young people leaving the Church, because they were led to doubt the authority of the Word of God as the result of such blatant compromise positions.

Peter Enns and *The Evolution of Adam*

While all the views of Adam and Eve I have discussed so far stray from the account of Scripture, Peter Enns surely holds the most egregious position on the historicity of the first couple. What does Enns believe? In short, he does not believe Genesis is even about our origins. And he does not believe Adam and Eve existed at all.

Enns taught at Westminster Theological Seminary in Pennsylvania from 1994 to 2008, and he is a former Senior Fellow with BioLogos. In 2012, Enns's book *The Evolution of Adam: What the Bible Does and Doesn't Say About Human Origins* was published, causing controversy among many Bible scholars and Christian leaders. In it, Enns makes two points in particular that are incredibly problematic for a historical reading of Genesis.[27]

Like so many other Bible scholars today, Enns uses ancient Near Eastern cosmologies to explain away the historical significance of Genesis. Now, it is important to understand that ancient Near Eastern cosmologies did play a role in the writing of the Pentateuch — they were errors that the Pentateuch corrected! When Moses authored the five books of the Bible, he presented the true version of the events at Creation, the Fall, the Flood, and so on. These inspired books not only shared truth given by God, but they also corrected the erroneous views of the surrounding nations. This is known as a polemic.

The first claim that causes problems for a historical reading of Genesis relates to how Enns treats ancient Near Eastern cosmologies. Enns goes a step too far, claiming that Genesis is no different from the origin stories of the surrounding nations:

> What bearing does the relationship between Genesis 1 and the *Enuma Elish* [a Babylonian creation myth] have on the evolution issue? It means that any thought of Genesis 1 providing a scientifically or historically accurate account of cosmic origins, and therefore being wholly distinct from the "fanciful" story in *Enuma Elish,* cannot be seriously entertained.[28]

---

27. For a full analysis of Peter Enns and *The Evolution of God*, see Lee Anderson, "A Response to Peter Enns's Attack on Biblical Creationism," *Answers Research Journal* 6 (2013): 117–135, http://www.answersingenesis.org/articles/arj/v6/n1/peter-enns-biblical-creationism.

28. Peter Enns, *The Evolution of Adam: What the Bible Does and Doesn't Say About Human Origins* (Grand Rapids, MI: Brazos Press, 2012), p. 40–41.

In other words, there is nothing special about the Bible — it is a product of its time, and we cannot trust that the history it presents is accurate. And if that is not clear enough in the above quote from Enns, he writes about the account of the global Flood, "The distinct theology of the biblical flood story, however, does not imply that it is of a higher historical or scientific order than the other ancient flood stories."[29] How does this sound to seminary students and church attendees? Enns is really saying, "You can't trust Genesis, but trust in Jesus" (whatever he means by that).

Now, Peter Enns is a type of theistic evolutionist, and his view of Genesis has clearly been influenced by his belief in evolutionary ideas. And his interpretation of the account of Adam and Eve and the Fall is no different. The way Enns chooses to read the account of Adam and Eve is as an account of Israel's origins. So instead of being literal history, Genesis 1–3 becomes a highly symbolic way of presenting the creation of the nation of Israel. Why would Enns choose this interpretation, when it clearly is not the most natural reading of the early chapters of Genesis? Here's how he explains it in his own words:

> I am not suggesting that the Adam story can only be read as a story of Israel's origins. It is, however, a compelling way to read it, **for it makes sense out of some well-known interpretive difficulties while also helping along the evolution discussion.** If the Adam story is not really a story of the beginning of humanity but of one segment of humanity, **at least some of the tensions between Genesis and evolution are lessened. . . .** [emphases added][30]

So really, Enns is concerned about meshing evolution and millions of years with Scripture. That is his real motivation! But he does even more than many compromised Bible scholars do today. He does not attempt to retain elements of the Genesis account; rather, he symbolizes the account of Adam and Eve entirely in order to make way for evolution!

But the second claim Enns makes that causes problems for a historical reading of Scripture actually relates to the Apostle Paul's references to Adam in the New Testament. In Romans 5:12, Paul explains that it was through Adam that sin entered the world:

---

29. Ibid., p. 49.
30. Ibid., p. 66.

> Therefore, just as through one man sin entered the world, and death through sin, and thus death spread to all men, because all sinned.

And in 1 Corinthians 15:21–22, God, through Paul, again asserts that it was through a literal, historical Adam that death and sin came into the world:

> For since by man came death, by Man also came the resurrection of the dead. For as in Adam all die, even so in Christ all shall be made alive.

Finally, in 1 Corinthians 15:45, the Apostle Paul references the creation of Adam in relation to the later incarnation of Christ on the earth:

> And so it is written, "The first man Adam became a living being." The last Adam became a life-giving spirit.

Now, just reading these passages in their plainest sense, what conclusion should we naturally come to? Do these verses indicate that Adam was not a historical person? Of course not! It is clear that the Apostle Paul believes Adam was real and that he was the progenitor of the entire human race.

So how does Dr. Enns handle these passages, in light of his belief that nothing in the account of Adam and Eve actually happened? The answer is shocking: Enns believes Paul was in error.

> Many Christian readers will conclude, correctly, that a doctrine of inspiration does not require "guarding" the biblical authors from saying things that reflect a faulty ancient cosmology. . . . when we allow the Bible to lead us in our thinking on inspiration, we are compelled to leave room for the ancient writers to reflect and even incorporate their ancient, mistaken cosmologies into their scriptural reflections.[31]

What Enns is really saying is that the Holy Spirit was not capable of producing an error-free Scripture — indeed, that the Holy Spirit even permitted the writers of Scripture to insert faulty and erroneous ideas into the inspired text. Thus, we cannot trust what Paul has to say about Adam. But if that is the case, why should we trust what he has to say about Christ — or about the Resurrection?

---

31. Ibid., p. 94–95.

In a 2011 Erasmus Lecture at Westmont College (a Christian college), Enns made a statement about Paul's use of Adam that is very telling:

> It's not so much that Genesis talks about an Adam; it's the fact that Paul talks about an Adam. That's the heart of the tension for Christians [concerning Genesis and evolution]. If Adam just stayed in the Old Testament where he belonged, we wouldn't have this problem. But Paul draws him out, and he uses him for a specific purpose. And for Paul, Adam is the first human being.[32]

I always ask what the real motivation is behind the compromised positions of Bible scholars and church leaders, and I believe Dr. Enns's real motive is clear here: he has lifted man's fallible ideas about our origins above God's Word and is now trying to make the Bible conform to evolutionary ideas. For Enns, Adam is not the first human, based on a belief in evolution, and so the Bible must be incorrect. What a sad state of affairs the Church is in.

The Culture Has Invaded the Church

I want to make sure readers understand that I do not call what one believes about Adam and Eve a salvation issue, but it is an authority issue. Disbelief in a historical Adam is a case of biblical authority being lost in the Church and culture. And one can tell immediately from these "academic" ideas and positions — like the ones Dembski and Enns are promoting — that are pervading the Church that something is clearly wrong. The Church is not touching the culture like it used to because we have allowed the culture to invade the Church. These varied compromise positions on Genesis are sadly being taught to most of the next generation of pastors, missionaries, and Bible scholars. No wonder we have such a mess in our world!

But such compromise is also a gospel issue. What does it mean for the gospel if there was no Fall? What does it mean for Christ's suffering and death if there has always been death and suffering in the world? What does it mean for the miracle of the Resurrection if the miracle of the special creation of man never occurred as written in God's Word? There are serious ramifications to giving up the Bible's account of man's origins. Are evolutionary ideas, whether geological, biological, astronomical, or anthropological worth

---

32. Peter Enns, "Lecture: Erasmus Lecture — Peter Enns, Feb. 9, 2011," Westmont TV (YouTube), http://www.youtube.com/watch?v=36T3tbygQgA&safety_mode=true&persist_safety_mode=1.

undermining the authority of the Word and the gospel of Jesus Christ? The answer is a resounding no. Pastors, teachers, Bible scholars — as you continue to read this book, I urge you to think carefully about the implications of compromising God's Word in Genesis with man's ideas of millions of years and evolution. Many in the Church are on the slippery slide from reinterpreting parts of Genesis to giving up a literal Adam and Eve and a literal Fall, to giving up Genesis altogether.

Chapter 10

Genesis — Scripture Interprets Scripture

As we think about the conflict between man's fallible ideas on our origins (evolution and/or millions of years), it is important to answer questions like these: Could God have created in six days? Did the entire human race descend from a single couple? Was there a literal Fall? Was the Flood of Noah's day a real, global event? Now, we can look to the evidence to see if it confirms the scriptural account — and it certainly does! — but I think it is paramount that we understand how to read Scripture on its own terms first.

Many people today have not been trained in proper, biblical apologetics. As a result, they doubt the truth of the Scriptures and walk away from the Church (as has been well documented in *Already Gone*). And while apologetics training should happen primarily in the home, the Church plays a role in that as well. But sadly, the Church is falling down in this area.

Not long ago, I came across a book written by Martin Thielen, a senior pastor in a United Methodist Church, titled *What's the Least I Can Believe and Still Be a Christian?* The title says it all, doesn't it? Now, I am sure this man loves the Lord and is sincere in his efforts to share the gospel with people. He writes that people "need to believe in Jesus — his life, teachings, example, death, and resurrection."[1] However, his book gives the entirely wrong impression about some very important issues.

He deals with biblical creation early, writing that while he respects creationists, biblical creation "has scientific problems. It denies virtually every branch of science."[2] He continues, "Not only does this literalist approach have scientific problems; it also has biblical problems. Contrary to what this view teaches, the Bible is not a science book."[3] Of course, I completely acknowledge that the Bible in not a science book in the sense of operational science — but it is a history book — a book of historical science! And as a history book, it tells us exactly how the universe came to be: God spoke it into existence.

But Pastor Thielen disagrees, writing, "Theistic evolution is a perfectly acceptable Christian belief."[4] And he keeps his own position on the matter no secret:

> Yes, I believe in creationism. And yes, I believe in evolution. I believe God created the world, but I believe God created through evolution.[5]

Thielen is the pastor of a church, shepherding believers as they grow (hopefully) into spiritual maturity. Wittingly or not, this shepherd is leading the sheep astray. What's worse is that Thielen is only one of many Christian leaders who have compromised on Genesis. We are truly facing an epidemic in our churches and Christian colleges and universities.

After reading such statements of compromise, the words of Jude often echo in my head: "Beloved, while I was very diligent to write to you concerning our common salvation, I found it necessary to write to you exhorting you to contend earnestly for the faith which was once for all delivered to the saints" (Jude 1:3). We need Christian men and women today who are prepared to be bold and unashamed of God's Word and the gospel. We need Christian men and women who are prepared to contend for the faith in this increasingly secularized culture and Church.

---

1. Martin Thielen, *What's the Least I Can Believe and Still Be a Christian?* (Louisville, KY: Westminster John Knox Press, 2011).

2. Ibid., p. 16.

3. Ibid.

4. Ibid., p. 18.

5. Ibid., p. 17.

The Creation Account on Its Own Terms

The way Scripture is intended to be read and understood is by reading it in its most natural sense and by allowing Scripture to interpret Scripture. When people perform *exegesis*, they are looking at Scripture and attempting to flesh out meaning based on the plain words, the genre, the context, other scriptural references, and so on. They are not necessarily trying to force their own views on the text — and certainly should not be.

But readers who commit *eisegesis* look at Scripture and use their own preconceived ideas, and ideas outside of Scripture, such as evolution and millions of years, to try to determine its meaning. Rather than finding biblically sound answers to their questions, these people end up twisting the words of the Bible to fit their own worldviews. Their starting point is not God's Word; it is man's word.

Even though we have covered some of this material in other chapters, I wanted to give some extra details to help us be equipped to be able to deal with the rampant compromise on Genesis across Christendom. I will summarize some of the arguments already used in this book concerning the literal days of creation, a global Flood, and a literal Adam and Eve, and then I will answer in detail some of the objections leveled at these positions. This will help readers to be more fully equipped to defend a literal Genesis.

So how should we read Genesis 1 using a proper approach to Scripture? Well, it is helpful to understand the definition of the Hebrew word for day, *yôm,* which we saw earlier in the book. *Yôm* can have a few different definitions based on context, but it is very clearly referring to a literal 24-hour day in Genesis 1 for the days of creation. Remember the first key principle of the historical-grammatical hermeneutic? We need to carefully observe the text of Scripture to better understand what it is saying. Let's look at part of Genesis chapter 1:

> Then God said, "Let there be light"; and there was light. And God saw the light, that it was good; and God divided the light from the darkness. God called the light Day, and the darkness He called Night. So the evening and the morning were the first day. Then God said, "Let there be a firmament in the midst of the waters, and let it divide the waters from the waters." Thus God made the firmament, and divided the waters which were under the firmament from

the waters which were above the firmament; and it was so. And God called the firmament Heaven. So the evening and the morning were the second day. (Genesis 1:3–8)

Now, just in these first few verses, do you notice the pattern? God creates something, names it, and then there was evening and there was morning, and it was the [insert number] day. Morning, evening, number, day. That's the pattern. So just from these opening verses, we can assume that the days were literal 24-hour days. If they were not, why would Moses have been so specific? But these are just the first two days of creation. Does the pattern carry on through the rest of the account of Creation Week? In fact, it does:

So the evening and the morning were the third day. (Genesis 1:13)

So the evening and the morning were the fourth day. (Genesis 1:19)

So the evening and the morning were the fifth day. (Genesis 1:23)

So the evening and the morning were the sixth day. (Genesis 1:31)

Evening, morning, number, day. In every instance in Genesis 1, that pattern in association with *yôm* indicates a normal-length day. But is there another passage we can turn to that will help us understand the meaning of *yôm* in Genesis 1?

Exodus 31:12 says that God commanded Moses to say to the children of Israel:

Work shall be done for six days, but the seventh is the Sabbath of rest, holy to the Lord. Whoever does any work on the Sabbath day, he shall surely be put to death. Therefore the children of Israel shall keep the Sabbath, to observe the Sabbath throughout their generations as a perpetual covenant. It is a sign between Me and the children of Israel forever; for in six days the Lord made the heavens and the earth, and on the seventh day He rested and was refreshed. (Exodus 31:15–17)

Where do we get our seven-day week? From Genesis 1. The above passage from Exodus shows clearly that the days of creation were thought of as normal-length days, and the workweek was modeled after Creation Week. "For in six days the Lord made the heavens and the earth" — that does not get much clearer.

Exodus 31:18 tells us that God gave Moses two tablets of stone upon which were written the commandments of God, written by the finger of God. Because God is infinite in power and wisdom, there is no doubt that He could have created the universe and its contents in no time at all, or six seconds, or six minutes, or six hours — after all, with God nothing will be impossible (Luke 1:37).

But that brings us to the question, why did God take so long? Why as long as six days? The answer is also given in Exodus 20:11, based on the Fourth Commandment:

> For in six days the LORD made the heavens and the earth, the sea, and all that is in them, and rested the seventh day. Therefore the LORD blessed the Sabbath day and hallowed it.

Outside of Scripture, a seven-day week has no basis. It finds its origin in the first book of the Bible. In Exodus 20, God commands His people, Israel, to work for six days and to rest for one — thus giving us one reason why He deliberately took as long as six days to create everything. God set the example for man in Genesis 1, and our week is patterned after this principle.

Consider this: if God had created everything in six thousand or even six million years, followed by a rest of one thousand or one million years, then we would have a very interesting week indeed!

Some say that Exodus 20:11 is just an analogy meant to communicate the idea that man is to work and rest — not that it was intended to communicate six literal 24-hour days followed by one literal 24-hour day. However, Bible scholars have shown that this commandment is not an analogy. No, it was a standard that was intended to be remembered by God's people. In other words, it was to be six literal days of work, followed by one literal day of rest, just as God worked for six literal days and rested for one.

Objections to Six Literal Days

Even after I present such a clear interpretation of Scripture, many times people will come to me and ask about or present objections to a literal six days. So I think it would be helpful to present some of those objections here along with clear biblical refutations to them. That way, you will be better equipped to respond to these claims when they are presented.

1. "Science" Proves the Earth Is Old. The first of these common objections is that "science" has supposedly shown the earth and universe to be billions of years old, so the days of creation must also be long periods of time. Of course, the age of the earth, as determined by man's fallible dating methods, is based on unproven assumptions — so it is not proven that the earth is billions of years old. What's more, this unproven age is being used to force an interpretation on the language of Scripture. In other words, man's fallible ideas are allowed to interpret God's Word, which undermines the use of language to communicate.

Another problem with this claim has to do with the fossil layers. Evolutionary scientists claim the fossil layers over the earth's surface date back hundreds of millions of years. As soon as one allows millions of years for the fossil layers, then one has accepted death, bloodshed, disease, thorns, and suffering before Adam's sin. But the Bible makes it clear that these things are a consequence of sin. In Genesis 1:29–30, God gave Adam and Eve and the animals plants to eat. Man was permitted to eat meat only after the Flood (Genesis 9:3). This makes it obvious that the statements in Genesis 1:29–30 were meant to inform us that man and the animals were vegetarian to start with.

After Adam disobeyed God, Scripture tells is that the Lord clothed Adam and Eve with "coats of skins" (Genesis 3:21). We believe this was the first animal death recorded in the Bible. The reason blood had to be shed can be summed up by Hebrews 9:22:

> And according to the law almost all things are purified with blood, and without shedding of blood there is no remission.

God requires the shedding of blood for the remission of sins. What happened in the Garden of Eden was a picture of what was to come in Jesus Christ, who shed His blood on the Cross as the Lamb of God who took away the sin of the world (John 1:29).

If the Garden were sitting on a fossil record of dead things millions of years old, then blood would have been shed before sin. This completely undermines the foundation of the Atonement. The Bible is clear: the sin of Adam brought death and suffering into the world. As Romans 8:19–22 tells us, all creation "groans" because of the effects of the Fall, and the creation will be liberated "from the bondage of corruption into the glorious liberty of the children of God" (Romans 8:21).

Revelation 21–22 makes it clear that there will be a "new heavens and a new earth" one day, where there will be "no more death" and "no more curse" — just like it was before sin changed everything. If there are to be animals as part of the new earth, obviously they will not be dying or eating each other, nor eating the redeemed people! Thus, adding these supposed millions of years to Scripture destroys the foundations of the message of the Cross.

2. Literal Days Limit God. Another objection I often hear is that when we insist that Creation Week was six solar days, we are limiting God, whereas allowing God billions of years does not limit Him. Actually, insisting on six ordinary days of creation is not limiting God, but limiting us to believing that God actually did what He tells us in His Word. What's more, if God created everything in six days, as the Bible says, this surely reveals the power and wisdom of God in a profound way — the Creator of the universe did not need eons of time. Billions of years, on the other hand, diminishes God by suggesting that God needed huge amounts of time to create. This limits God's power by imposing fallible man's word on God's Word. As I said to someone once who used this objection, "I don't limit God; I limit myself. I let God tell me what He did — I don't tell God what He supposedly did."

3. Genesis 1 and 2 Contradict Each Other. Many people, including professing Christians, claim that Genesis 2 is a different account of creation, with a different order, so Genesis 1 cannot be accepted as teaching six literal days. But really, Genesis 2 is not a different account of creation. Most of it is a more detailed account of Day 6 of creation. Chapter 1 is an overview of the whole of creation in chronological order; chapter 2 gives details surrounding the creation of the Garden of Eden, the first man and his activities on Day 6, and the creation of the first woman. We see this pattern of an overview followed by a more detailed explanation in other accounts, such as the Flood and the Tower of Babel.

Between the creation of Adam and the creation of Eve, the King James Version says, "Out of the ground the LORD God formed every beast of the field and every fowl of the air" (Genesis 2:19). This seems to say that the land beasts and birds were created between the creation of Adam and Eve. However, Jewish scholars did not recognize any such conflict with the account in chapter 1, where Adam and Eve were both created after the beasts and birds (Genesis 1:23–25). There is no contradiction, because in Hebrew the precise tense of a verb is determined by the context. It is clear from chapter 1 that the beasts and birds were created before Adam, so Jewish scholars would have understood the verb "formed" to mean "had formed" or "having formed" in Genesis 2:19. If we translate verse 19, "Now the Lord God had formed out of the ground all the beasts of the field," the apparent disagreement with Genesis 1 disappears completely.

4. Seventh Day Is Not Literal. Some people make the claim that because there is no "evening and morning" for the seventh day of Creation Week (Genesis 2:2), we must still be in the "seventh day," meaning that none of the days were ordinary days.

But look again at my explanation above on interpreting Genesis 1. Exodus 20:11 clearly refers to seven literal days — six for work and one for rest. What's more, God stated that He "rested" from His work of creation — not that He is resting! The fact that He rested from His work of creation does not preclude Him from continuing to rest from this activity. God's work now is different — it is a work of sustaining His creation and of redemption because of man's sin.

Furthermore, in arguing that the seventh day is not an ordinary day because it is not associated with "evening and morning," proponents are tacitly agreeing that the other six days are ordinary days because they are defined by an evening and a morning. Regardless, the seventh day does have a number (seven) with the word *day* — which makes it clear it is an ordinary day.

Some have argued that Hebrews 4:3–4 implies that the seventh day is continuing today:

> For we who have believed do enter that rest, as He has said: "So I swore in My wrath, 'They shall not enter My rest,' " although the works were finished from the foundation of the world. For He has spoken in a certain place of the seventh day in this way: "And God rested on the seventh day from all His works. . . ."

However, verse 4 reiterates that God rested (past tense) on the seventh day. If someone says on Monday that he rested on Friday and is still resting, this would not suggest that Friday continued through to Monday! Also, only those who have believed in Christ will enter that rest, showing that it is a spiritual rest, which is compared with God's rest since the Creation Week. It is not some sort of continuation of the seventh day (otherwise everyone would be "in" this rest).

Hebrews does not say that the seventh day of Creation Week is continuing today, merely that the rest He instituted is continuing. God had rested from His work of creation, and now His work is one of reconciliation and redemption.

A Literal Reading of the Flood Account

The account of the global Flood of Noah's day has come under attack both in the secular world and in the Church. What is the source of these attacks? Evolutionary thinking about the fossil record. Now, Genesis 6–8 offers a straightforward account of the Flood, but those who contest that account usually want to trust the ideas of evolutionary historical science over Scripture.

Besides an outright denial that the Flood ever happened, one of the most common claims is that the Flood was regional or local. But what does God's Word say about the Flood?

The description of the Flood in Scripture is not difficult to understand. Prior to the Flood, God gives Noah incredibly specific instructions on building an Ark:

> And God said to Noah, "The end of all flesh has come before Me, for the earth is filled with violence through them; and behold, I will destroy them with the earth. Make yourself an ark of gopherwood; make rooms in the ark, and cover it inside and outside with pitch. And this is how you shall make it: The length of the ark shall be three hundred cubits, its width fifty cubits, and its height thirty cubits. You shall make a window for the ark, and you shall finish it to a cubit from above; and set the door of the ark in its side. You shall make it with lower, second, and third decks."
> (Genesis 6:13–16)

The Ark's measurements are convincing for two reasons: the proportions are like that of a modern cargo ship, and it is about as large as a wooden ship can be built. The cubit gives us a good indication of size.[6] According to research done by Tim Lovett, who has studied the Flood and the Ark for over a decade, "With the cubit's measurement, we know that the Ark must have been at least 450 feet (137 m) long, 75 feet (23 m) wide, and 45 feet (14 m) high. In the Western world, wooden sailing ships never got much longer than about 330 feet (100 m), yet the ancient Greeks built vessels at least this size 2,000 years earlier. China built huge wooden ships in the 1400s

---

6. The cubit was defined as the length of the forearm from elbow to fingertip. Ancient cubits vary anywhere from 17.5 inches (45 cm) to 22 inches (56 cm), the longer sizes dominating the major ancient constructions. Despite this, even a conservative 18-inch (46 cm) cubit describes a sizeable vessel.

that may have been as large as the Ark. The biblical Ark is one of the largest wooden ships of all time — a mid-sized cargo ship by today's standards."[7]

Noah and his family would have been brilliant engineers. When God created Adam and Eve, everything was "very good," including their minds. Now, as time has gone on, man has lost more and more of the great intellectual capabilities we had in the beginning. But Noah and his family would have understood how to construct an Ark of wood just as well — and probably better! — as we do today. If we take God at His Word, then we have to trust that they could and did build an Ark.

The account in Genesis 7 explains that God commanded Noah to take representatives of every kind of land-dwelling animal, in order to preserve them:

> Then the LORD said to Noah, "Come into the ark, you and all your household, because I have seen that you are righteous before Me in this generation. You shall take with you seven each of every clean animal, a male and his female; two each of animals that are unclean, a male and his female; also seven each of birds of the air, male and female, to keep the species alive on the face of all the earth. (Genesis 7:1–3)

Now, if the Flood had been local, why would Noah have needed to build an Ark and take representatives of the land-dwelling animals? Couldn't he and his family have simply journeyed outside of the area that would be flooded? A local flood does not make sense when examined against the scriptural account. And what's more, observational science confirms the Bible's history of a global, catastrophic Flood.

Secular geologists believe the fossil-bearing rock layers took millions of years to form. They claim that numerous sea creatures dwelled on shallow sea floors and were slowly buried, to be replaced by new sea creatures growing on the seafloors. In the evolutionary view, these rock layers we see today supposedly came about over longs ages of sea creatures being buried.

Uniformitarianism is the idea that "the present is the key to the past," meaning that the geologic processes we see today, in the ways they operate today, are all we need to explain the rock layers. And while catastrophes such as local floods and volcanic eruptions are allowable because we see them

---

7. For a more detailed explanation of how the Ark could have been built, see Ken Ham and Tim Lovett, "Was There Really a Noah's Ark and Flood?" in *The New Answers Book 1*, Ken Ham, gen. ed. (Green Forest, AR: Master Books, 2006), p. 125–140.

today, secular geologists reject the global Flood before the evidence is even examined.

But Genesis 7:11 tells us that "all the fountains of the great deep were broken up, and the windows of heaven were opened." And we learn in verse 24 that "the waters prevailed on the earth one hundred and fifty days." Just how far-reaching was the Flood? Well, the result was that the waters rose so high, they covered even the highest hills:

> Now the flood was on the earth forty days. The waters increased and lifted up the ark, and it rose high above the earth. The waters prevailed and greatly increased on the earth, and the ark moved about on the surface of the waters. And the waters prevailed exceedingly on the earth, and all the high hills under the whole heaven were covered. The waters prevailed fifteen cubits upward, and the mountains were covered. (Genesis 7:17–20)

The *entire* earth was covered by the floodwaters — even the mountains. The Flood was so catastrophic, Genesis tells us, that all the living creatures (on the land) and all the humans — save Noah, his family, and the animals on the Ark — died.

> And all flesh died that moved on the earth: birds and cattle and beasts and every creeping thing that creeps on the earth, and every man. All in whose nostrils was the breath of the spirit of life, all that was on the dry land, died. So He destroyed all living things which were on the face of the ground: both man and cattle, creeping thing and bird of the air. They were destroyed from the earth. Only Noah and those who were with him in the ark remained alive. (Genesis 7:21–23)

With such a clear description of what happened during this real historical event, it is very rational to expect to find evidence today of billions of dead animals and plants buried in rock layers composed of water-deposited sand, lime, and mud all around the earth. And indeed, that's exactly what we do find — billions of dead things buried in rock layers laid down by water all over the earth.

Instead of taking millions of years to form, most of the fossil-bearing rock layers could have formed rapidly during the year-long global catastrophic

Flood of Noah. We cannot have it both ways. Most of the rock layers are either a testimony of the global Flood, or they are the record of millions of years of history. We cannot consistently believe in both, because those supposed long ages do not fit into the year-long Flood of Noah.

Besides the scientific confirmation of the global Flood, the biblical account of the Flood shares the same genre and context as Genesis 1–2. The Flood account is historical narrative and the context forces us to understand it as a historical account of a global catastrophe. Is the Flood account confirmed as history in the New Testament?

Jesus Christ, in the gospel of Luke, referenced the Flood as a historical event:

> And as it was in the days of Noah, so it will be also in the days of the Son of Man: They ate, they drank, they married wives, they were given in marriage, until the day that Noah entered the ark, and the flood came and destroyed them all. Likewise as it was also in the days of Lot: They ate, they drank, they bought, they sold, they planted, they built; but on the day that Lot went out of Sodom it rained fire and brimstone from heaven and destroyed them all. Even so will it be in the day when the Son of Man is revealed. (Luke 17:26–30)

The Apostle Peter also referenced the Flood as literal history when he warned about scoffers in the last days who would willfully forget that after the earth was created by God, it perished, "being flooded with water" (2 Peter 3:6). When we examine Scripture and the scientific evidence without trying to make way for evolutionary ideas, the conclusion is clear: the Flood of Noah was a real, catastrophic, global event.

Adam and Eve as Historical Figures

In Genesis 1–3, we find the accounts of the creation of Adam and Eve and the Fall of man due to Adam's sin. The importance of these accounts to the foundation of the gospel has already been hinted at earlier, but I want to expand on that with a proper historical-grammatical reading of these accounts.

Now, the accounts of Adam and Eve in Genesis 1–3 are straightforward and establish some important theological points. Without this literal history, the very foundation of the gospel message is undermined. Of course, as I have said many times before, a belief in a literal Adam is not necessary for salvation, but denial of the truth of Genesis 1–3 is a biblical authority issue. So, what does the text say about Adam and Eve?

The first chapter of Genesis explains that God created man in His own image:

> Then God said, "Let Us make man in Our image, according to Our likeness; let them have dominion over the fish of the sea, over the birds of the air, and over the cattle, over all the earth and over every creeping thing that creeps on the earth." So God created man in His own image; in the image of God He created him; male and female He created them. (Genesis 1:26–27)

Once again, our first step here is to carefully observe the text. Scripture is clear that God specially created human beings — and He made them *in His image*. What should we make of the claims of those who claim that there was a large group of "neo-lithic farmers" or ape-like creatures from which God chose some to be in relationship with Him? Such claims simply are not in the text!

What's more, these claims mar the idea of the image of God. God created man, according to Genesis 1, as a special creation that was different from the animals. The text does *not* say that God turned some ape-like creatures into human beings or that He added His image to ape-like creatures sometime later. The context of this passage is the creation of the universe and everything in it, and its genre is historical narrative. There is no reason why we cannot trust that Genesis 1 means exactly what it says — Adam and Eve were specially created in the image of God.

In Genesis 2, we find a more detailed account of the creation of Adam and Eve:

> And the Lord God formed man of the dust of the ground, and breathed into his nostrils the breath of life; and man became a living being. . . . And the Lord God caused a deep sleep to fall on Adam, and he slept; and he took one of his ribs, and closed up the flesh in its place. Then the rib which the Lord God had taken from man He made into a woman, and He brought her to the man. And Adam said: "This is now bone of my bones and flesh of my flesh; she shall

be called Woman, because she was taken out of Man." (Genesis 2:7, 21–23)

Much to the dismay of theistic evolutionists and others who do not accept the miraculous creation of man, God has given us an account of how He created Adam — from the dust of the earth. Literally, God formed Adam from the dust and breathed into him life. Could the text be any clearer? Eve, the account tells us, was created from Adam's side. It does not take any academic training to understand the plain meaning of this passage. So then, why do some Bible scholars, Christian academics, and church leaders attempt to explain how they think God "really" created Adam and Eve? Theistic evolutionists are especially committed to finding a biological explanation for the miraculous creation of human beings, even though Genesis makes it obvious that the creation of man was a *miraculous* work of God.

Furthermore, Genesis 2 establishes that Adam and Eve were the original two humans — and thus, they were the progenitors of the entire human race. According to Scripture, we are all related to Adam and Eve (and to Noah) in some way. But secular ideas about human origins — which are founded on evolution and millions of years — tell us that this is impossible.

Sadly, more and more professing Christians are rejecting the idea that Adam and Eve were the original two humans, based on secular evolutionary views. As I mentioned in an earlier chapter, when I began my ministry over 25 years ago, I predicted that if compromise on Genesis continued to spread in the Church, the Church would eventually give up an historical Adam. Unfortunately, I was correct. Today, we are seeing a growing number of Bible scholars and church leaders denying a literal Adam and Eve as they attempt to mix evolutionary ideas with Scripture — and they are teaching their students and congregations these same compromise positions!

Now, there is one more crucial part of the account of Adam and Eve that has to be considered: the Fall. Genesis 3 recounts how the serpent (Satan) tempted Eve in the Garden of Eden to eat from the one tree that God had commanded Adam and Eve not to eat from. The serpent uses an argument that has never faded from man's rebellious heart — "Did God really say . . ?" (Genesis 3:1, NIV). He causes Eve to doubt God's Word, and the text tells us about the rebellious actions that followed:

So when the woman saw that the tree was good for food, that it was pleasant to the eyes, and a tree desirable to make one wise, she took of its fruit and ate. She also gave to her husband with her, and he ate. (Genesis 3:6)

Once Adam had eaten of the tree of the knowledge of good and evil, sin and death entered the world. For the first time, Adam and Eve felt shame, "and they sewed fig leaves together and made themselves coverings" (Genesis 3:7).

As a consequence of Adam and Eve's disobedience, the Lord God places the Curse on creation:

> Then to Adam He said, "Because you have heeded the voice of your wife, and have eaten from the tree of which I commanded you, saying, 'You shall not eat of it':
> "Cursed is the ground for your sake;
> In toil you shall eat of it
> All the days of your life.
> Both thorns and thistles it shall bring forth for you,
> And you shall eat the herb of the field.
> In the sweat of your face you shall eat bread
> Till you return to the ground,
> For out of it you were taken;
> For dust you are,
> And to dust you shall return." (Genesis 3:17–19)

Because of their sin, Adam and Eve (and all their descendants — the entire human race) would experience toil, thorns, suffering, disease, and death. Does the world around us confirm what the Bible says about the state of things? Yes, it absolutely does. We do not live in a beautiful world; no, we live in a world filled with death, disease, and destruction and a remnant of the beauty. And we know this is not "natural"!

So why is it so important that the account of Adam and Eve be true? Because their existence is foundational to the gospel! Now, I want to make very clear that belief in a historical Adam and Eve is not, as I have said many times, a salvation issue per se, but it is a biblical authority issue and a gospel issue. When we deny the existence of Adam and Eve, then how do we explain the origin of sin and death in the world? And if we cannot explain how sin and death came into the world — or if we believe that it was always here — then what was the purpose of Christ's death and Resurrection? Why was the Atonement even necessary?

Genesis 3 also records what we believe to be the first animal sacrifice in Scripture: "Also for Adam and his wife the LORD God made tunics of skin, and clothed them" (Genesis 3:21). We know from Hebrews that without blood being shed, there is no forgiveness of sins (Hebrews 9:22). The animal sacrifice in Genesis 3 foreshadows the eventual death of Jesus Christ on the Cross for our sins — the only hope and solution for fallen man. The gospel of Jesus Christ makes a literal Adam and Eve and a literal Fall necessary for our sinful state to make sense.

The Apostle Paul confirms that all of creation is no longer "very good," as it was before Adam's sin:

> For the creation was subjected to futility, not willingly, but because of Him who subjected *it* in hope; because the creation itself also will be delivered from the bondage of corruption into the glorious liberty of the children of God. For we know that the whole creation groans and labors with birth pangs together until now. (Romans 8:20–22)

Christ died and rose again to provide the one way to salvation for sinful man. But if sin and death did not actually enter the world through Adam, but was just always here as part of God's "very good" creation, why did Christ need to die? The Atonement becomes meaningless in such a worldview.

The problem with mixing evolution and or millions of years with Scripture is that it undermines the very foundation of the gospel. While a person can still be a Christian even while denying the existence of a literal Adam and Eve, such a belief makes Genesis 1–3 untrustworthy. And from there, it's a slippery slope to making even the gospel untrustworthy. We can trust God's Word when He tells us that Adam and Eve were the first humans. It may not necessarily affect one's salvation if one rejects a literal Adam and Eve as recorded in Genesis, but it does affect how those one influences (e.g., the coming generations) view Scripture itself — and that is the issue!

Exegesis, Not Eisegesis

The Bible, when read with the plain meaning of the words in mind, makes sense. When we understand the Bible on its own terms, there is no need for man's fallible ideas to be mixed with Scripture to supposedly make sense of the world. God's Word provides answers to life's questions, including the question of how the universe came to be, where many of the rock layers and fossils came from, and how man came to be in his current sinful state. It also provides us with the hope of the gospel of Jesus Christ — the one way that we can be saved from our sin problem and ourselves. But if we cannot trust the first 11 chapters of Genesis to mean what they say, how then can we have confidence in any of God's Word? The solution is clear: we have to take God at His Word from the very first verse.

Chapter 11

 Implications of Accepting
Evolutionary Ideas

Throughout this book, I have dealt primarily with the major forms of compromise in regard to the Book of Genesis found in the Church today. Numerous Bible scholars, Christian academics, church leaders, and church attendees have made an effort to integrate evolutionary ideas (in geology, astronomy, biology, and anthropology) with biblical truth. But these are two sets of contradictory ideas!

Now, however, I want to focus on the implications of placing man's evolutionary ideas (even if it is just accepting the supposed millions of years for the age of the earth/universe) above the Word of God. When Christians accept man's fallible opinions about the origin of the universe, they are — unwittingly or not — accepting a belief system based on death and hopelessness. As I have said throughout this book, molecules-to-man evolution or adaptations of it are inevitably founded on millions of years. Specifically, they are founded on millions of years of death, disease, and suffering.

In this chapter, I want to deal more fully with just some of the implications for Christians of mixing evolutionary ideas and/or millions of years with Scripture. While there are many issues with such compromise positions, only three will be discussed here: the impact on death and suffering, on morality, and on the message of the gospel. As I have said over and over, such compromise is not necessarily a salvation issue, but it is an authority issue and a gospel issue. Even though I have covered these topics previously, in this chapter I want to give more details concerning the three topics mentioned above, for the sake of more powerfully equipping the reader to defend a literal Genesis and to be able to counter the rampant compromise in the Church.

When God created the universe and everything in it, He called it all "very good" (Genesis 1:31). Clearly, the mixture of evolution and millions of years with Scripture would mean that God was referring to death and suffering as "very good." This is because as soon as one accepts the supposed millions of years, then one has no option but to accept death, disease, and suffering before man — as the millions of years idea comes from the belief that most of the fossil record was laid down millions of years before man.

But let me be clear: God did *not* call death, disease, and suffering good. Death was not part of the original creation — not according to God's Word.

How is a pastor or Christian academic who has compromised with evolution supposed to explain the origin of death and suffering to a hurting, sinful world? How can he explain the origin of morality? How are believers to trust the full gospel message when they cannot even trust that the first 11 chapters of the Bible are true? That is a difficult thing to do when your belief system requires you to treat death as something that God calls "very good" — and that therefore God is responsible for death!

Death and Suffering — A Daily Reminder

Tragedies are in the news constantly. We hear about many large-scale, "senseless" disasters that claim the lives of numerous people. These include such terrible events as the 9/11 terrorist attacks on New York's World Trade Center and the Pentagon; the Boston Marathon bombing; and school shootings across the country. Natural disasters add to these death tolls, such as Hurricane Katrina in the Gulf Coast or the Asian tsunami that took the lives of over 170,000 people.

In an evolutionary worldview, how can people explain such events when they have no basis for hope? Atheist Richard Dawkins summed up this view of life succinctly in an interview with Tony Jones on the Australian television show, *Q & A*. When asked about the afterlife, Dawkins explains that he does not believe there is one:

> Well, the answer to the question of what's going to happen
> when we die depends on whether we're buried, cremated or give

our bodies to science. . . . The brain is going to rot. That is all there is to it.[1]

Such an outlook on the world certainly does not make atheism sound appealing, does it? But what about the answers that former U.S. Presidents George H.W. Bush and Bill Clinton gave in 2005 in response to the 2004 tsunami tragedy. They were interviewed by Larry King, who asked them questions concerning their religious faith and how people should understand what happened in Asia in terms of the existence of a loving God. Generic statements such as "life isn't easy" were uttered. And both presidents said that such tragedies strengthened their "faith" (though what this "faith" entails was not defined on the program). Sadly, no real answers were provided.

These men, who at one time held the most powerful office in the world, chose not to use the Bible and its very first book to present an answer. Indeed, it is in the Bible's first three chapters where Christians can offer a questioning world the explanation of the meaning of death and suffering — and why a loving God allows death and suffering to happen.

But what happens when evolutionary thinking (which includes millions of years) is mixed with the opening chapters of Genesis? Simply put, those answers are muddled or even lost all together. Tragedies happen on a daily basis. Now, without taking anything away from the anguish and grief that result from terrible catastrophes, in an ultimate sense they are a consequence of an event described in Genesis 3 — an event that occurred on the saddest day in the history of the universe: when the first man Adam rebelled against the Creator, bringing sin and death into a once-perfect world. And because we are descendants of Adam, when he sinned, we sinned. Thus death and suffering is our fault — we caused it. It is not God's fault. God stepped into human history to save us from what we did.

That is the explanation a Christian should be able to offer concerning the origin of death and suffering. When a major tragedy captures global attention, there is usually much discussion in the media concerning how such things can be understood in terms of a loving God. Atheists will often chime in and claim that there cannot be a loving God because of such a horrible

---

1. Richard Dawkins, interview by Tony Jones, "Religion and Atheism," *Q&A: Adventures in Democracy*, ABC1 (Australia), April 9, 2012, http://www.abc.net.au/tv/qanda/txt/s3469101. htm.

calamity. And what about the Christian leader who accepts evolution and millions of years? What can he say about the origin of death and suffering? According to his compromise position, to be consistent he would have to say that these things are "very good." He would have to say that God created death and suffering and made death our foundation.

But you see, death and suffering are *not* "very good." No, they are painful reminders of sin's entrance into the world and the effects of the Curse on creation. And the Christian who takes God at His Word in the first three chapters of Genesis can consistently teach this point.

Darwin on Death

How did Charles Darwin deal with death and suffering? It has been written that his daughter "Annie's cruel death destroyed Charles's tatters of beliefs in a moral, just universe. Later he would say that this period chimed the final death-knell for his Christianity. . . . Charles now took his stand as an unbeliever."[2]

When Darwin wrote his famous book *On the Origin of Species*, he was in essence writing a history (his supposed history) concerning death and struggle. In the conclusion of his chapter entitled "On the Imperfections of the Geological Record," Darwin wrote: "Thus, from the war of nature, from famine and death, the most exalted object which were are capable of conceiving, namely, the production of the higher animals, directly follows."[3]

From his evolutionary perspective on the origin of life, Darwin recognized that death had to be a permanent part of the world. Undoubtedly, he struggled with this issue as he sought to reconcile some sort of belief in God with the death and suffering he observed all around him, and which he believed had gone on for millions of years.

This struggle came to a climax with the death of his daughter Annie — claimed to be "the final death-knell for his Christianity."

Belief in evolution and millions of years necessitates that death has been a part of history since life first appeared on this planet. The fossil layers (containing billions of dead things) supposedly represent the history of life over

2. Adrian Desmond and James Moore, *Darwin: The Life of a Tormented Evolutionist* (New York: W.W. Norton and Co., 1991), p. 387.

3. Charles Darwin, *On the Origin of Species* (Cambridge, MA: Harvard University Press, 1964), p. 490.

millions of years. As the late Carl Sagan is well known to have said, "The secrets of evolution are time and death."[4]

Sin and Death According to the Bible

The Bible puts sin and death together, not time and death.

From the perspective of the literal history of the Book of Genesis, there was a perfect world to start with — described by God as "very good" (Genesis 1:31) — but it was marred because of Adam's rebellion. Sin and its consequence of death (along with suffering and disease) entered the world that was once a paradise (Romans 5:12 and following). The death of man and the animals was not part of the original creation.

The true history of death, as understood from a literal Genesis, actually enables us to recognize a loving Creator who hates death. So which history do you accept? Is it the one that makes God an ogre responsible for millions of years of death, disease, and suffering?

Belief in evolution and millions of years requires a belief that death has always been present, ever since life first appeared on the earth. If you believe that the fossil record (which contains billions of dead things) represents the history of life over millions and millions of years before man, it is a very ugly record.

Sagan's phrase that the "secrets of evolution are time and death" encapsulates the most widely accepted history of death in the world. According to the evolutionary view of the world, death, disease, and suffering over millions of years led to man's emergence, exist in the present world, and will continue into the future. The evolutionary view of death makes it a permanent part of our history — our evolutionary *ally* in the "creation" of life.

Evolution's Impact on Suffering

If a person believes in millions of years, then from that perspective, our world has *always* been a deadly place. But the question we have to ask is what caused the cancer, disease, and violence represented in the fossil record?

Now, Christians who have attempted to mix long ages of earth history with the Bible's account of creation have a serious problem. God's Word

---

4. Carl Sagan, *Cosmos*, part 2: "One Voice in the Cosmic Fugue," produced by the Public Broadcasting Company, Los Angeles, with affiliate station KCET, and first aired in 1980 on PBS stations throughout the United States.

clearly states that God is the Creator, and He called *everything* that He had made before the Fall of Adam and Eve "very good."

As soon as Christians, such as Bible scholars and church leaders, allow for death, suffering, and disease before Adam's sin (which they automatically *must* if they believe in millions of years), then they have raised a serious question about the gospel message. If death has always been present, then what exactly has sin done to the world?

The Apostle Paul tells us that death is the penalty for sin (Romans 6:23) — a fact that is foundational to the gospel of Jesus Christ (1 Corinthians 15:21–22, 45)! Moreover, how can all things be "restored" to a state with no death, pain, or tears in the future (Revelation 21:4) if there never was a time free of death and suffering?

A God of . . . Death?

The sinless, "very good" creation was marred by the rebellion of the first man, Adam. His sin brought an intruder into the world — death. God had to judge sin with death, as He warned Adam that He would (Genesis 2:17; cf. 3:19).

As a result of God's judgment on the world, He has given us a taste of life without Him — a world that is running down; a world full of death and suffering. The Apostle Paul tells us that the creation "groans" over this:

> For the creation was subjected to futility, not willingly, but because of Him who subjected it in hope; because the creation itself also will be delivered from the bondage of corruption into the glorious liberty of the children of God. For we know that the whole creation groans and labors with birth pangs together until now. (Romans 8:20–22)

God Himself subjected the creation to processes of decay, as a consequence of man's sin.

When Christians accept the evolutionary view of the world, they also must explain how they can find a God of love amid the groaning of creation. By understanding Genesis as a literal account of the Fall, we know we are looking at a fallen, sin-cursed world.

From the Bible's perspective, death is an enemy, not an ally. In 1 Corinthians 15:26, the Apostle Paul describes death as the "last enemy." Death was *not* part of God's original creation. Based on a straightforward reading of Genesis, it is clear that death entered the world when Adam sinned and that death will be no more in the future, when the creation is restored to a perfect state as it used to be.

The first book of the Bible, Genesis, is crucial to begin to deal with death, disease, and suffering, because the origin of death itself is outlined in the first chapters of this book. When Christians give up the first 11 chapters of Genesis in favor of evolution and millions of years, they are without a way to explain where death, disease, and suffering came from, except that God must be responsible and called such "very good."

Did Our Morals "Evolve"?

Another issue that many Christians who have compromised on Genesis fail to take into account is the origin of morality. The evolutionary view of morality is a failed attempt at explaining the origin of morality. Basically, the secular view of morals is that they evolved over time and in many ways are culturally constructed.

According to one prominent secularist, "We only live once. . . . So why not try to be nice to each other?"[5] The man who said that was Michael De Dora, the director of the Center for Inquiry's Office of Public Policy. This organization is "dedicated to fostering secular society," and De Dora is, not surprisingly, an atheist.

Now, in an interview, De Dora tries to explain where people should turn for a moral framework outside of the Bible. He fails to do so adequately

According to the interviewer, the Center for Inquiry "aims to put an end to religion's influence on public policy." So how does De Dora defend his statement that we should be "nice" to each other? Unsurprisingly, he gives all the credit for morality to evolution. He says, "There's plenty of evidence, once you accept the theory of evolution, that morality is developed over a long period of time so we can live together without wanting to kill each other all the time."

The question we should be asking is obvious: If morals evolved slowly over time through chance processes, how do we know they evolved the right way? Why should we trust "morals" that evolved by chance? And how did the animal world make it past the first kinds? Shouldn't they have been so devoid of morals that they killed each other off completely? The foundation

5. Liz Essley, "Credo: Michael De Dora," *Washington Examiner*, October 26, 2012, http://washingtonexaminer.com/credo-michael-de-dora/article/2511838.

of evolutionary ideas is death. There is no way to reasonably expect morals to simply emerge among organisms by chance.

De Dora goes on:

> We're all born with a basic moral sense, and it's our duty to refine that. . . . You have to look at thousands of years of writing to try to reason through and use our consciences and decide what's right and wrong to find out how we should treat other people and animals.

Actually, we *are* all born with a basic moral sense:

> for when Gentiles, who do not have the law, by nature do the things in the law, these, although not having the law, are a law to themselves, who show the work of the law written in their hearts, their conscience also bearing witness, and between themselves their thoughts accusing or else excusing them. (Romans 2:14–15)

God's Word clearly outlines our moral framework. But those writings that De Dora recommends looking to for morality include Aristotle, Plato, and Socrates — all fallible, fallen men. So instead of allowing God's Word, where our moral framework comes from, to influence public policy, De Dora would rather rely on fallible philosophical writings. And De Dora's position on the origin of morality is indicative of most evolutionists' views.

Now, earlier in the interview De Dora said it is "necessary" to show hostility toward those who try to make him live according to their "religious dogmas." But he ends the interview by saying, "Each human being has the duty and the obligation to treat their fellow creatures as best and as nicely as possible." Over the years, I've pointed out the inconsistency of the atheistic worldview — and this is another example! By saying that I have a "duty" to treat people and animals well, De Dora is pushing his own religious dogma on me. In the atheistic worldview, who has the authority to give such an "obligation" to humanity? No one! Without the Bible, everything comes down to man's changing opinions. De Dora just wants his religious dogma imposed on people.

The inconsistency doesn't end there, however. De Dora says, "I think that everyone has to find their own meaning in life." But, I assume, a meaning within the parameters of this "duty" to be nice to people. But what if I find that my meaning is totally opposite of being nice to people? Within the atheistic framework, what stops me from doing whatever I want, regardless of how it may affect others?

Really, what De Dora has done is defined his own moral framework, imposed it on everyone who reads this interview, and then said, "But don't try to push your views on me!" But he wants to push his ideas on everyone else! It is not possible to have a consistent worldview without the absolute authority and truth of God's Word as a foundation.

Morality in a secular worldview is incredibly problematic: on the one hand, secularists either want to make Nature a higher power or they want to be a power unto themselves, but on the other hand, secularists do not want to live in a world where there is no morality to govern our actions — that would result in anarchy (only explained by man's sin nature!).

Morality in a Compromised Biblical Worldview

So what about the Christian who has compromised with evolutionary ideas? What can he say about morality?

Well, the first chapter of Genesis teaches us that man is made in God's image:

> Then God said, "Let Us make man in Our image, according to Our likeness; let them have dominion over the fish of the sea, over the birds of the air, and over the cattle, over all the earth and over every creeping thing that creeps on the earth." So God created man in His own image; in the image of God He created him; male and female He created them. (Genesis 1:26–27)

Because we are all created in God's image, no human being (including the unborn!) has any more or less value than another. And as part of God's special creation of man, he gave us a moral sense (Romans 2:15). That moral sense had to be there from the very beginning. Clearly, it was — Adam knew it was wrong to disobey God, but he did so in spite of that. And God punished Adam's sin in the way He said He would — with death (spiritual and physical).

But the Christian who rejects the Genesis accounts of Creation and the Fall cannot consistently say that morality was given to us by God — at least not in the way the Bible teaches. And after all, it is the Bible's account that matters! Now, theistic evolutionists will try to say that God guided man's evolution and that with that guidance came morality. But none of that is found in the text of Genesis — so it is a compromise position attempting to force a secular idea onto Scripture.

The Bible offers the clearest explanation of how morality came about: morality was given to us by God, and its framework is found in the pages of Scripture.

Evolution and Millions of Years — A Gospel Issue!

Ever since I first started giving talks on the creation/evolution controversy and biblical authority, I have said that if our foundation in the Church is not the Bible, from the very first verse, we will end up losing the culture. Furthermore, I would argue that the message of the gospel in churches that have compromised on Genesis has been harmed as a result, as God's Word has been undermined, adversely affecting the coming generations in the Church in regard to how they view Scripture — and this has had a devastating effect on the culture as well.

The harmful effects of this compromise on the gospel were aptly demonstrated in an article by BioLogos guest writer Mike Beidler. Now, Beidler, like others at BioLogos, is a theistic evolutionist. In his article series, he claims that the Genesis account of creation is mythical and that believers today should not take it literally. Beidler attempts to show Christians that they should have no fears about losing biblical authority or the gospel, in an effort to help them feel better about accepting evolution and millions of years. What is significant about this article series is that Beidler is very honest about the implications of theistic evolution.

Beidler's view places man's word in authority over God's Word — it adds to the decline of biblical authority that is so prevalent in today's culture. But Beidler's goal in his series is to lessen believers' fears of losing biblical authority if they compromise on the Genesis account of creation.

In the third article in his series, titled "Losing Our Savior,"[6] Beidler further explains his position on Genesis. Over the years, I have often argued that if we cannot trust one part of the Bible (such as Genesis) then it raises doubts about many other parts of Scripture, including the reliability of the Gospel accounts — and often puts people on a slippery slide of unbelief.

---

6. Mike Beidler, "Confronting Our Fears, Part 3: Losing Our Savior," BioLogos, http://biologos.org/blog/confronting-our-fears-part-3.

But Beidler disagrees. Even though Genesis is not that much older than the Gospels, he falsely claims, "The life of Jesus as presented in the four Gospels is nothing like the etiological myths encountered in Genesis 1–11; we can safely treat the Gospels as a *reliable source* for knowing how the early Church viewed the historical person of Jesus of Nazareth . . . " (emphasis mine).

So, the Gospels are reliable — but Genesis is not, despite the fact that through a detailed statistical analysis of the Hebrew language, Genesis has been shown to be historical narrative? What a low view of inerrancy.

Of course, the next step in Beidler's argument is to explain away Adam and Eve — and he does just that. He writes that sin is still a reality even without a historical Adam and Eve. "In fact," he writes, "one could argue that evolutionary biology provides an even more powerful paradigm for explaining the source of mankind's sinful nature in our day than the biblical text does." What a shocking conclusion from a professing Christian — evolution explains man's sinful nature better than the Word of God, the Creator of the universe. As you have seen throughout this book, this is the nonsense that is pervading the Church more and more — no wonder the Church and the nation as a whole is in trouble.

As if that was not bad enough, let's examine Beidler's potential explanation for the origin of our sin nature in the evolutionary creationists' worldview. He states, "Our inherited evolutionary baggage [was] borne [*sic*] of an instinctual (and once necessary) need to preserve one's self by means of selfish acts." In other words, our sinful nature supposedly had its origin in our evolutionary ancestral past, which, according to Beidler, was directed by God. If that is the case, then God is responsible for our sinful nature rather than our rebellion in a real Adam (and thus a real historical Fall).

Beidler's treatment of the Apostle Paul is just as bad. Now, Paul (and really, God through Paul, since this is the Word of God) treated Adam as a very real historical figure in Romans 5 and 1 Corinthians 15. When we take these Scriptures at face value, there is no doubt that Paul believed in an historical Adam. But Beidler explains away Paul's statement, saying that Paul was not trying to argue for an historical Adam — he was arguing for a "literal Savior." He compares Paul's use of Adam in that verse to a character in a parable — parables did not contain real people, so why should Paul's statement?

But you know, the main problem with Beidler's view is that, just as Genesis is clearly historical narrative, parables are clearly parables. Listeners then and readers now know that parables typically do not contain historical figures. But Paul's teaching in Romans 5 and 1 Corinthians 15 is not a parable! There is no reason to think that he believed Adam was mythical. And besides, the first time the gospel is preached is in Genesis 3:15 — if that is mythical, then the gospel itself is mythical.

Paul also referred to the literal creation and fall of Adam and Eve in 1 Timothy 2:13–14 while discussing ideas about authority in the Church. He wrote, "For Adam was formed first, then Eve. And Adam was not deceived, but the woman being deceived, fell into transgression." Once again, there is no doubt that Paul viewed Adam, Eve, and their sin as part of literal history. Are we supposed to assume that this passage was a parable as well?

Beidler even says that one should expect Paul to believe in a literal Adam and Eve due to his Jewish upbringing and Pharisaical training. However, the implication from Beidler is that Paul was mistaken, and he even cites Peter Enns as a source readers can look to "for other possible ways to understand Paul's understanding of Adam." As we saw in an earlier chapter, not only does Enns deny the existence of Adam and Eve entirely, he also argues that not only Paul, but also Jesus, accommodated the errors of their day. In other words, according to Enns, Jesus knowingly or unknowingly taught errors about the first man and woman. And I need to emphasize again — even though Paul wrote these passages being referred to — he was inspired by the Holy Spirit to write what God wanted to reveal to us. As we read in Thessalonians: "For this reason we also thank God without ceasing, because when you received the word of God which you heard from us, you welcomed it not as the word of men, but as it is in truth, the word of God, which also effectively works in you who believe" (1 Thessalonians 2:13). These compromisers certainly have a very different view of what Scripture is than I do — or than what Scripture itself clearly claims!

BioLogos has no way to defend these positions scripturally. What I think has happened here is that the people at BioLogos have approached the Bible with the requirement that evolution and millions of years must fit into Scripture. What Beidler is teaching here is not a viable alternative to biblical creation based on any kind of textual evidence. No, he is attempting to use clever academic arguments and terms to subvert the authority of God's Word so that man's fallible, changing ideas are treated as the truth about our origins. Sadly, this destructive approach is at epidemic proportions in our Church culture today.

Evolution's Impact on the Gospel

How do the compromise views of Christians like those at BioLogos impact the message of the gospel? The answer may sound harsh, but I think it is important to be up front about this: their version of events makes God the author of sin and a god of death. What's more, it makes the Bible untrustworthy.

The evolutionary worldview has an anti-supernatural bias. Theistic evolutionists are determined to explain the origin of the universe and man through God-guided, naturalistic means. But the creation was the first miracle recorded in Scripture! If the first miracle was not really a miracle at all, what's to stop us from rejecting the miracle of the Resurrection as well? The Apostle Paul wrote that the miracle of the Resurrection is central to our faith:

> Now if Christ is preached that He has been raised from the dead, how do some among you say that there is no resurrection of the dead? But if there is no resurrection of the dead, then Christ is not risen. And if Christ is not risen, then our preaching is empty and your faith is also empty. Yes, and we are found false witnesses of God, because we have testified of God that He raised up Christ, whom He did not raise up — if in fact the dead do not rise. For if the dead do not rise, then Christ is not risen. And if Christ is not risen, your faith is futile; you are still in your sins! Then also those who have fallen asleep in Christ have perished. If in this life only we have hope in Christ, we are of all men the most pitiable. (1 Corinthians 15:12–19)

Without the Resurrection, in other words, we are without hope. When we preach the good news of the gospel, we tell people of the Savior Christ, fully God and fully man, who walked the earth, lived a perfect life, died a criminal's death, and *rose again* on the third day. In rising again, Jesus Christ defeated death, the "last enemy."

The Resurrection is the key! If Christ did not actually rise miraculously from the dead, then, as the Apostle Paul writes, "your faith is also empty."

To put it plainly, our ability to fully trust God's promise of salvation relies upon our ability to trust everything He says about history from beginning to end. So it is right for believers to fear that the mixture of evolution and millions of year will harm the message of the gospel. As I have said many times before, we can trust God's Word, from the very first verse.

Epilogue

 Returning to the
Authority of God's Word

If the foundations are destroyed, what can the righteous do? (Psalm
11:3).

A s I wrote at the beginning of this book, my prayer is that as a result of
reading this book, many more Christians (including Christian leaders)
will speak with authority and give that "certain sound" concerning God's
Word beginning in Genesis. Throughout this book, I have outlined a problem in our churches, seminaries, and Christian colleges today: the authority
of God's Word is being challenged when it comes to the accounts of Creation, the Fall, and the Flood in Genesis. It is the Genesis 3 attack of our
day!

But it is not enough to point out a problem. We have to find a solution
as well. For over 25 years, I have been speaking and writing about the cre-
ation/evolution debate and the continual erosion of the authority of God's
Word in the Church and culture. And in all that time, the solution to the
problem has not changed. What is it?

First, our Christian leaders must return to the authority of God's Word
in *every* area, including the origin of the universe and everything in it.
Numerous Bible scholars, Christian academics, and church leaders have
compromised on Genesis 1–11. I urge you to challenge them lovingly and
firmly to reconsider their views and to take God at His Word. Try to get

them to understand that for many of them they are using eisegesis on Genesis 1–11 and exegesis on the rest of Scripture.

Second, equip yourselves and your families with sound, biblically based apologetics to counter the Genesis 3 attack of our day. You may be getting solid teaching on Genesis in your church or Sunday school classroom (though most Christians are not), but you and your family can have that solid teaching in your home as well. At Answers in Genesis, our goal is to provide you with equipping resources so that you will be able to respond to the skeptical questions and attacks of our day. For example, our *Answers Bible Curriculum,* designed for the entire family, is a perfect resource both for homeschool families and churches to use in teaching people to trust what God says in His Word. Thousands of churches are now using our *Answers Bible Curriculum* for their Sunday school programs.

Let me reiterate an example I used earlier. It is my analogy to explain the role of apologetics in teaching God's Word and the gospel. This is based on John 11: Jesus comes to the tomb of Lazarus. Lazarus is dead. A non-Christian is "dead in trespasses and sin." Only God can raise the dead—only God's Word can save a person dead in trespasses and sin.

At the tomb of Lazarus, Jesus says, "Take away the stone" (John 11:39):

> Jesus said, "Take away the stone." Martha, the sister of him who was dead, said to Him, "Lord, by this time there is a stench, for he has been dead four days." Jesus said to her, "Did I not say to you that if you would believe you would see the glory of God? " Then they took away the stone from the place where the dead man was lying. And Jesus lifted up His eyes and said, "Father, I thank You that You have heard Me. And I know that You always hear Me, but because of the people who are standing by I said this, that they may believe that You sent Me." Now when He had said these things, He cried with a loud voice, "Lazarus, come forth!" (John 11:39–43)

Now Jesus could have moved the stone with one word — but what humans can do, He gets them to do. They moved the stone. What humans could not do, He did — He raised the dead to life.

Our job is to move the stone — to take away the stumbling block. That is the role of apologetics — moving the stone. We give answers to defend the Christian faith, but not just for the sake of answers — we must point people to the Word of God. Remember, "faith comes by hearing and hearing by the Word of God" (Romans 10:17). It is God's Word that saves. We must do the best we can to defend the Christian faith — but also to point people to the Word, to the gospel that saves.

Finally, faithfully share the gospel! In Matthew 28:19–20, Christ gives believers what is called the Great Commission:

> Go therefore and make disciples of all the nations, baptizing them in the name of the Father and of the Son and of the Holy Spirit, teaching them to observe all things that I have commanded you; and lo, I am with you always, even to the end of the age.

As we call the Church back to the authority of God's Word, we must also be diligent in sharing the good news of the gospel with the lost. And one of the most effective ways to do that is to start in the same place the Bible does — at the beginning.

In an increasing number of instances, it has become apparent that before we can effectively proclaim the message of Christ, we must establish the foundation of the Creation and the Fall. It is on this foundation that the rest of the gospel is built — and that is exactly why the mixture of evolutionary ideas is so harmful to that message.

Evolution and/or millions of years can be a barrier to the gospel for many people, because what is commonly regarded as "science" has so convinced people that the universe is billions of years old and therefore Genesis cannot be taken as history — in a straightforward way. This causes them to doubt the authority of God's Word — and that doubt can lead to unbelief in the rest of the Scriptures. Many people need those barriers removed before they will even listen to the truth of the gospel. Starting with God's Word in Genesis, we can show them answers to the skeptical questions that have caused them to doubt. This serves to help remove those barriers. The message is quite simple really — the history in the Bible is true, and the gospel based in that history is true.

Pastors, seminary professors, Bible scholars, Christian college and university professors, church leaders, lay people — I want to challenge you to think carefully about what you have read in this book. If you have accepted man's fallible ideas about the origin of the universe, consider the implications that has on the view of death and suffering, on the gospel message, and on the trustworthiness of Scripture. Even though this may not affect your salvation, I suggest it is affecting the way those you influence view Scripture itself.

We serve a God who cannot lie. Why shouldn't we trust His account of creation, the Fall, and the Flood? I urge you to return to the foundation of Scripture.

Appendix A

How Should We Interpret the Bible, Particularly Genesis 1–11?

Tim Chaffey[1]

Introduction

A popular seminary professor recently wrote the following about the creation of Adam and Eve:

> Any evils humans experience outside the Garden before God breathes into them the breath of life would be experienced as natural evils in the same way that other animals experience them. The pain would be real, but it would not be experienced as divine justice in response to willful rebellion. Moreover, once God breathes the breath of life into them, we may assume that the first humans experienced an amnesia of their former animal life: Operating on a higher plane of consciousness once infused with the breath of life, they would transcend the lower plane of animal consciousness on

---

1. This article was originally published in *How Do We Know the Bible Is True?* Vol. 1, eds. Ken Ham and Bodie Hodge (Green Forest, AR: Master Books 2011).

which they had previously operated — though, after the Fall, they might be tempted to resort to that lower consciousness.[2]

So according to this professor, Adam and Eve were animals before God breathed the breath of life into them. At that point, they experienced "amnesia of their former animal life" so that they would no longer remember their animal past.

How does this line up with the Word of God, which states that God made Adam from the dust of the ground (Genesis 2:7) and Eve from Adam's rib (Genesis 2:22)? Has the professor made a plausible interpretation of God's Word? Is his interpretive work what Paul had in mind when he advised Timothy to be diligent in his efforts to accurately interpret the Word of Truth (2 Timothy 2:15)?

The example above highlights the importance of being able to properly interpret the Bible. In this post-modern age, bizarre interpretations are accepted because people believe they have the right to decide for themselves what a passage means. In other words, meaning is in the eye of the beholder, so you can decide truth for yourself.

This ideology flies in the face of Christ's example. He routinely rebuked those who twisted the words of Scripture or mis-applied them. The Bible is God's message to man. We can have perfect confidence that God is capable of accurately relaying His Word to us in a way that we can understand. As such, it is crucial that we learn how to interpret properly so that we can determine the Author's Intended Meaning (AIM) rather than forcing our own ideas into the text. A given document means what the author intended it to mean. The alternative would make communication futile. There would be no point in writing anything if the readers are simply going to take what they want from the passage, rather than what the writer intends. All communication is predicated on the presupposition that language conveys the author's or speaker's intention (unless, of course, the person is trying to deceive us, which is something God does not do since He wants us to understand His Word).

Interpretation

Hermeneutics (from the Greek word *hermēneuō*, which means to explain or interpret) is the branch of theology that focuses on identifying and applying sound principles of biblical interpretation. While the Bible is generally plain

---

2. William A. Dembski, *The End of Christianity: Finding a Good God in an Evil World* (Nashville, TN: Broadman & Holman Publishing Group, 2009), p. 155.

in its meaning, proper interpretation requires careful study and is not always an easy task. Consider that the Bible was written over a period of roughly 2,000 years by 40 or more authors using three languages (Hebrew, Aramaic, and Greek). The authors wrote in different genres and had different vocabularies, personalities, cultural backgrounds, and social standings. The Holy Spirit moved each of these men to produce His inspired, inerrant, and infallible Word (2 Timothy 3:16; 2 Peter 1:20–21), but He allowed their various writing styles and personalities to be expressed in its pages. It was written in a culture very different from our modern world and has been translated from its original languages. These are just some of the factors that must be taken into account as we interpret.

In fact, Bible colleges and seminaries often require their students to complete a course in hermeneutics. Numerous books have been written to explain these principles, and while Bible-believing Christians may disagree over particulars, there is general agreement about the major rules required to rightly divide the Word of Truth.

This is not to claim that only the scholarly elite can correctly interpret the Bible. Various groups have wrongly held this position. William Tyndale lived in the early 16th century when only certain people were allowed to interpret the Bible, which was only available in Latin, not the language of the common man. He sought to bring God's Word to the average person by translating it into English. Tyndale is credited with telling a priest that he could make a boy who drove a plow to know more of the Scripture than the priest himself.[3] The Bible was penned so that in its pages all people, even children, can learn about God and what He has done so that we can have a personal relationship with Him.

We must also battle against our pride, which tempts us to think that our own views are always right or that the beliefs of a particular teacher are necessarily right. We must strive to be like the Bereans who were commended by Luke for searching the Old Testament Scriptures daily to make sure that what Paul taught was true (Acts 17:11).

God desires for His people to know and understand His Word — that's why He gave it to us and instructed fathers to teach it to their children in the home (Deuteronomy 6:4–9). However, we must keep in mind several important points.

---

3. http://www.tyndalesploughboy.org, accessed January 7, 2011.

First, Christians must seek the guidance of the Holy Spirit while study-ing the Bible. It's not that the Bible requires any "extra-logical" or mystical insight to understand it. But we are limited in our understanding and often hindered by pride. We need the Holy Spirit to help us to think correctly, lest we distort the Scriptures (2 Peter 3:16).

Second, a person can spend his or her entire life and still never come close to mining the depths of Scripture. The Bible is written in such a mar-velous way that a child can understand the basic message, and yet the most educated theologians continue to learn new things from the Bible as they study it. There is always much more to learn, so we must humbly approach the Word of God.

Third, God has given the Church learned men and gifted teachers who have devoted their lives to studying God's Word. While these people are certainly not infallible, we shouldn't automatically reject the work of those who have gone before us.

Finally, since the Bible consists of written data, then in order to under-stand it, we must follow standard rules of grammar and interpretation. We will examine some of these rules and principles later, especially as they relate to Genesis.

Because people often confuse the two concepts, it must be pointed out that interpretation is different than application, although they are related. Interpretation answers the questions, "What does the text say?" and "What does the text mean?" Application follows interpretation and answers the question, "How can I apply this truth in my life?" After all, the goal of studying the Bible is not to simply fill one's head with information but to learn what God wants us to know so that we can live how He wants us to live.

Which Method Do We Use?

Bible-believing Christians generally follow a method of interpretation known as the historical-grammatical approach. That is, we try to find the plain (literal) meaning of the words based on an understanding of the his-torical and cultural settings in which the book was written. We then follow standard rules of grammar, according to the book's particular genre, to arrive at an interpretation. We seek to perform careful interpretation or exegesis — that is, to "read out of" the text what the author intended it to mean. This is in contrast to eisegesis, which occurs when someone "reads into" the text his own ideas — what the reader wants the text to mean. In other words, exegesis is finding the AIM (Author's Intended Meaning) of the passage because its true meaning is determined by the sender of the message, not the recipient.

This hermeneutical approach has several strengths. It can be demonstrated that the New Testament authors interpreted the Old Testament in this manner. Also, it is the only approach that offers an internal system of "checks and balances" to make sure one is on the right track. As will be shown, other views allow for personal opinion to sneak into one's interpretation, which does not truly reflect what the text means.

Finally, this approach is consistent with how we utilize language on a daily basis while interacting with others. For example, if your best friend says, "I am going to drive to work tomorrow morning," you can instantly understand what he means. You know that he has a vehicle that he can drive to his place of employment, and that's exactly what he plans on doing early the next day.

If the post-modern approach is accurate and meaning is determined by the recipient of the message, then perhaps your friend is really just telling you that he likes pancakes. Communication becomes impossible in such a world, and it gets even worse if your friend was talking to you and several other buddies. One friend might think he was talking about his favorite color, another interpreted his words to mean that he doesn't believe in air, and another thought he meant that he was going to walk to work ten years later.

Words have a particular meaning in a particular context. When they are placed together in sentences and paragraphs, then a person must follow common-sense rules in order to derive the appropriate meaning. The sender of the message had a reason for choosing the words he did and putting those words together in a particular order and context. The same is true with the Bible. God had a reason for moving the writers of the Bible to use the words they did in the order they did. Our goal must be to ascertain the AIM.

Principles of Interpretation

Since the goal of interpreting the Bible is to determine the Author's Intended Meaning, we must follow principles derived from God's Word. The following principles do not comprise an exhaustive list but are some of the major concepts found in the majority of books on interpretation. Following a survey of these principles, we will examine the quote from the introduction of this chapter to see if it properly applies these standards.

Carefully Observe the Text

It may seem rather obvious, but this principle is often overlooked. We must carefully observe what the text actually states. Many mistakes have been made by people who jump into interpretation based on what they think the text states rather than what it really does state.

As you read a particular verse or passage, pay close attention to different types of words that make up a sentence. Is the subject singular or plural? Is the verb tense past, present, or future? Is the sentence a command, statement of fact, or question? Is the statement part of a dialogue? If so, who is the speaker, and why did he make that comment? Can you note any repetition of words, which perhaps shows emphasis? What ideas are compared or contrasted? Can you identify any cause and effect statements or questions and answers? What is the tone of the passage; are emotional words used?

Failure to carefully observe the text has resulted in numerous misconceptions about the Bible. For example, many Christians have taught that Adam and Eve used to walk with God in the cool of the day. While it is possible that they did take walks with God in the garden, the Bible never claims this. Instead, God's Word reveals that *after* they had sinned, Adam and Eve "heard the sound of the LORD God walking in the garden in the cool of the day," and they hid themselves from Him (Genesis 3:8).

Carefully observing the text can also protect you from making another common mistake. Just because the Bible contains a statement does not mean that it affirms the statement as godly. For example, much of the Book of Job consists of an ongoing dialogue between Job and four of his friends (Bildad, Eliphaz, Zophar, and Elihu). Some people have been careless by quoting certain verses from this book to support their own ideas, but we have to keep in mind that God told Eliphaz that what he, Bildad, and Zophar had spoken about Him was not right (Job 42:7). This ties in perfectly with our next principle.

Context Is Key

Perhaps no principle of interpretation is more universally agreed upon than the idea that understanding the context of the word, phrase, or passage is absolutely essential. *Context* is defined as "the parts of a discourse that surround a word or passage and can throw light on its meaning."[4]

You may have heard someone say that a particular verse has been pulled out of context. Skeptics of Scripture often take verses out of context when they attack the Bible. The reason is that they can make the Bible "say" just about anything if they do not provide the context. For example, the skeptic might ask, "Did you know that the Bible says, 'There is no God'?" Then he may go on to claim that this contradicts other passages, which certainly teach that God does exist.

How do we handle such a charge? We look at the context of the quoted words, which in this case comes from Psalm 14:1 (and is repeated in Psalm 53:1). It states, "The fool has said in his heart, 'There is no God.' " So, it's true that the Bible states, "There is no God," but it attributes these words to a foolish person. So the Bible is not teaching both the existence and non-existence of God, as the skeptic asserts.

If I asked you what the word "set" means, would you be able to provide me with the correct answer? No, it would be impossible because the word has more than 70 definitions in the 11th edition of *Merriam-Webster's Collegiate Dictionary*, and can be used as a verb, noun, and an adjective. Now, if I asked you what the word "set" meant in the following sentence, you could easily figure it out: "His mind was *set* on solving the problem." In this sentence, the word means "intent" or "determined." But without the context, you would not know this.

The same thing is true with the Bible or any other written communication. The context clarifies the meaning of the word, phrase, sentence, etc. With the Bible, it is important to know the context of the particular passage you are studying. It is also important to understand the context of the entire book in which the passage is found and how that book fits into the context of Scripture.

We also need to recognize where the passage fits into the flow of history. It makes a huge difference in determining the writer's intent if we note whether the passage was pre-Fall, pre-Flood, pre-Mosaic Law, after the Babylonian exile, during Christ's earthly ministry, after His Resurrection, or after Pentecost. This is especially important when we reach the point of application. For example, just because God commanded Israel to sacrifice

---

4. Frederick C. Mish, editor in chief, *Merriam-Webster's Collegiate Dictionary*, 11th Edition (Springfield, MA: Merriam-Webster, 2008), s.v. "Context."

lambs at Passover doesn't mean we should do the same today. Jesus died on the Cross as our Passover Lamb (1 Corinthians 5:7) and was the ultimate fulfillment of the Passover sacrifice. Since the Bible was revealed progressively, there are instances where later revelation supersedes earlier revelation.

Ron Rhodes summarized these truths by stating, "No verse of Scripture can be divorced from the verses around it. Interpreting a verse apart from its context is like trying to analyze a Rembrandt painting by looking at only a single square inch of the painting, or like trying to analyze Handel's 'Messiah' by listening to a few short notes."[5]

Clarity of Scripture

Since the Bible is God's Word to man, He must expect us to understand it. As such, it makes sense that He would communicate His message to us in such a way so that we can indeed comprehend it if we are serious about wanting to know the truth. The Apostle Paul told the Corinthians:

> Rather, we have renounced secret and shameful ways; we do not use deception, nor do we distort the word of God. On the contrary, by *setting forth the truth plainly* we commend ourselves to every man's conscience in the sight of God. (2 Corinthians 4:2, NIV, emphasis added) Proverbs 8:9 states that God's words "are all plain to him who understands, and right to those who find knowledge."

This principle was one of the key differences between the Reformers and Roman Catholics. The Reformers believed in the perspicuity (clearness) of Scripture, especially in relation to its central message of the gospel, and they believed each believer had the right to interpret God's Word. Roman Catholic doctrine held (and still holds) that Scripture can only be interpreted by the Magisterium (teaching office of the church).

Consider the words of Psalm 119, which is by far the longest chapter in the entire Bible, and every one of its 176 verses extols the superiority of God's Word. "Your word is a lamp to my feet and a light to my path" (Psalm 119:105). "The entrance of Your words gives light; it gives understanding to the simple" (Psalm 119:130). God's Word should be a lamp to our feet and a light to our path, giving understanding to the simple. How could it be or do any of these things if it is not clear?

---

5. Ron Rhodes, "Rightly Interpreting the Bible," from http://home.earthlink.net/~ron-rhodes/Interpretation.html. Accessed January 12, 2011.

The principle of the clarity of Scripture does not mean that every passage is easily understood or that one does not need to diligently study the Word of God, but it does teach that the overall message of the Word of God can be understood by all believers who carefully and prayerfully study it. The principle also means that we should not assume or look for hidden meanings but rather assess the most straightforward meaning. Two of Christ's favorite sayings were "It is written" and "Have you not read?" Then He would quote a verse from the Old Testament. By these sayings, He indicated that the Scriptures are generally clear.

Compare Scripture with Scripture

Another key principle of hermeneutics is that we should use Scripture to interpret Scripture. Known by theologians as the "analogy of faith" or "analogy of Scripture," this principle is solidly based on the Bible's own teachings. Since the Bible is the Word of God and God cannot lie or contradict Himself (Numbers 23:19; Hebrews 6:18), then one passage will never contradict another passage. This principle is useful for several reasons.

First, not all Bible passages are equally clear. So a clear passage can be used to shed light on a difficult, not-so-clear passage. There are a number of obscure verses in Scripture, where you might wish the writer had provided more details. First Corinthians 15:29 is a classic example. Right in the middle of the chapter on the Resurrection of Jesus and the future resurrection of believers, Paul asked, "Otherwise, what will they do who are baptized for the dead, if the dead do not rise at all? Why then are they baptized for the dead?" (1 Corinthians 15:29). Several ideas have been suggested to explain what Paul meant about baptism for the dead, but because this is the only verse in all of Scripture that mentions this concept, we may not be able to reach a firm conclusion about its meaning.

However, by comparing this verse with other Scripture, we can reach definite conclusions about what it *does not* teach. We know that Paul did not instruct the Corinthians to baptize people for the dead,[6] because Paul and other biblical writers unequivocally taught that salvation is only by God's grace and can only be received through faith alone in Christ alone (Ephesians 2:8–9). We can also be sure that those who practice such a thing are

---

6. The Latter-Day Saints (Mormons) have developed an entire doctrine called baptism by proxy in which current members of the group are baptized in place of the dead. They use this verse to support this practice.

not accomplishing what they hope to accomplish — the salvation of an unbeliever who has already died. Hebrews 9:27 states, "it is appointed for men to die once, but after this the judgment."

Second, by comparing Scripture with Scripture, we have a system of checks and balances to help us stay on the right track. There will likely be times when, for whatever reason, we incorrectly interpret a given passage. By studying other passages that shed light on the same issue, we can recognize our error. Many people are unwilling to change their original interpretation and hold on to contradictory beliefs. Some will even claim that the Bible contradicts itself when, in reality, they have misinterpreted one or both of the passages. It is crucial for us to humbly approach Scripture and realize that if we believe we have found a contradiction, then it is our interpretation that is flawed, not God's Word.

Since this principle provides a system of checks and balances, it can provide us with great certainty concerning a given interpretation. If we interpret a passage and then discover that every other passage on the topic seems to teach the same truth, we can be confident in the accuracy of our interpretation.

Classification of Text

While interpreting the Bible, we must never forget to understand the genre (literary style) of the passage we are studying. The Bible contains numerous types of literature, and each one needs to be interpreted according to principles befitting its particular style. Following is a chart identifying the basic literary style of each book of the Bible. Note that some books contain more than one style. For example, Exodus is written as history, but chapter 15 includes a song written in poetic language. Also, the books are sometimes divided into more categories, but for our purposes "History" includes the books of the Law, the historical books, and the four gospels; "Poetry" includes the Psalms and wisdom literature; "Prophecy" includes the prophetic books; and "Epistles" are the New Testament letters written to an individual or church or groups of churches.

These distinctions are important to keep in mind while interpreting the Bible. Each classification uses language in a particular way. Historical books are primarily narratives of past events and should be interpreted in a straightforward manner. This does not mean that they never utilize figurative language. For example, after Cain killed his brother Abel, God said to Cain, "What have you done? The voice of your brother's blood cries out to Me from the ground. So now you are cursed from the earth, which has

History	Poetry	Prophecy	Epistles
Genesis	Job	Isaiah	Romans
Exodus	Psalms Jeremiah	1 Corinthians	
Leviticus	Proverbs	Lamentations	2 Corinthians
Numbers	Ecclesiastes	Ezekiel	Galatians
Deuteronomy	Song of Solomon	Daniel	Ephesians
Joshua		Hosea	Philippians
Judges		Joel	Colossians
Ruth		Amos	1 Thessalonians
1 Samuel		Obadiah	2 Thessalonians
2 Samuel		Jonah	1 Timothy
1 Kings		Micah	2 Timothy
2 Kings		Nahum	Titus
1 Chronicles		Habakkuk	Philemon
2 Chronicles		Zephaniah	Hebrews
Ezra		Haggai	James
Nehemiah		Zechariah	1 Peter
Esther		Malachi	2 Peter
Matthew		Revelation	1 John
Mark			2 John
Luke			3 John
John			Jude
Acts			

opened its mouth to receive your brother's blood from your hand" (Genesis 4:10–11). There are two obvious instances of figurative language in this passage: the ground "opened its mouth" and Abel's "blood cries out" from it. Nevertheless, these figures of speech are perfectly legitimate in historical writing, and it is easy to understand what they mean.

Poetry, prophecy, and the New Testament epistles all have their own particular nuances and guidelines for proper interpretation. Space does not permit a full treatment here, so just remember to recognize the book's (or passage's) genre and interpret accordingly.[7]

---

7. For a detailed contrast between poetic and narrative genres in the Bible, see Tim Chaffey, "Parallelism in Hebrew Poetry Demonstrates a Major Error in the Hermeneutic of Man Old-Earth Creationists," available at <http://www.answersingenesis.org/articles/arj/v5/n1/hebrew-parallelism>.

Church's Historical View

Finally, it is important to know how those who have gone before us have interpreted a passage in question. Although our doctrine must be based squarely on the Word of God and not on tradition or what some great leader believed, we should allow ourselves to be informed by the work of others who have spent long hours studying God's Word. Most doctrines have been discussed, debated, and formulated throughout Church history, so we should take advantage of that resource.

Imagine studying a passage and reaching a conclusion only to discover that no one else in history has ever interpreted those verses in the same way. You would not necessarily be wrong, but you would certainly want to re-examine the passage to see if you had overlooked something. After all, you need to be very careful and confident in your interpretation before proposing an idea that none of the millions of interpreters have ever noticed before.

While Bible scholars and pastors often have access to resources that permit them to search out the teachings of our spiritual forefathers, this information can also be obtained by the average Christian. Consider borrowing a commentary from a pastor or taking advantage of some of the Bible software on the market, which allows you to quickly search for this information.

Application of the Hermeneutical Principles

Let's consider how well Professor Dembski's quote from the introduction fits the description of the creation of Adam and Eve as described in Genesis 2. Was he careful to observe the text, examine the context, assume the clarity of Scripture, compare Scripture with Scripture, properly classify the text, and compare his conclusions with those who have gone before him?

Here is the quote again:

> Any evils humans experience outside the Garden before God breathes into them the breath of life would be experienced as natural evils in the same way that other animals experience them. The pain would be real, but it would not be experienced as divine justice in response to willful rebellion. Moreover, once God breathes the breath of life into them, we may assume that the first humans experienced an amnesia of their former animal life: Operating on a

higher plane of consciousness once infused with the breath of life, they would transcend the lower plane of animal consciousness on which they had previously operated — though, after the Fall, they might be tempted to resort to that lower consciousness.[8]

Shortly before this quote, Dembski proposed that the world was full of death and suffering but that God created an oasis of perfection (the Garden of Eden) in which Adam and Eve were allowed to live.[9] Is this consistent with Scripture? Did he *carefully observe the text*?

In Genesis 2:7, the verse which describes the creation of Adam, we immediately run into a problem. It states, "And the LORD God formed man [Hebrew: *'adam*] of the dust of the ground, and breathed into his nostrils the breath of life; and man became a living being." The following verse, Genesis 2:8, reveals that after God made Adam, He created the Garden of Eden and put Adam in it. So Dembski is right that Adam came from outside the garden and was subsequently moved into it. However, contrary to Dembski's claims, Adam was already fully human while he was still outside the garden. The immediate **context** reveals that Adam was made from the "dust of the ground," so he did not evolve from ape-like ancestors.

There are some other problems. According to Genesis 2:21–22, the first woman (Eve) was made from Adam's rib once Adam was in the garden and *after* he named the animals. She was not an animal who came from outside the garden, nor did she become fully human when she entered the garden or receive amnesia about the past the moment she entered it. So this interpretation does not pay attention to the details of the text of Genesis 2. Also, in the context, Genesis 1:31 indicates that everything God had made was "very good." This sharply contrasts with Dembski's view of a world that was already full of pain and "natural evils."

Dembski's interpretation also runs counter to the **clarity of Scripture** (at least in the early chapters of Genesis). A plain reading of the text reveals that Adam was made from the dust of the ground, placed in the garden, told to name the animals, and put in a deep sleep during which God made the first woman from Adam's rib.

When we **compare Scripture with Scripture**, we find other reasons why Dembski's interpretation fails. The Bible consistently shows that death

---

8. Dembski, *The End of Christianity*, p. 155.
9. Ibid., p. 153.

did not exist prior to Adam's sin.[10] Also, in Genesis 3:18–19 God explained that, as a result of Adam's sin and God's Curse, the ground would bring forth thorns and thistles (the ground that was cursed was outside the garden from which Adam and Eve were expelled), making Adam's work more difficult, and that Adam would eventually die. Yet, since Dembski apparently accepts a view of theistic evolution (the notion that God used evolutionary processes to bring man into existence),[11] he promotes the idea that thorns and death pre-existed Adam by hundreds of millions of years. He seeks to solve this dilemma by claiming that Adam's sin was retroactively applied to all of creation.[12] Nowhere does the Bible state anything like this. Throughout its pages, the Bible reveals there was no death before sin because death was brought into the world by man.

The literary style of Genesis, based on the **classification of the text**, was also ignored by Dembski. As will be demonstrated in the next section, Genesis was written as historical narrative, and it should be interpreted as such. Although many claim to believe in the historicity of the events in Genesis 1–11, they simply reclassify the text as something other than history. For example, some view it as poetic or mythological.[13] It is not enough to simply claim that one believes Genesis is historically accurate. One must also recognize that it was written as historical narrative and interpret accordingly. The strange ideas proposed by Dembski reveal he does not interpret the early chapters as historical narrative.

Dembski's interpretation of these chapters is rather unique. It certainly has not been a standard or well-accepted position throughout **Church history**, and I only know of one other person who has discussed something

---

10. See Dr. Terry Mortenson's article "Young-Earth Creationist View Summarized and Defended" at http://www.answersingenesis.org/articles/aid/v6/n1/yec-view-summary, accessed February 16, 2011.

11. Actually, Dembski is very confusing in his section on Adam and Eve (p. 155–159). Some statements seem to reject evolution, but many other statements seem to accept it. At the very least, he seems to indicate that theistic evolution is compatible with the theodicy he is proposing.

12. For a full refutation of Dembski's view, see Terry Mortenson's article "Christian Theodicy in Light of Genesis and Modern Science: A Young-Earth Creationist Response to William Dembski" at http://www.answersingenesis.org/articles/arj/v2/n1/dembskis-theodicy-refuted, accessed January 26, 2011.

13. Tim Chaffey and Bob McCabe, "Framework Hypothesis" in Ken Ham and Bodie Hodge, *How Do We Know the Bible Is True?* Vol. 1 (Green Forest, AR: Master Books, 2011), p. 189–199.

similar.[14] While this principle of considering the Church's historical view does not disprove his view by itself, it illustrates the need to carefully examine his beliefs before accepting them.

Also, we should ask why Dembski has come up with this novel view. Dembski answered that question when he wrote, "The young-earth solution to reconciling the order of creation with natural history makes good exegetical and theological sense. Indeed, the overwhelming consensus of theologians up through the Reformation held to this view. I myself would adopt it in a heartbeat *except that nature seems to present such strong evidence against it.*"[15]

This statement reveals his motives. The young-earth creationist position is clearly presented in the text of Scripture, but he does not accept it because he believes scientists have shown the earth and universe to be billions of years old. As such, he does not allow the Bible to be the authority in this area. Instead, he has placed man's ever-changing views in a position to override the plain words of the God who knows all things, cannot lie, and has revealed to us how and when He created. By his interpretation, Dembski is reading into (eisegesis) the Bible what he would like it to mean, rather than reading out (exegesis) of the Bible what it actually teaches.

Several other problems could be cited, but these are sufficient to show that Dr. Dembski has failed to accurately interpret the passage about the creation of man. The early chapters of Genesis are written as historical narrative. When you follow the well-accepted principles of interpretation, then it is easy to see why, until the onslaught of old-earth philosophy in the early 1800s, Christians have predominantly believed that God created everything in six days approximately six thousand years ago.[16]

Interpreting Genesis 1–11

By allowing man's ever-changing ideas about the past to override the plain words of Scripture, many people have proposed that Genesis 1–11 should

---

14. Because he also sought to reconcile the ideas of long ages and the biblical teaching that death came as a result of Adam's sin, Charles Spurgeon once briefly stated as a possibility the concept of death as a result of Adam's sin being retroactively applied to the death of animals for long periods of time prior to the Fall. Charles H. Spurgeon, "Christ, the Destroyer of Death" (preached on December 17, 1876), *The Metropolitan Tabernacle Pulpit*, Vol XXII (Pasadena, TX: Pilgrim, 1981), p. 698–699.

15. Dembski, *The End of Christianity*, p. 55.

16. For more information on this dramatic shift in interpretation of Genesis 1–11 in the early 1800s, see Terry Mortenson, *The Great Turning Point: The Church's Catastrophic Mistake on Geology — Before Darwin* (Green Forest, AR: Master Books, 2004).

be viewed as mythical, figurative, or allegorical, rather than as historical narrative. Since these people believe in millions and billions of years of death, suffering, disease, and bloodshed prior to Adam's sin, they search for ways to reinterpret the Bible's early chapters in a manner that will allow their views. As a result, the accounts of Creation, the Fall, the Flood, and the Tower of Babel are often reinterpreted or dismissed.

We must remember that our goal is to discover the AIM (Author's Intended Meaning) of the biblical text. Did God intend for these chapters to be understood in a figurative, mythical, or allegorical manner, or did He intend to tell us precisely (though not in all the detail we might want) what He did in the beginning and in the early history of the earth? The Bible provides abundant support for the conclusion that these chapters are indeed historical narrative.

First, although many commentators have broken Genesis into two sections (1–11 and 12–50), such a distinction cannot be found in the text. Some have even argued that the first 11 chapters represent primeval history and should be interpreted differently than the final 39 chapters. There are several problems with this approach. Genesis 12 would make little sense without the genealogical background provided in the previous chapter. Further, since chapter 11 includes the genealogy of Shem (which introduces us to Abraham), this links it to the genealogy in Genesis 10, which is tied to the one found in Genesis 5.

Second, Todd Beall explained another link between chapters 11 and 12, which demonstrates one should not arbitrarily insert a break in the text at this point. He wrote, "Genesis 12 begins with a *waw* consecutive verb, *wayomer* ('and he said'), indicating that what follows is a continuation of chapter 11, not a major break in the narrative."[17] Also, chapter 11 ends with mention of Abraham, and chapter 12 begins with Abraham.

Third, Genesis seems to be structured on the recurrence of the Hebrew phrase *eleh toledoth* ("This is the book of the genealogy of . . ." or "This is the history of . . ."). This occurs 11 times throughout the book: 6 times in Genesis 1–11 and 5 times in chapters 12–50. Clearly, the author intended that both sections should be interpreted in the same way — as historical narrative.

---

17. Todd S. Beall, "Contemporary Hermeneutical Approaches to Genesis 1–11" in Terry Mortenson and Thane H. Ury, *Coming to Grips with Genesis: Biblical Authority and the Age of the Earth* (Green Forest, AR: Master Books, 2008), p. 145.

Fourth, the New Testament treats Genesis 1–11 as historical narrative. At least 25 New Testament passages refer directly to the early chapters of Genesis, and they are always treated as real history. Genesis 1 and 2 were cited by Jesus in response to a question about divorce (Matthew 19:4–6; Mark 10:6–9). Paul referenced Genesis 2–3 in Romans 5:12–19; 1 Corinthians 15:20–22, 45–47; 2 Corinthians 11:3; and 1 Timothy 2:13–14. The death of Abel recorded in Genesis 4 is mentioned by Jesus in Luke 11:51. The Flood (Genesis 6–9) is confirmed as historical by Jesus (Matthew 24:37–39) and Peter (2 Peter 2:4–9, 3:6), and in Luke 17:26–29, Jesus mentioned the Flood in the same context as he did the account of Lot and Sodom (Genesis 19). Finally, in Luke's genealogy of Christ, he includes 20 names found in the genealogies of Genesis 5 and 11 (Luke 3:34–38).

Conclusion

These are just some of the reasons why Genesis 1–11 should be understood as literal history. Jesus and the New Testament authors viewed it as such,[18] and the internal consistency of Genesis demonstrates its historical nature. Consequently, to interpret Genesis 1–11 in the same way Jesus did, you must treat the passage as historical narrative and follow the standard principles of interpretation. When you do this, it is clear that God created everything in six normal-length days approximately six thousand years ago.

18. For more on Christ's and the Apostles' view of Genesis 1–11, see chapters 11 and 12 in Mortenson and Ury, *Coming to Grips with Genesis*.

Appendix B

Why Should We Believe in the Inerrancy of Scripture?

By Brian Edwards[1]

Introduction

You don't really believe the Bible is true, do you?"

The shock expressed by those who discover someone who actually believes the Bible to be without error is often quite amusing. Inevitably, their next question takes us right back to Genesis. But what does the Christian mean by "without error," and why are we so sure?

Inspiring or Expiring?

Let's start by understanding what we mean when we talk about the Bible as "inspired," because that word may mislead us. The term is an attempt to translate a word that occurs only once in the New Testament, and it's not the best translation, even though William Tyndale introduced it back in 1526. The word is found in 2 Timothy 3:16, and the Greek is *theopneustos*. This term is made from two words, one being the word for God (*theos*, as in theology) and the other referring to breath or wind (*pneustos*, as in pneumonia and pneumatic). It is significant that the word is used in 2 Timothy 3:16 passively.

---

1. This article was originally published in *How Do We Know the Bible Is True?* Vol. 1, eds. Ken Ham and Bodie Hodge (Green Forest, AR: Master Books, 2011).

In other words, God did not "breathe into" (inspire) all Scripture, but it was "breathed out" by God (expired). Thus, 2 Timothy 3:16 is not about how the Bible came to us but where it came from. The Scriptures are "God-breathed."

To know how the Bible came to us, we can turn to 2 Peter 1:21 where we discover that "holy men of God spoke as they were moved by the Holy Spirit." The Greek word used here is *pherō*, which means "to bear" or "to carry." It was a familiar word that Luke used of the sailing ship carried along by the wind (Acts 27:15, 17). The human writers of the Bible certainly used their minds, but the Holy Spirit carried them along in their thinking so that only His God-breathed words were recorded. The Apostle Paul set the matter plainly in 1 Corinthians 2:13: "These things we also speak, not in words which man's wisdom teaches but which the Holy Spirit teaches."

The word "inspiration" is so embedded in our Christian language that we will continue to use it, though we now know what it really means. God breathed out His Word, and the Holy Spirit guided the writers. The Bible has one Author and many (around 40) writers.

With these two acts of God — breathing out His Word and carrying the writers along by the Spirit — we can come to a definition of inspiration:

> The Holy Spirit moved men to write. He allowed them to use their own styles, cultures, gifts, and character. He allowed them to use the results of their own study and research, write of their own experiences, and express what was in their minds. At the same time, the Holy Spirit did not allow error to influence their writings. He overruled in the expression of thought and in the choice of words. Thus, they recorded accurately all God wanted them to say and exactly how He wanted them to say it in their own character, styles, and languages.

The inspiration of Scripture is a harmony of the active mind of the writer and the sovereign direction of the Holy Spirit to produce God's inerrant and infallible Word for the human race. Two errors are to be avoided here. First, some think inspiration is nothing more than a generally heightened sensitivity to wisdom on the part of the writer, just as we talk of an inspired idea or invention. Second, some believe the writer was merely a mechanical dictation machine, writing out the words he heard from God. Both errors fail to adequately account for the active role played by the Holy Spirit and the human writer.

How Much Is Inerrant?

If "inspired" really means "God-breathed," then the claim of 2 Timothy 3:16 is that all Scripture, being God-breathed, is without error and therefore can be trusted completely. Since God cannot lie (Hebrews 6:18), He would cease to be God if He breathed out errors and contradictions, even in the smallest part. So long as we give *theopneustos* its real meaning, we shall not find it hard to understand the full inerrancy of the Bible.

Two words are sometimes used to explain the extent of biblical inerrancy: plenary and verbal. "Plenary" comes from the Latin *plenus,* which means "full," and refers to the fact that the whole of Scripture in every part is God-given. "Verbal" comes from the Latin *verbum,* which means "word," and emphasizes that even the words of Scripture are God-given. Plenary and verbal inspiration means the Bible is God-given (and therefore without error) in every part (doctrine, history, geography, dates, names) and in every single word.

When we talk about inerrancy, we refer to the original writings of Scripture. We do not have any of the original "autographs," as they are called, but only copies, including many copies of each book. There are small differences here and there, but in reality they are amazingly similar. One 18th-century New Testament scholar claimed that not one thousandth part of the text was affected by these differences.[2] Now that we know what inerrancy means, let's cover what it doesn't mean.

- Inerrancy doesn't mean everything in the Bible is true. We have the record of men lying (e.g., Joshua 9) and even the words of the devil himself. But we can be sure these are accurate records of what took place.

- Inerrancy doesn't mean apparent contradictions are not in the text, but these can be resolved. At times, different words may be used in recounting what appears to be the same incident. For example, Matthew 3:11 refers to John the Baptist *carrying* the sandals of

---

2. Bishop Brook Foss Westcott, *The New Testament in the Original Greek* (London, MacMillan, 1881), p. 2.

the Messiah, whereas John 1:27 refers to him *untying* them. John preached over a period of time, and he would repeat himself; like any preacher he would use different ways of expressing the same thing.

- Inerrancy doesn't mean every extant copy is inerrant. It is important to understand that the doctrine of inerrancy only applies to the original manuscripts.

Inerrancy does mean it is incorrect to claim the Bible is only "reasonably accurate," as some do.[3] That would leave us uncertain as to where we could trust God's Word.

What Does the Bible Claim?

Is it true, as John Goldingay stated, that this view of inerrancy "is not directly asserted by Christ or within Scripture itself"?[4] Let's look at what the Bible says about itself.

The View of the Old Testament Writers

The Old Testament writers saw their message as God-breathed and therefore utterly reliable. God promised Moses He would eventually send another prophet (Jesus Christ) who would also speak God's words like Moses had done. "I will raise up for them a Prophet *like you* from among their brethren, and will put My words in His mouth, and He shall speak to them all that I command Him" (Deuteronomy 18:18, emphasis added). Jeremiah was told at the beginning of his ministry that he would speak for God. "Then the Lord put forth His hand and touched my mouth, and the Lord said to me: 'Behold, I have put My words in your mouth' " (Jeremiah 1:9).

The Hebrew word for prophet means "a spokesman," and the prophet's message was on God's behalf: This is what the Lord says. As a result, they frequently so identified themselves with God that they spoke as though God Himself were actually speaking. Isaiah 5 reveals this clearly. In verses 1–2 the prophet speaks of God in the third person (*He*), but in verses 3–6 Isaiah changes to speak in the first person (*I*). Isaiah was speaking the very words of God. No wonder King David could speak of the Word of the Lord as "flawless" (2 Samuel 22:31; see also Proverbs 30:5, NIV).

---

3. John Goldingay, *Models for Scripture* (Toronto: Clements Publishing, 2004), p. 282.
4. Ibid., p. 273.

The New Testament Agrees with the Old Testament

Peter and John saw the words of David in Psalm 2, not merely as the opinion of a king of Israel, but as the voice of God. They introduced a quotation from that psalm in a prayer to God by saying, "who by the mouth of Your servant David have said: 'Why did the nations rage, and the people plot vain things?' " (Acts 4:25).

Similarly, Paul accepted Isaiah's words as God Himself speaking to men: "The Holy Spirit spoke rightly through Isaiah the prophet to our fathers" (Acts 28:25).

So convinced were the writers of the New Testament that all the words of the Old Testament Scripture were the actual words of God that they even claimed, "Scripture says," when the words quoted came directly from God. Two examples are Romans 9:17, which states, "For the Scripture says to the Pharaoh," and Galatians 3:8, in which Paul wrote, "the Scripture, foreseeing that God would justify the Gentiles by faith, preached the gospel to Abraham beforehand. . . ." In Hebrews 1, many of the Old Testament passages quoted were actually addressed to God by the Psalmist, yet the writer to the Hebrews refers to them as the words of God.

Jesus Believed in Verbal Inspiration

In John 10:34 Jesus quoted from Psalm 82:6 and based His teaching upon a phrase: "I said, 'You are gods.' " In other words, Jesus proclaimed that the words of this psalm were the words of God. Similarly, in Matthew 22:31–32 He claimed the words of Exodus 3:6 were given to them by God. In Matthew 22:43–44 our Lord quoted from Psalm 110:1 and pointed out that David wrote these words "in the Spirit," meaning he was actually writing the words of God.

Paul Believed in Verbal Inspiration

Paul based an argument upon the fact that a particular word in the Old Testament is singular and not plural. Writing to the Galatians, Paul claimed that in God's promises to Abraham, "He does not say, 'And to seeds,' as of many, but as of one, 'And to your Seed,' who is Christ" (Galatians 3:16). Paul quoted from Genesis 12:7; 13:15; and 24:7. In each of these verses, our translators used the word *descendants*, but the Hebrew word is singular. The same word is translated "seed" in Genesis 22:18. Paul's argument here is that God was not *primarily* referring to Israel as the offspring of Abraham, but to Christ.

What is significant is the way Paul drew attention to the fact that the Hebrew word in Genesis is singular. This demonstrates a belief in verbal inspiration because it mattered to Paul whether God used a singular or plural in these passages of the Old Testament. It is therefore not surprising Paul wrote that one of the advantages of being a Jew was the fact that they "have been entrusted with the very words of God" (Romans 3:2, NIV). Even many critics of the Bible agree that the Scriptures clearly teach a doctrine of verbal inerrancy.

Self-authentication

To say the Bible is the Word of God and is therefore without error because the Bible itself makes this claim is seen by many as circular reasoning. It is rather like saying, "That prisoner must be innocent because he says he is." Are we justified in appealing to the Bible's own claim in settling this matter of its authority and inerrancy?

Actually, we use "self-authentication" every day. Whenever we say, "I think" or "I believe" or "I dreamed," we are making a statement no one can verify. If people were reliable, witness to oneself would always be enough. In John 5:31–32 Jesus said that self-witness is normally insufficient. Later, when Jesus claimed, "I am the light of the world" (John 8:12), the Pharisees attempted to correct Him by stating, "Here you are, appearing as your own witness; your testimony is not valid" (John 8:13, NIV). In defense, the Lord showed that in His case, because He is the Son of God, self-witness is reliable: "Even if I bear witness of Myself, My witness is true . . ." (John 8:14). Self-witness is reliable where sin does not interfere. Because Jesus is God and therefore guiltless (a fact confirmed by His critics in John 8:46), His words can be trusted. In a similar manner, since the Bible is God's Word, we must listen to its own claims about itself.

Much of the Bible's story is such that unless God had revealed it we could never have known it. Many scientific theories propose how the world came into being. Some of these theories differ only slightly from each other, but others are contradictory. This shows no one can really be sure about such matters because no scientist was there when it all happened. Unless the God who was there has revealed it, we could never know for certain. The same is true for all the great Bible doctrines. How can we be sure of God's anger against sin, His love for sinners, or His plan to choose a people for Himself, unless God Himself has told us? Hilary of Poitiers, a fourth century theologian, once claimed, "Only God is a fit witness to himself" — and no one can improve upon that.

Who Believes This?

The belief the Bible is without error is not new. Clement of Rome in the first century wrote, "Look carefully into the Scriptures, which are the true utterances of the Holy Spirit. Observe that nothing of an unjust or counterfeit character is written in them."[5] A century later, Irenaeus concluded, "The Scriptures are indeed perfect, since they were spoken by the Word of God and his Spirit."[6]

This was the view of the early Church leaders, and it has been the consistent view of evangelicals from the ancient Vaudois people of the Piedmont Valley to the 16th-century Protestant Reformers across Europe and up to the present day. Not all used the terms "infallibility" or "inerrancy," but many expressed the concepts, and there is no doubt they believed it. It is liberalism that has taken a new approach. Professor Kirsopp Lake at Harvard University admitted, "It is we [the liberals] who have departed from the tradition."[7]

Does It Matter?

Is the debate about whether or not the Bible can be trusted merely a theological quibble? Certainly not! The question of ultimate authority is of tremendous importance for the Christian.

Inerrancy Governs Our Confidence in the Truth of the Gospel

If the Scripture is unreliable, can we offer the world a reliable gospel? How can we be sure of truth on any issue if we are suspicious of errors anywhere in the Bible? A pilot will ground his aircraft even on suspicion of the most minor fault, because he is aware that one fault destroys confidence in the complete machine. If the history contained in the Bible is wrong, how can we be sure the doctrine or moral teaching is correct?

The heart of the Christian message is history. The Incarnation (God becoming a man) was demonstrated by the Virgin Birth of Christ.

---

5. Clement of Rome First letter to the Corinthians XLV.

6. Irenaeus, *Against Heresies*, XVII.2.

7. Kirsopp Lake, *The Religion of Yesterday and Tomorrow* (Boston, MA: Houghton, Mifflin Co., 1926), p. 62.

Redemption (the price paid for our rebellion) was obtained by the death of Christ on the Cross. Reconciliation (the privilege of the sinner becoming a friend of God) was gained through the Resurrection and Ascension of Christ. If these recorded events are not true, how do we know the theology behind them is true?

Inerrancy Governs Our Faith in the Value of Christ

We cannot have a reliable Savior without a reliable Scripture. If, as many suggest, the stories in the Gospels are not historically true and the recorded words of Christ are only occasionally His, how do we know what we can trust about Christ? Must we rely upon the conflicting interpretations of a host of critical scholars before we know what Christ was like or what He taught? If the Gospel accounts are merely the result of the wishful thinking of the Church in the second or third centuries, or even the personal views of the Gospel writers, then our faith no longer rests upon Jesus but upon the opinions of men. Who would trust an unreliable Savior for their eternal salvation?

Inerrancy Governs Our Response to the Conclusions of Science

If we believe the Bible contains errors, then we will be quick to accept scientific theories that appear to prove the Bible wrong. In other words, we will allow the conclusions of science to dictate the accuracy of the Word of God. When we doubt the Bible's inerrancy, we have to invent new principles for interpreting Scripture that for convenience turn history into poetry and facts into myths. This means people must ask how reliable a given passage is when they turn to it. Only then will they be able to decide what to make of it. On the other hand, if we believe in inerrancy, we will test by Scripture the hasty theories that often come to us in the name of science.

Inerrancy Governs Our Attitude to the Preaching of Scripture

A denial of biblical inerrancy always leads to a loss of confidence in Scripture both in the pulpit and in the pew. It was not the growth of education and science that emptied churches, nor was it the result of two world wars. Instead, it was the cold deadness of theological liberalism. If the Bible's history is doubtful and its words are open to dispute, then people understandably lose confidence in it. People want authority. They want to know what God has said.

Inerrancy Governs Our Belief in the Trustworthy Character of God

Almost all theologians agree that Scripture is in some measure God's revelation to the human race. But to allow that it contains error implies God
has mishandled inspiration and has allowed His people to be deceived for
centuries until modern scholars disentangled the confusion. In short, the
Maker muddled the instructions.

Conclusion

A Church without the authority of Scripture is like a crocodile without
teeth; it can open its mouth as wide and as often as it likes — but who cares?
Thankfully, God has given us His inspired, inerrant, and infallible Word.
His people can speak with authority and boldness, and we can be confident
we have His instructions for our lives.

Appendix C

Millions of Years and the Downfall of the Christian West

By Dr. Terry Mortenson

Most people have heard that:

- the idea of long ages of evolutionary change originated with Charles Darwin;

- Christians started to reject the literal accounts of a worldwide flood and the creation after Darwin;

- no serious scientist today doubts that the earth is millions/billions of years old.

In this brief article, we will show that these widely held beliefs are actually wrong. We will reveal that:

1. the idea of a very old earth was popular in scientific circles even before Darwin;

2. many scientists (including many professing Christians) started to reject a straightforward reading of Genesis many decades before Darwin's *Origin of Species* was published;

3. there are thousands of practicing scientists today who believe in a young age for the earth.

Most people today, including many who attend church, take for granted that the earth and universe are millions and millions (even billions) of years old. But it has not always been that way, and it is important in today's "culture wars" to understand how this change took place and why.

Geology's Early Beginnings

Geology (the study of rocks and fossils) as a separate field of science[1] is only about 200 years old.

Going back to ancient Greek times, people had noticed fossils in rock layers. Many believed that the fossils were the remains of former living things turned to stone. Many early Christians (including Tertullian, Chrysostom, and Augustine) attributed them to Noah's Flood.

Prior to 1750 one of the most important geological thinkers was Nicolaus Steno (1638–1686), a Dutch anatomist and geologist. He established the principle of "superposition," namely, that sedimentary rock layers are deposited in a successive, essentially horizontal fashion (that is, a lower stratum was deposited before the one above it).

In his book *Forerunner* (1669), Steno expressed belief in a roughly 6,000-year-old earth and that fossil-bearing rock strata were deposited by Noah's Flood. Over the next century, several authors wrote books essentially reinforcing that view.

In the latter decades of the 18th century, several prominent Frenchmen contributed to the development of the idea of an earth that is millions of years old. One of these respected scientists was Comte de Buffon. In his 1779 book *Epochs of Nature*, he imagined that the earth was once like a hot molten ball that had cooled to reach its present state over 75,000 years ago (though his unpublished manuscript says about 3,000,000 years).

In Scotland, James Hutton was developing a different theory of earth history. In 1788 he published a journal article and in 1795 a book, both with the title *Theory of the Earth*. He proposed that the continents were being slowly eroded into the oceans. Those sediments were gradually hardened by the internal heat of the earth and then raised by convulsions to become new land masses, which would later be eroded into the oceans, hardened and elevated.

---

1. Geology involves systematic field studies, collection and classification of rocks and fossils, and development of theoretical reconstructions of the historical events that formed those rock layers and fossils. Some people studied rocks and fossils before the 19th century, but that is when geology developed as a separate branch of science.

So in Hutton's view, earth history was cyclical, and he stated that he could find no evidence of a beginning in the rock record, making earth history indefinitely long.

The "Catastrophist-Uniformitarian" Debate

Hutton did not pay much attention to the fossils. However, in 1812 Georges Cuvier, the famous French vertebrate palaeontologist, published his *catastrophist* theory of earth history in his *Discourse on the Revolutions of the Surface of the Globe.*

Cuvier believed that over the course of untold ages, many catastrophic floods of continental or nearly global extent periodically had destroyed and buried many creatures in sediments. He believed that all but one of these catastrophes occurred before the creation of man.

A massive blow to this idea of catastrophism came during the years 1830 to 1833, when Charles Lyell, a lawyer by training, published his influential three-volume work, *Principles of Geology.* Reviving and expanding on the ideas of Hutton, Lyell explained in *Principles* how he thought geologists should interpret the rocks.

Lyell's theory was radical *uniformitarianism,* in which he insisted that only present-day processes of sedimentation and erosion at *present-day rates of intensity and magnitude* should be used to interpret the rock record of past geological activity. Geological processes of change, he argued, have been uniform throughout earth history, hence the term *uniformitarianism.* No continental or global catastrophic floods (like Noah's Flood in the Bible) have ever occurred, insisted Lyell.

In the late 1830s only a few catastrophists remained, but they believed Noah's Flood was geologically insignificant. Uniformitarianism became the ruling dogma in geology. By the end of the 19th century, the age of the earth was considered by all geologists to be in the hundreds of millions of years. Radiometric dating methods began to be developed in 1903, and over the course of the 20th century, the supposed age of the earth expanded to about 4.5 billion years.

Christian Responses to Old-Earth Geology

During the first half of the 1800s, the Church responded in various ways to these old-earth theories of the catastrophists and uniformitarians. A number of writers in Great Britain (and a few in America), who became known as "scriptural geologists," raised biblical, geological, and philosophical arguments against the old-earth theories.

Some of the scriptural geologists were scientists, and some were clergy. Some were both ordained and scientifically well informed, as was common in those days. Many of them were geologically very competent by the standards of their day, both by reading and by their own careful observations out among the rocks and fossils.

The scriptural geologists believed that the biblical accounts of creation and Noah's Flood explained the rock record far better than the old-earth theories.[2]

Other Christians in the early 1800s quickly accepted the idea of millions of years and tried to fit all this time somewhere into the Bible's Book of Genesis, even though the uniformitarians and catastrophists were still debating, and geology was in its infancy as a science.

For example, in 1804 Thomas Chalmers, a young Presbyterian pastor, began to preach that Christians should accept the concept of millions of years, and in an 1814 review of Cuvier's book, he proposed that all the time could fit between Genesis 1:1 and 1:2. By that time, Chalmers was becoming a highly influential evangelical leader and consequently his "gap theory" became very popular. In 1823 the respected Anglican theologian George Stanley Faber began to advocate the day-age view, namely that the days of creation were not literal but figurative of long ages.

Looking at the Flood Differently

To accept these geological ages, Christians also had to reinterpret Noah's Flood. In the 1820s, John Fleming, a Presbyterian minister, contended that Noah's Flood was so peaceful it left no lasting geological evidence. John Pye Smith (1774–1851), a Congregational theologian, preferred to see it as localized flooding in the Mesopotamian valley (modern-day Iraq).

Liberal theology, which by the early 1800s was dominating the Church in Europe, was beginning to make inroads in Britain and North America in the 1820s. The liberals considered Genesis 1–11 to be as historically unreliable and unscientific as the creation and flood myths of the ancient Babylonians, Sumerians, and Egyptians.

---

2. See Terry Mortenson, *The Great Turning Point: the Church's Catastrophic Mistake on Geology — before Darwin* (Green Forest, AR: Master Books, 2004) for a full discussion of these men and the battle they fought against these developing old-earth theories and Christian compromises.

In spite of the efforts of the scriptural geologists, these various old-earth reinterpretations of Genesis prevailed so that by about 1845, all the commentaries on Genesis had abandoned the biblical chronology and the global Flood, and by the time of Darwin's *Origin of Species* (1859), the young-earth view had essentially disappeared within the Church.

From that time onward, most Christian leaders and scholars of the Church have accepted the idea of millions of years and have insisted that the age of the earth is not important. Many godly men soon accepted evolution also. Space allows us to mention only a few examples.

The Baptist "prince of preachers," Charles Spurgeon of England, uncritically accepted the old-earth geological theory (though he never explained how to fit the long ages into the Bible). In an 1855 sermon he said,

> Can any man tell me when the beginning was? Years ago we thought the beginning of this world was when Adam came upon it; but we have discovered that thousands of years before that God was preparing chaotic matter to make it a fit abode for man, putting races of creatures upon it, who might die and leave behind the marks of his handiwork and marvelous skill, before he tried his hand on man.[3]

The great Presbyterian theologian at Princeton Seminary in New Jersey, Charles Hodge (1779–1878), insisted that the age of the earth was not important. He favored the gap theory initially and switched to the day-age view later in life. His compromise contributed to the eventual victory of liberal theology at Princeton about 50 years after his death.[4]

C.I. Scofield put the gap theory in his notes on Genesis 1:2 in his 1909 *Scofield Reference Bible*, which has been used for nearly a hundred years by millions of Christians around the world. More recently, a respected evangelical Old Testament scholar reasoned:

> From a superficial reading of Genesis 1, the impression would seem to be that the entire creative process took place in six twenty-four-hour days. If this was the true intent of the Hebrew author . . .

---

3. C.H. Spurgeon, "Election" (1855), *The New Park Street Pulpit*, vol. 1 (Pasadena, TX: Pilgrim Publ. 1990), p. 318. Spurgeon made other similar concessions to old-earth theory later in life, but never showed evidence of really studying the issue carefully.

4. See Joseph Pipa and David Hall, eds., *Did God Create in Six Days?* (Whitehall, WV: Tolle Lege Press, 2005), p. 7–16, for some of the documentation of this sad slide into apostasy.

this seems to run counter to modern scientific research, which indicates that the planet Earth was created several billion years ago. . . .[5]

Numerous similar statements from Christian scholars and leaders in the last few decades could be quoted to show that their interpretation of Genesis is controlled by the fact that they *assume* that the geologists have proven millions of years. As a result, most seminaries and Christian colleges around the world are compromised.

The irony of all this compromise is that in the last half of the 20th century, the truth of Genesis 1–11 was increasingly being vindicated, often unintentionally, by the work of evolutionists. Since the 1970s a number of secular "neo-catastrophist" geologists have increasingly challenged Lyell's "slow-and-gradual" assumptions and argued that much of the rock record shows evidence of rapid catastrophic erosion or sedimentation, drastically reducing the time involved in the formation of many geological deposits.

These neo-catastrophist re-interpretations of the rocks have developed along with a resurgence of "Flood geology," a view of earth history very similar to that of the 19th-century scriptural geologists and a key ingredient to young-earth creation (which was essentially launched by the publication of *The Genesis Flood* by Drs. John Whitcomb and Henry Morris in 1961). This movement is now worldwide in scope, and the sophistication of the scientific model is rapidly increasing with time.

Disastrous Consequences of Compromise

The scriptural geologists of the 19th century opposed old-earth geological theories not only because the theories reflected erroneous scientific reasoning and were contrary to Scripture, but also because they believed that the Christian compromise with such theories would eventually have a catastrophic effect on the health of the Church and her witness to a lost world.

Accordingly, Henry Cole, an Anglican minister, wrote in 1834:

> Many reverend Geologists, however, would evince their reverence for the divine Revelation by making a distinction between its *historical* and its *moral* portions; and maintaining, that the latter only is inspired and absolute Truth; but that the former is not so;

---

5. Gleason Archer, *A Survey Of Old Testament Introduction* (Chicago, IL: Moody Press, 1985), p. 187.

and therefore is open to any latitude of philosophic and scientific interpretation, modification or denial! . . .What the consequences of such things must be to a revelation-possessing land, time will rapidly and awfully unfold in its opening pages of national skepticism, infidelity, and apostasy, and of God's righteous vengeance on the same![6]

Cole and other opponents of the old-earth theories rightly understood that the historical portions of the Bible (including Genesis 1–11) are foundational to the theological and moral teachings of Scripture. Destroy the credibility of the former, and sooner or later you will see rejection of the latter — both inside and outside the Church. If the scriptural geologists were alive today and saw the castle diagram shown in chapter 1 of this book, they would say: "That pictures *exactly* what we were concerned about!"

The history of the once-Christian nations in Europe and North America has confirmed the scriptural geologists' worst fears about the Church and society. Abortion, homosexual behavior, divorce, teen pregnancy, drug abuse, pornography, adultery, school violence, etc., have skyrocketed. As a whole, these nations have become more resistant to the gospel and the Bible's authority — and more atheistic in their education and media, which justifies the label of being "post-Christian" countries.

To be sure, the teaching of evolution and millions of years has not caused these moral and spiritual problems — the cause is the rebellious hearts of men. But the evolutionary old-earth theory has powerfully undermined the credibility and authority of the Bible and therefore its cultural influence. And as churches and their educational institutions have compromised on the teachings of Genesis 1–11, they have become increasingly spiritually weak (or dead) and ineffective in taking the gospel to a lost and dying world. In fact, the gospel message itself is undermined if you believe there was death for millions of years before the Fall of Adam into sin.

It is time for the Church, especially her leaders and scholars, to stop ignoring the question about the age of the earth and the scientific evidence that increasingly vindicates the Word of God. The Church must repent of her compromise with millions of years and once again believe and preach the literal truth of Genesis 1–11.

---

6. Henry Cole, *Popular Geology Subversive of Divine Revelation* (London: Hatchard and Son, 1834), p. ix–x, 44–45 footnote.

At the same time, the idea of a young earth is becoming more widely accepted in many countries. In fact, a respected reporter with the highly influential *Washington Post* newspaper wrote in 2005 that the young-earth creation movement in America was growing "stronger day by day."[7] There are now literally thousands of scientists (hundreds with earned PhDs from respected secular universities) worldwide who reject evolution and long ages in favor of the teaching of the Word of God — that the earth and all that is in it was made about 6,000 years ago.[8] And their number is growing rapidly.

With ongoing research, like the important RATE project (that has cast serious doubts on radiometric dating methods),[9] an increasing number of teaching conferences on a literal Genesis, the opening of the Creation Museum near Cincinnati (2007), and other intensive endeavors by creationists, the controversy over the age of the earth that began before Darwin will only intensify.

---

7. "In Evolution Debate, Creationists Are Breaking New Ground," Michael Powell (New York City bureau chief with the *Washington Post*), *Washington Post*, September 25, 2005, p. A3.

8. For example, the Creation Research Society has about 600 member scientists/engineers. See also www.answersingenesis.org/Home/Area/bios.

9. See Don DeYoung, *Thousands . . . Not Billions* (Green Forest, AR: Master Books, 2005) and the DVD documentary by the same title.